Visionary Encounters

Visionary Encounters

*The Dzogchen Teachings of
Bönpo Treasure-Revealer Shense Lhaje*

COMPILED, INTRODUCED, AND
TRANSLATED FROM THE TIBETAN BY
Adriano Clemente

SNOW LION
BOULDER
2016

Snow Lion
An imprint of Shambhala Publications, Inc.
4720 Walnut Street
Boulder, Colorado 80301
www.shambhala.com

© 2016 by Adriano Clemente
All rights reserved. No part of this book may be reproduced in any form or by any means, electronic or mechanical, including photocopying, recording, or by any information storage and retrieval system, without permission in writing from the publisher.

9 8 7 6 5 4 3 2 1

First Edition
Printed in the United States of America

⊗ This edition is printed on acid-free paper that meets the American National Standards Institute z39.48 Standard.
✿ Shambhala makes every effort to print on recycled paper.
For more information please visit www.shambhala.com.

Distributed in the United States by Penguin Random House LLC and in Canada by Random House of Canada Ltd

LIBRARY OF CONGRESS CATALOGING-IN-PUBLICATION DATA
Names: Clemente, Adriano, compiler, translator. | Gshen-gsas, Lha-rje, 1215–1268? Works. Selections. English.
Title: Visionary encounters : the Dzogchen teachings of Bönpo treasure-revealer Shense Lhaje / Compiled, introduced, and translated from the Tibetan by Adriano Clemente.
Description: First edition. | Boulder : Snow Lion, 2016. | Includes bibliographical references and index.
Identifiers: LCCN 2015048411 | ISBN 9781559394321 (paperback)
Subjects: LCSH: Rdzogs-chen. | Gshen-gsas, Lha-rje, 1215–1268?—Teachings. | BISAC: RELIGION / Buddhism / Tibetan. | RELIGION / Buddhism / Sacred Writings. | RELIGION / Buddhism / Rituals & Practice.
Classification: LCC BQ7662.4 .C53 2016 | DDC 294.3/420423—dc23
LC record available at https://lccn.loc.gov/2015048411

Contents

Preface	ix
Introduction	1
Dzogchen in the Bön Tradition	1
The Basic Principles of Dzogchen	4
Trenpa Serdam: The Golden Teaching of Trenpa Namkha	7
Trenpa Namkha	8
Shense Lhaje	10
The Visionary Dimension	24
The Origins of *The Golden Teaching*	28
Editions of *The Golden Teaching*	32
The Translated Texts	33
Note on the Translation	34

Four Texts from The Golden Teaching

1. Visionary Encounters with Knowledge-Holders and Dakinis	39
2. Clarifying the Real Nature: The Upadesha That Reveals Nakedly the Wisdom of Clear Insight	83
3. The Garland of Nectar: Orally Transmitted Advice from Eighty Knowledge-Holders in the Form of Questions and Answers	97
4. The Precious Golden Lamp: Advice from Eighty Dakinis	123

Appendices

1.	The *Dran pa gser gdams* in the Various Editions	151
2.	The Previous Lives of Gshen sras lha rje	163
3.	Iconographical Details of Knowledge-Holders and Ḍākinīs	167
4.	Names of Knowledge-Holders with Spelling Variants	171
5.	Names of Ḍākinīs with Spelling Variants	175
6.	The Translated Texts' Main Textual Variants in Two Editions of the *Dran pa gser gdams*	179
7.	A List of Gshen sras lha rje's Works in the Bönpo Canon	193

Glossary of Tibetan Terms and Expressions	197
Notes	201
Bibliography	223
Index of Tibetan, Sanskrit, and Zhang Zhung Names and Terms	231

> Look at your mind, and you will see everything!
> Search inside you, and you will find everything!
> Take hold of your natural place, and you will reach the land of bliss!
>
> —The dakini Wöden Barma to Shense Lhaje

> Were it not better to believe Vision with all our might and strength, tho' we are fallen and lost?
>
> —William Blake, *The Ghost of Abel*

Chögyal Namkhai Norbu, Dzogchen master and an authority on Tibetan culture and history. Photo taken by Nina Robinson in 1994. Used with permission.

Preface

In 1981, when I was a student at the Istituto Universitario Orientale of Naples, Italy, my Dzogchen master Chögyal Namkhai Norbu, at that time professor of Tibetan Language and Literature, suggested for my graduation thesis that I study a Dzogchen text from the Bön tradition. He chose the *Trenpa Serdam* (*Dran pa gser gdams*) or *The Golden Teaching of Trenpa Namkha*, a cycle of teachings rediscovered by the thirteenth-century Bönpo Shense Lhaje, an important tertön or treasure-revealer in this tradition. In particular he pointed out the text called *Advice from Eighty Dakinis*, which he found especially interesting. I had no idea, apart from the need to research into the Dzogchen teaching in the Bön tradition, the reason why he chose this particular text, which is little known in comparison to famous cycles such as *The Oral Transmission of Shang Shung* (*Zhang zhung snyan rgyud*). Later I came to understand that Chögyal Namkhai Norbu himself has a rich visionary life in his dreams of clarity, through which he has received an important cycle of Dzogchen teachings.[1] This for me became a link for appreciating even more the extraordinary life-stories and teachings of Shense Lhaje, and for relating them to the dream experiences of my master.

Chögyal Namkhai Norbu, a pioneer in spreading the Dzogchen teaching in the West and an accomplished scholar in all the fields of Tibetan culture, started to inquire into the origins of Tibetan culture in the early seventies, identifying in the ancient Bön tradition and the Shang Shung kingdom[2] the source of Tibetan civilization. As a result of his research he wrote two books, *The Necklace of Jewels* and *The Necklace of Zi*,[3] which, because of the original ideas, the bold outlook, and the honest questioning about the real sources of Tibetan culture and history, fell like bombs among the Tibetan refugees living in India. Consequently, at that time many narrow-minded lamas accused him of being a Bönpo, while in fact he had never received any Bönpo education. The only indirect connection was that his root guru, Changchub Dorje (1863–1961), among the many Dzogchen masters he had followed, had also received essential teachings from the great Bönpo Dzogchen master Shardza Trashi Gyaltsen (1859–1934).[4] Later Chögyal Namkhai Norbu completed his research with two books that have become milestones in Tibetan studies: *Drung, Deu and Bön*,[5] focusing mainly on the ancient traditions of Bön, and *The Light of Kailash*, on the history and culture of the kingdoms of Shang Shung and Tibet.[6]

When he toured India and Nepal in 1978 with some Italian assistants to shoot *Arura*, a documentary film on Tibetan medicine, he had the chance to visit the Bönpo settlement and monastery Menri Sarpa in Dolanji, Himachal Pradesh. There he spent a few weeks with Yongdzin Lopön Tenzin Namdak, the highest authority in the Bön tradition, and through this connection he started to send some of his students to this monastery in order to research the Bönpo teachings and traditions.

In 1981, two of my colleagues, the Tibetologists Giacomella Orofino and Enrico Dell'Angelo, left for the Bönpo monastery, where they spent some months studying with Lopön Tenzin Namdak. In February 1982 I also left for India, and after a short visit to holy places such as Varanasi and Bodhgaya, I headed for the Bönpo settlement of Dolanji. Living in India was an abrupt change from my life in Naples, although Naples was and still is the most Asian among Italian cities. When I reached the monastery, I was welcomed by the Khenpo, H.H. Sangye Tenzin Jongdong, who kindly assigned me a monk's room. Life in the monastery was quiet and absolutely frugal. No toilet, and no potable water to drink. Mineral water did not exist in India at that time.

After the first few days, I got accustomed to the place and the people, and was warmly received by Lopön Tenzin Namdak, who was busy with the ongoing sacred dances after the Losar celebrations, and advised me to practice meditation for some days. When the dances were over, he called me and said, "Namkhai Norbu has written to me that you should study the *Trenpa Serdam*. Get the text from somebody and we will start!"

When I obtained the text from a monk living nearby and brought it to Lopön, he opened it slowly and said, "Oh! There is a section that tells of the visionary accounts of Shense Lhaje—it is very nice, and we shall read it together!"

From that day, every afternoon around two o'clock Lopön, on the way to the monastery, would stop and knock at my room and say, "*Signora!*"

LOPÖN TENZIN NAMDAK AND ADRIANO CLEMENTE.
PHOTO TAKEN BY TENZIN WANGYAL AT THE BÖNPO SETTLEMENT OF DOLANJI,
HIMACHAL PRADESH, IN FRONT OF LOPÖN'S HOUSE, AUGUST 1982.

("lady," but meant to be *signore*, "gentleman"). Then he would sit on my bed close to me and read one or two pages of the text called *Visionary Encounters with Knowledge-Holders and Dakinis*. He did not allow me to record it, so I had to write everything down while he spoke. This went on for about two months. The rest of the time I would review the translation and transcribe, with the help of a monk, the difficult cursive *ume* script of this book, containing many *duyig* or abbreviated words, into the letters of *uchen* (capital script).

During those months I became acquainted with Lopön's simple way of living and his down-to-earth manner of communicating, displaying some of the noblest qualities of a human being: humbleness and simplicity. He used to teach in the monastery in the mornings, while in the afternoons he would stay in his room or outside in the garden, receiving occasional visitors or people seeking help or advice. I started to spend much time with him and his closest students at his house. He would often joke with us and tease me about the stories that I told about my life in Italy, and since I was wearing a beard "like yak's hair," he gave me the affectionate nickname "Gyari Pusob" (the shaggy bearded one).

In the meantime, I had become friends with Geshe Tenzin Wangyal, at that time still known as Tsering Phuntsok. He had also received a letter from Chögyal Namkhai Norbu asking him to help me. He was a young, bright monk, and a Dzogchen practitioner, and the only one who could speak good English, so we got along very well from the beginning. He would often invite me to his house where his mother prepared delicious Tibetan dishes, to have a break from the boredom of the monastery. We spent a lot of time together, and he helped me record Tibetan folk songs in the village from singers of various parts of Tibet. We also had much fun. I remember once we went for lunch in the town of Solan, and when the waiters brought us the warm water with lime used to wash the hands after eating, we, who did not know what to do with it, drank it in one gulp. Another time one of his relatives prepared chang, the Tibetan beer, for me, but as I was living in a monk's room I had to hide it under my bed. One night a monk arrived and, smelling the vapors of the chang, asked innocently, "I smell something like a medicine, what is it?" Of course, I could not explain.

We also conversed about the Dzogchen teaching and spiritual matters, and even though he was younger than I, he was always the smartest. Once I was playing the sarod, an Indian stringed instrument, for him, and when I finished, I asked him, "Do you like this music?" "Yes," he said, "it is very peaceful." "It's music for meditation," I continued, but he added, "Well, it sounds more like music for *chingwa* (a sleepy state of meditation)!"

Geshe Tenzin Wangyal, now a Dzogchen teacher in his own right and founder of the Ligmincha Institute, in the late eighties asked Chögyal Namkhai Norbu to be invited to Italy by the Dzogchen Community to continue his academic research, but once he arrived in Italy he was requested by members of the Dzogchen Community to give Dzogchen teachings. I acted as his interpreter when he gave his first Dzogchen teaching in the West in Milan, 1989.

After some months, I left the monastery to visit Nepal, and while I was there, I began to read other chapters of *The Golden Teaching*, when my attention fell on a short but essential teaching on Dzogchen, *Clarifying the Real Nature*. When I went back to Dolanji in August, I asked Lopön if he would teach it to me, and he gave an oral translation of this beautiful text. When I left the monastery in October I felt sad having to part from the teacher and all the new friends I had made.

Back in Italy I prepared my dissertation and wrote a thesis in Italian called *La dottrina rdzogs chen nel ciclo di insegnamenti visionari "Dran pa gser gdams,*" which I defended in the summer of 1983. The thesis contained an introduction to the Bön Dzogchen tradition and to the *Trenpa Serdam* cycle, plus some excerpts from the *Visionary Encounters with Knowledge-Holders and Dakinis*, and the whole *Clarifying the Real Nature*.

After that, at the suggestion of Chögyal Namkhai Norbu and with his precious help, I translated *Advice from Eighty Dakinis* and *Advice from Eighty Knowledge-Holders*. A small booklet containing excerpts from the four texts was later published by Shang Shung Edizioni as *Shense Lhaje, Visionary Encounters and Dzogchen Teachings from the Golden Advice* in 1995.

The present book is partly based on my original thesis, but the four texts here are translated in their entirety. Moreover, many parts of the translation have been revised thanks to a second edition of the *Trenpa Serdam* published in the Bönpo Katen. As for the introduction, a large quantity of material on Dzogchen Bön and Bönpo history, at the time of my dissertation virtually nonexistent, is now available, and the reader is kindly asked to refer to Dan Martin's *Unearthing Bon Treasures: Life and Contested Legacy of a Tibetan Scripture Revealer, with a General Bibliography of Bon* (Brill's Tibetan Studies Library), 2001, and of course to the many other publications especially on Bön Dzogchen issued in the last years.

In September 2014, from the nineteenth to the twenty-third, Lopön Tenzin Namdak transmitted part of the *Trenpa Serdam* at the Buddhas Weg, Siedelsbrunn, Germany. The text he chose was *Advice from Eighty Dakinis*, and he gave Dzogchen instructions on the basis of the teachings of the first nineteen dakinis. On that occasion I had the chance to clarify some points of translation that were still unresolved. Moreover I learned that another edition of the *Trenpa Serdam* had been found in the Tengyur collection from the Khyungpo Tengchen monastery (Khyung po steng chen), which I have not had the chance to examine in its entirety, and that a new edition had been published in Sichuan in 2013. Khenpo Tenpa Yungdrung taught part of "Pointing-Out Instructions on Primordial Wisdom," the first chapter of the *Trenpa Serdam* upadesha, and he kindly helped me in clarifying several obscure passages, besides providing me a copy of the Tengchen edition of the four texts translated here. I sincerely thank him for all this.

Lastly in September 2015, from the eleventh to the thirteenth, Lopön Tenzin Namdak transmitted the rest of the instructions contained in the *Advice from Eighty Dakinis* in Shenten Dargye Ling, France, and I had the occasion to revise that translation once again.

I wish to thank H.H. Sangye Tenzin Jongdong for giving me hospitality at the Dolanji settlement in 1982 and in later years; Jeffrey Cox at Snow Lion Publications who believed in this project from the beginning; Susan Kyser for reviewing the manuscript and correcting my English; Dan Martin and Jean-Luc Achard for generous information on historical and literary issues, and for useful suggestions; Gerd Manusch for providing me with invaluable digital texts; Anapola Couchonnal and her family for sponsoring my work in the final stages; Kurt Keutzer, Migmar Tsering, and all those who contributed directly or indirectly to the outcome of this book.

Regarding the spelling of Tibetan and Sanskrit terms, in the main text a phonetic transcription system has been used in which, by and large, consonants are pronounced as in English and vowels as in Italian. In the notes and in the appendices, except for terms like Bön and Dzogchen, the formal orthography has been used. The Wylie transliteration of Tibetan names and terms can be found in the index at the end of the book.

This book would never have seen the light without the direction and inspiration provided by Chögyal Namkhai Norbu, who opened my eyes to the knowledge of the incomparable spiritual transmission of Dzogchen. The little that I know about Dzogchen is due to his generous and unremitting flow of transmissions and explanations in the course of forty years.

I also feel immense gratitude for Lopön Tenzin Namdak, who kindly sat with me for hours with his saintly presence and sharp wit, and who, each time we have met over the years, has patiently asked me, "What about the *Trenpa Serdam*, have you finished it?"

Adriano Clemente
Isla Margarita, April 2013
Bugnanino, Italy, October 2015

Lopön Tenzin Namdak, supreme holder of the Bön tradition.
Photo taken by Adriano Clemente in 1997.

Trenpa Namkha. Thangka from Dolpo, artist unknown.
Owned by Adriano Clemente. Photo courtesy of Alex Siedlecki.

Introduction

Dzogchen in the Bön Tradition

Dzogchen, a Tibetan word that means "total perfection" or "absolute completeness," is the name of a spiritual teaching found in both the Bön and the Ancient Buddhist traditions of Tibet, where it is considered the highest path of realization, due to its direct and clear presentation of the nature of mind as the source of all phenomena of existence and to its special methods for accomplishing its potentiality.

The meaning of Dzogchen refers to this real, self-perfected nature of each individual, whether a buddha or a sentient being in samsara, and the scope of this teaching is to reveal directly and experientially the state of "Dzogchen" so that this knowledge becomes wholly integrated in one's life and behavior. A Dzogchen master is a being who has realized his or her real nature and is able to lead others to do so by means of traditional methods and personal advice. A Dzogchen student first has to discover the state of "dzogchen," and once this is done, the main task is to gain familiarity with the state transmitted by the master until all dualistic limitations are overcome.

In the Buddhist tradition, the origin of Dzogchen is attributed to Garab Dorje, a master from Oddiyana[1] who lived some centuries after the parinirvana of Buddha Shakyamuni. His transmission passed on to various siddhas from Oddiyana and India, until it reached Tibet in the eighth century thanks to the masters Vimalamitra and Padmasambhava, and to the Tibetan translator Vairochana. The teachings of these masters then converged into the Nyingma or Ancient tradition of Tibetan Buddhism, whose transmission has been kept alive up to the present day by many realized teachers.[2]

Bön is the name of the autochthonous religion of Tibet. Originally it denoted a variety of ritual traditions akin to shamanism, whose characteristic feature was the importance of reciting (*'bon pa*) mantras. At a certain point, with the appearance of the master Shenrab Miwo, twelve of these traditions were reformed and integrated with the teachings of this master who founded the so-called Yungdrung Bön, or Immortal Bön.³ According to the research of Chögyal Namkhai Norbu, Shenrab Miwo could have lived two thousand years B.C.E., concurrently with the arising of the kingdom of Shang Shung in Western Tibet.⁴

It is difficult to ascertain which of the teachings contained in the present Bönpo canon were actually taught by Shenrab Miwo, since many sutra and tantra teachings similar to those present in the Buddhist canon are found in it. Nevertheless, we can have no doubt that Dzogchen was part of these teachings, as there is an unbroken line of Dzogchen transmission known as the Oral Transmission of Shang Shung (*Zhang zhung snyan rgyud*), which was probably put into writing in the seventh or eighth century but dates back much earlier in its origins.

Dzogchen in Bön historical literature is also known as "the series of the Mind" (*sems phyogs*) or "the Bön of the utterly pure Mind" (*yang dag pa'i sems bon*). Tradition says that it was first taught by Chime Tsugphü,⁵ an earlier incarnation of Shenrab Miwo, who had received it directly from the deity Shenla Wökar. In any case, it is undoubtedly part of the teachings transmitted by the great master himself and later spread from Shang Shung into Tibet and other countries.

According to the most widespread classification of Shenrab Miwo's teaching, found in his extensive biography *Zijid*,⁶ all the teaching of Bön are contained in nine vehicles (*theg pa rim dgu*): four vehicles of the cause and five vehicles of the result. The four Bön of the cause are

1. the vehicle of the Shen of Cha (*Phywa gshen theg pa*), containing methods of divination, astrological calculations, medicine, and rituals to remove negativities;
2. the vehicle of the Shen of the Phenomenal Universe (*Snang gshen theg pa*), containing rites of protection, exorcism, and ransom;
3. the vehicle of the Shen of Magical Power (*'Phrul gshen theg pa*), containing wrathful rites of "liberating" destruction (*bsgral*) of evil entities; and
4. the vehicle of the Shen of Existence (*Srid gshen theg pa*), containing various funerary rites and methods dealing with the after-death.

The five Bön of the result are

5. the vehicle of the Virtuous (*Dge bsnyen theg pa*), containing rules of conduct for lay practitioners;
6. the vehicle of the Ascetic (*Drang srong theg pa*), containing rules of monastic discipline;
7. the vehicle of the White A (*A dkar theg pa*), containing tantric teachings dealing with transformation;
8. the vehicle of the Primordial Shen (*Ye gshen theg pa*), containing further and higher tantric teachings; and
9. the supreme, unsurpassable vehicle (*Yang rtse bla med theg pa*), containing Dzogchen teachings.

As we can see, the four vehicles of the cause mainly contain various kinds of ritual traditions and branches of knowledge such as medicine, astrology, divination, and so forth. The first four of the vehicles of the result contain the equivalent of the Buddhist sutric and tantric teachings. The last, the supreme vehicle, is Dzogchen.

Another traditional classification of Bön is the one known as the Four Portals and the Fifth, the Treasury (*Sgo bzhi mdzod lnga*). They are

1. Pönse (*Dpon gsas*), or the Masters, containing Dzogchen teachings;
2. Chabnag (*Chab nag*), or the Black Waters, dealing with rituals to remove negativities, methods of divination, astrology, and so forth;
3. Phenyul (*'Phan yul*), containing teachings on the Prajñaparamita;
4. Chabkar (*Chab dkar*), or the White Waters, containing tantric teachings; and
5. Dzö (*Mdzod*), or the Treasury, dealing with the essence of the previous four.[7]

According to the latter, Dzogchen teachings are identified as the Masters (*Dpon gsas*). In *The Treasury of Good Sayings* (*Legs bshad mdzod*), written by the renowned master Shardza Trashi Gyaltsen, concerning the first propagation of Bön teachings, we find the following subdivision of Dzogchen into three different systems:[8]

1. The Four Cycles of Transmission (*Bka' brgyud skor bzhi*), belonging to the Oral Transmission of Shang Shung (*Zhang zhung snyan rgyud*), the most ancient and authentic cycle of Dzogchen teachings, orally transmitted by a lineage of buddhas[9] and knowledge-holders to the master Tapihritsa and from the latter to Gyerpung

Nangzher Löpo, a historical personage who lived around the seventh or eighth century[10]

2. The Three Cycles of Propagation (*Bsgrags pa skor gsum*), comprising three cycles of teachings respectively spread in the realms of the devas, of human beings, and of the nagas. They were originally taught by the siddha Nyachen Lishu Tagring[11] and later rediscovered as termas, or textual treasures, in the eleventh century.

3. The Nine Lesser Cycles on the Mind (*Sems smad sde dgu*), a cycle of teachings better known as the Nine Hidden Cycles on the Enlightened Nature of Mind (*Byang chub sems gab pa dgu skor*), a terma rediscovered several times[12]

The present and more commonly accepted subdivision of the Dzogchen teachings, known as A Dzog Nyen Sum (*a rdzogs snyan gsum*), is the following:

1. The Instructions on the A (*A khrid*), teachings originating from Gongdzö Ritrö Chenpo (1038–1096)[13] and later arranged into a system by Druchen Gyalwa Yungdrung (1242–1296).[14] This system derives from the Nine Lesser Cycles of the Mind mentioned above.
2. The Dzogchen system, based on the *Yangtse Longchen*, a cycle of teachings attributed to Nyachen Lishu Tagring and rediscovered by Zhötön Ngödrub Tragpa in Lhodrag in 1088.[15] This system derives from the Three Cycles of Propagation mentioned above.
3. The Oral Transmission of Shang Shung, the most important cycle of Dzogchen teachings transmitted uninterruptedly from master to student up to the present day.

THE BASIC PRINCIPLES OF DZOGCHEN

The foundation of the Dzogchen view in the Bönpo tradition[16] is the notion of a primordial base (*gdod ma'i gzhi*), the original condition of existence, which is also called the all-ground (*kun gzhi*), the enlightened nature of mind as pure and total consciousness (*byang chub kyi sems*), and the basic space of existence (*bon nyid kyi dbyings*). This condition, ineffable and inconceivable, pervades equally every form of existence and transcends both samsara and nirvana. It is comparable to space or to a cloudless sky, whose boundaries cannot be found.

From this universal condition, in the same way as the sun rises in the sky, the individual consciousness of pure awareness (*rang rig, rig pa*)[17] arises, nondual awareness beyond subject and object, whose nature is the inseparability of emptiness (*stong pa*) and clarity (*gsal ba*). Just as the sun naturally manifests its rays, original consciousness is endowed with the energy function of primordial wisdom (*rig pa'i ye shes kyi rtsal*), which manifests in the appearance of five lights (*'od lnga*), archetypes of every form of existence of both samsara and nirvana.
The General View in Twelve Chapters says:

> Before the division into samsara and nirvana, not even the names "buddha" and "sentient being" exist. The supreme consciousness, universal source, pervades all without being touched by any limitation. According to whether the nature of this source is understood or not, it becomes the basis of both buddhas and sentient beings. Just as the sun shines in the clear, immaterial space, although the essence of the mind is nothing whatsoever, it manifests clearly in manifold ways without interruption. In the same way that, for example, luminous rays spread in every direction from the disk of the sun, the totally luminous self-awareness possesses rays of light.[18]

If there is recognition (*rtogs pa, rig pa*) of this manifestation as the projection of one's own mind (*rang snang*), that is, the natural emanation of one's energy (*rtsal*), the state of enlightenment is attained in the self-perfected or naturally existing (*lhun grub*)[19] three kayas or dimensions (*sku gsum*).[20] They are dharmakaya, the dimension of the essential condition (*bon sku*); sambhogakaya, the dimension of perfection (*rdzogs sku*); and nirmanakaya, the dimension of manifestation or emanation (*sprul sku*).
The General View in Twelve Chapters says:

> Although this is the condition of the original all-ground, there is a great difference in whether it is recognized or not. For example, just as the darkness naturally vanishes when the light of the sun appears in the sky, when there is recognition the kayas and pure dimensions of enlightenment arise self-perfected and without any effort. Sentient beings who have no understanding are similar to a light gone out in the dark. Because of not recognizing, for

sentient beings the illusory vision of the experience of suffering arises.[21]

And:

> At that time for [the primordial buddha] Samantabhadra,[22] without having performed a grain of sesame's worth of virtue, the wisdom of self-originated awareness manifests through the simultaneous arising of his sharp awareness. When the natural light of the energy of awareness arises in all directions, he understands it to be the energy manifestation of [his own] awareness.[23]

If there is no recognition (*ma rig pa*) of the real nature, because of mistaken or illusory considerations (*'khrul pa*) concerning what is perceived as something outside, separated from oneself (*gzhan snang*), wisdom is obscured. In this dualistic condition of the mind (*sems* or *blo*), the dimension of samsara or transmigration appears in the six states of existence or classes of beings (*rigs drug*).[24]

The General View in Twelve Chapters says:

> Without having committed a single hair of negative actions, sentient beings of the three worlds are deceived by the original base. When the five lights of the purity of one's vision appear, through the simultaneous arising of ignorance caused by dull faculties, they do not recognize them as their own vision but consider them as objects outside. When the thoughts of ego-grasping become bigger and coarser, mind and mental events, and wrong ideas manifest so that the self-appearing five lights are perceived as outer objects. As a consequence the vision of light is destroyed, and the five lights are conceived as fire, water, earth, air, and space. The yellow is perceived as earth, the green as air, the red as fire, the blue as water, the white as space. With the delusion of an outer dimension, just as a lake freezes and becomes ice, the illusory vision of ignorance is naturally formed. Believing the illusory vision to be a real object, from the pure essences of the five lights the illusory material body is produced as the impure part.[25]

Self-liberation (*rang grol*) is the essence of Dzogchen practice, based on the main point of continuing the state of instant presence which represents the authentic nature of the mind introduced by the teacher. Unlike the sutra path where the emotions have to be abandoned or the tantric path where they have to be transformed, the Dzogchen practitioner, without rejecting or accepting them, recognizes them as the energy of one's own primordial state and is no longer conditioned or hindered by them. In this way, thoughts and emotions dissolve by themselves or self-liberate without any effort.

The aim of Dzogchen practice is the stable recognition of one's real nature of nondual, pure awareness or instant presence, and the complete reabsorbing of the energy originally emanated from this state into the basic space of existence (*dbyings*),[26] with the realization of the naturally perfected three kayas, or in some cases, of the rainbow body of light (*'ja' lus*), a special achievement for a Dzogchen practitioner.[27]

TRENPA SERDAM: THE GOLDEN TEACHING OF TRENPA NAMKHA

The *Trenpa Serdam*, or *The Golden Teaching of Trenpa Namkha*, is a collection of Dzogchen teachings put into writing by Shense Lhaje (Gshen sras lha rje or Gshen gsas lha rje),[28] a Bönpo master who lived in the thirteenth century. The title of the entire collection derives from its main cycle of teaching, originally taught by the great siddha Trenpa Namkha, one of the most important figures in Bön history, to his son Tsewang Rigdzin, and from the latter transmitted to Shense Lhaje. The remaining texts in the collection contain autobiographical stories and teachings received from other masters or composed by Shense Lhaje himself.

In the subdivision of the Bönpo canon by Nyima Tendzin, examined by Per Kvaerne in his 1974 article "The Canon of the Tibetan Bönpos," this text is classified in the secret section of the Tengyur,[29] with the title *The Golden Teaching on Dzogchen* (*Rdzogs chen gser gdams*). It belongs to the category of *nyengyü*, or oral transmission,[30] a term that refers to scriptures orally revealed through visions or dreams[31] by realized beings such as knowledge-holders, siddhas, and dakinis, female manifestations of the energy of the primordial state. This kind of sacred literature began to appear in the Bönpo tradition around the twelfth century, two centuries after the rediscovery of termas, or treasures, had started.[32] *Termas* are texts or objects hidden in a particular period of time due to various reasons such as the unsuitability of the circumstances for spreading a specific teaching, religious persecutions, and so forth, which are then rediscovered, even many centuries later, by means of predictions and instructions delivered to specially destined and qualified individuals known as *tertöns*, or treasure-discoverers.

Terma scriptures, whose importance is paramount also in the Ancient or Nyingma tradition of Tibetan Buddhism,[33] are broadly subdivided into two categories: earth treasures (*sa gter*), sacred objects or texts discovered in rocks and other material places, and mind treasures (*dgongs gter*), teachings that gush out spontaneously from the expanse of contemplation of the tertön's mind. The latter category is very close to that of the oral transmission in the Bönpo tradition, and it is difficult to establish a clear line of demarcation between the two, inasmuch as there are various forms of transmissions of the texts in both of them.[34]

Traditionally the first text belonging to the category of "oral transmission" is considered to have been transmitted by Trenpa Namkha to Gyermi Nyiwö.[35] Bönpo literature contains a large number of these texts, such as, for example, the *Zijid* (*Gzi brjid*), the largest biography of Shenrab Miwo.

The main authors and sources of this kind of treasure text are a number of knowledge-holders extremely important in the history of Bön, such as Trenpa Namkha, his son Tsewang Rigdzin, Tongyung Thuchen, and Mutsa Gyerme, all of whom were active in the task of spreading and translating the Bönpo scriptures from the language of Shang Shung into Tibetan, in a period of time broadly stretching from the first propagation of Bön to the kingdom of Trisong Deutsen (742–797) in the eighth century.[36]

Trenpa Namkha

According to oral information provided by Lopön Tenzin Namdak, three different masters with the name Trenpa Namkha have existed. The first was miraculously born in a lotus flower in Tagzig, a semilegendary land that is the birthplace of Bön according to traditional sources.[37] There is no historical information about him, and his name is mainly found in ritual texts.

The second Trenpa Namkha, from Shang Shung, is the most relevant in Bön, and the one who transmitted the *Trenpa Serdam*. He was active during the time of the eighth Tibetan king Trigum Tsenpo and is considered to be still alive in his rainbow body.

The third Trenpa Namkha was born in southern Tibet at the time of the Tibetan king Trisong Deutsen. According to a well-known anecdote, at the time of the persecution of Bön, when he was twenty-six years of age, he preferred to shave his head and wear the Buddhist monks' robe rather than go into exile, affirming that there is no difference between Bön and Buddhism inasmuch as they have the same aim of attaining enlightenment.[38] He is also counted among the twenty-five disciples of Padmasambhava.

A summary of the second Trenpa Namkha's life follows.[39]

Trenpa Namkha was born in the Garuda Valley or Khyunglung, one of the capitals of the ancient kings of Shang Shung,[40] in the town called Deden Wöntro, in the castle Shelle Dzongphug. His father was Gyungyar Mukhö and his mother Chatsün Kungma. He was the only son and was called Gyungyar Khöpung, and also Trenpa Namkha (Sky of Memory), by virtue of his capacity to remember five hundred past lives.

When he was thirteen he said to his parents, "In my previous life my father was called was Tsensher Gyerchen and my mother Luza Thingtsün. My name was Trigyer Tongnam. I studied four hundred thousand Böns, I applied the knowledge of the *Treasury Source of Existence* (*Srid pa'i mdzod phug*),[41] made the *Kha Long Ying*[42] of Dzogchen my ultimate goal, and practiced the Khangying cycle of deities.[43] Now I am going to resume my practice from former lives. On the fifteenth day of the first month of spring, the eight scholars[44] will be examined by the learned Thami Theke.[45] I also want to go there to be examined."

The eight scholars then authorized him to practice the tantric cycle of Chipung related to the teachings on the Shitro, or Peaceful and Wrathful Manifestations,[46] and he did so in the place known as Nyigong Yungdrung. Thus he attained the clear knowledge of the essence of all the outer, inner, and secret tantras of Bön, as if looking into a crystal ball in the palm of his hand.

Afterward, at the time of the first persecution of Bön by the eighth Tibetan king Trigum Tsenpo (around the first century), Trenpa Namkha was particularly active in preserving and hiding a large number of Bönpo texts. After Trigum Tsenpo died, his son and heir Pude Kungyal confessed in front of the Bönpos and resumed relations with them, especially with Trenpa Namkha, of whom he requested a special Bön teaching as his personal practice. Trenpa Namkha transmitted to him the Chipung cycle.

Then Trenpa Namkha went to practice in the Yarlha Shampo cave in central Tibet. As he was having no success in his spiritual progress, one day he invoked intensely the lineage masters from the dharmakaya buddha Samantabhadra to his own teacher. Early the next morning he heard a voice predicting that he would find help in the town of Tagzig. He was amazed at hearing this, transformed himself into a young garuda bird and flew to Tagzig where he met a Bönpo who told him, "Son, if you want to attain spiritual realization, you have first of all to find a dakini as mudra (consort),[47] otherwise you will not succeed. Therefore, go and look for her!" and pointed his finger to the four directions. He was the knowledge-holder Khanam Kyolpo.

Then Trenpa Namkha headed for the eight charnel grounds searching for a consort. After a long period of ascetic practices, the siddhas and the deities of the tantric cycle of the Peaceful and Wrathful Manifestations appeared to him, and, among many other signs of spiritual accomplishment, an eye appeared miraculously on his left foot.[48]

Afterward he traveled to India, to the town of Bhisha, where he thought he would find a consort for his practice. Then he heard a cuckoo saying from the sky, "Great Lama! If you want to teach the teachings of Shenrab, you must first of all search for a blessed mudra called Norzangmo who lives in the Utpala Dzepa charnel ground, and for a mudra of action, the daughter of a brahmin, whose mother is Kunga Zangmo. Her name is Nyima Wöden."[49]

Thus, he went to the Utpala Dzepa charnel ground and found the dakini Norzangmo, whom he took as his blessed mudra. When he went back to Bhisha, on his way he met seven girls walking together, and the last of them told him, "Great Lama! You and I have a spiritual connection from former lives to practice karmamudra. I will serve you, but please bless me, as I am a dakini of action and haven't yet reached the level of wisdom."

Trenpa Namkha blessed her, gave her initiations, and took her as his consort. Later she bore twin children. The first was white in color and peaceful, and enjoyed being alone. He was called Yungdrung Tönsal or Tsewang Rigdzin,[50] and was a famous siddha in the Bönpo tradition. The second was red in color, with a fierce face, and was called Padma Thongdrol. He was also known as Padmasambhava in the Buddhist tradition.[51]

Shense Lhaje

No biography of Shense Lhaje has ever appeared, and we can have no certainty that it was ever written. In the recently published Bönpo Katen there is a small text called *The Lives of Wangden Shense (Dbang ldan gshen gsas kyi skyes tshogs)*,[52] but it contains only a list of the previous rebirths of the master and no actual details of his life. We can find biographical details scattered here and there in his works and rediscovered texts, as he is considered an important tertön in the Bön tradition. He is also known as Kode Phagpa Yungdrung Yeshe (Go lde[53] 'phags pa g.yung drung ye shes), Kode Phag Gom Yungdrung Yeshe (Go lde 'phags sgom g.yung drung ye shes), Wangden Shense (Dbang ldan gshen sras), Nyö Nyima Sherab (Gnyos nyi ma shes rab), and Horshig Lhaje (Hor shig lha rje). His importance as a tertön is unquestionable, as he is numbered among the hundred main Bönpo tertöns.[54]

Since in his autobiographical writings he styles himself "the beggar from Ling,"[55] we can assume that he was born in Ling or Lingtsang, the ancient kingdom celebrated in the Gesar epic, which in the thirteenth century included a large part of Kham but was later incorporated into Derge. His birth year has been given as 1215,[56] which corresponds to the Wood-Pig year of the fourth rabjung, or sixty-year cycle, and he probably spent part of his life in the Meshö area of Derge,[57] since this is the place where the first half of his visionary encounters take place, while in the second half another place, called Lag, is mentioned.[58] We have no knowledge of the teachers he met and followed, although he states the exact time when he was introduced to the Great Vehicle of Bön:

> Having left incomplete the benefit for others, I had to enter again and again the womb of a mother endowed with material senses, and I took the body of a beggar in this life, like a nonhuman being. Until I was twenty-one my thoughts were only for samsaric things. When I was twenty-two I was introduced to the supreme vehicle, and as a result the practice I had done in the past reawakened. When I reached twenty-three years of age I concretely realized my state of instant presence, and bliss became continuous.[59]

As we can see, he does not mention the name of any human teacher but simply states that he had already practiced the spiritual path in his previous lives. When he tells about how he resumed it in this life, he particularly mentions the special connection he had with a siddha of the past, Tongyung Thuchen:[60]

> When I met Tongyung, king of the knowledge-holders, doors opened in every direction through his kindness and all the sugatas[61] of the mind lineage, the knowledge-holders, the deities, and the mother dakinis gave me advice, showed me their faces, and bestowed upon me the supreme and common siddhis,[62] and the outer, inner and secret initiations of Bön.[63]

It is certain that he achieved realization through the Dzogchen path, as he writes in one of his visionary accounts:

> I am a beggar and a liar who knows nothing.
> Without looking anywhere, I recognized my real state.
> Without meditating, I achieved concrete realization.
> Without seeking, I found the precious jewel.
> Without applying any practice, I attained the great aim.
> Without embarking on a journey, I reached my final destination.[64]

And also:

> For me, a stupid and uncontrived person,
> The karmic traces of my practice in former lives have now reawakened.
> Without studying the scriptures of Bön
> I resolved the outer and inner doubts in my mind.
> Without enduring hardship on the mountains
> I realized the root of the unborn essence.
> Without exerting myself in the practice
> I met all the knowledge-holders and dakinis.[65]

As is the case with most tertöns, it seems that he was not a fully ordained monk: he often styles himself as *tsünchung*, a term that might imply only the observance of basic precepts, but we do not find details of any of his consorts, except the nonhuman dakini Nyima Wöden, about whom he says in his visionary accounts:

> Nyima Wöden, sovereign lady of all dakinis,
> From you, compassionate rays spread in all regions,
> Your face is white and luminous like the full moon . . .

Your body has no specific form, you can show any miraculous transformation.

By virtue of past karmic connections, you have been my secret consort.[66]

Many aspects of his life and traits of his character are clearly shown in his autobiographical account *Visionary Encounters with Knowledge-Holders and Dakinis*, an example of a type of Tibetan literature that is widespread in the biographies and visionary accounts of tertöns and highly realized masters.[67]

In the first part of his stories, we find a young Tibetan Khampa busy grazing his donkey and taking care of other ordinary duties. At the same time, he experiences a dimension beyond dualistic concepts in his encounters with various knowledge-holders and dakinis, who spur him into pursuing real knowledge of his natural state by abandoning worldly life and devoting himself to meditation.

In the second part we find a mature master with a following of students, to whom he bestows teachings and initiations without partiality. Although sometimes he pays homage to the "root guru" (*rtsa ba'i bla ma*) at the beginning of his writings, there is no mention of any of his human teachers, and he only names the knowledge-holders and dakinis with whom he was continuously in contact for all of his life. We have the names of some of his students though, as they are mentioned in the colophons of his works.[68] His main student seems to have been Khyungpo Nangchen Tragpa,[69] as his name is often given as the first recipient of many of Shense Lhaje's termas. Moreover, in his autobiographical account of past lives mentioned above, Shense Lhaje at the end of the list of his previous incarnations says:

I am Shense Lhaje, and extracted important termas in Eastern Tibet. Together with one called Khyungpo Tragpa, who was blessed by great scholars and translators, I guided beings through compassionate energy and turned the wheel of Bön of the Great Vehicle.[70]

Another direct student that we find in the colophon of many texts of the Katen edition of the *Trenpa Serdam* is Sherab Pal, but I have not been able to identify him further.

Shense Lhaje's rediscoveries belong to the textual treasures of Kham,[71] although he is also accredited with termas from a rock in northern Tsang, central Tibet. He is traditionally recognized as one of the emanations of Trenpa Namkha, as declared by the great master himself in his eight-volume biography:[72]

> My emanation will have the name Wangden Shense.[73]

However, the earliest historical source in which Shense Lhaje appears, under the name Wangden Shense, is the *Register of the Lineage of Existence* (*Srid pa rgyud kyi kha byang*), attributed to Trenpa Namkha and rediscovered by Khöpo Lodrö Thogme (born in 1280) in 1310, where, among many other realized masters, his birth and role as a tertön is predicted. In this book Trenpa Namkha declares:

> A supreme emanation of mine will appear
> Who will be called Wangden Shense.
> With uninterrupted conduct like an ornament,
> Through the Bön of secret series he will guide beings to liberation.[74]

The History of the Origin of the Teaching, written by the Bönpo master Kundrol Tragpa (born in 1700), mentions the tertön under the name Kode Nyima Sherab (Go bde nyi ma shes rab) and gives more details about his rediscoveries:

> Kode Nyima Sherab, from the Karu stupa in China (*rgya yi mchod rten ka ru*) and from Kophu Ragtrom in Kham discovered *The Supreme Subjugator for Taming the Za* [*Class of Beings*] (*Gza' dul gtso mchog rnam 'joms*), *The Long and Short Versions of the Dharanis of Nampar Gyalwa* (*Rnam par rgyal ba'i gzungs che chung*), *The Sadhana of Namgyal According to the Chinese System* (*Rnam rgyal rgya nag ma'i sgrub pa*), [and] ten different tantric cycles. He received *The Golden Teaching of Trenpa* (*Dran pa gser gdams*), the *Bhumis and Paths* (*Sa lam*),[75] and so forth as orally transmitted Dzogchen. Concerning his Buddhist discoveries, from the place known as Chagöshang he extracted the *Vaishravana Bearing a Red Spear* (*Rnam sras mdung dmar can*) and so forth, as explained in the histories of Buddhist termas.[76]

In the *Treasury of Good Sayings* by Shardza Trashi Gyaltsen, Shense Lhaje is mentioned in connection with the rediscovery of the two ritual cycles pertaining to the manifestation of Shenrab Miwo known as Nampar Gyalwa, or Namgyal. He writes:

> The history of the rediscovery of the *Chinese Cycle of Namgyal* (*Rnam rgyal rgya nag ma*)[77] and *Shang Shung Cycle of Namgyal* (*Rnam rgyal zhang zhung ma*) has four parts.
>
> First, how they were hidden. At the time of the decline of the teaching, the *Shang Shung Cycle of Namgyal* was hidden into treasure by Gyimtsa Machung[78] at Ragtrom. The *Chinese Cycle* was hidden by the Chinese Legtang Mangpo at the Karu stupa in China and other places.
>
> Second, how they were extracted. Trenpa Namkha said:
>
> > A supreme emanation of mine will appear,
> > He will be called Wangden Shense.
> > He will display a conduct of nonattachment
> > And through the Bön of secret treasures will guide beings to liberation.[79]
>
> The prophesied tertön Kode Phagpa, a.k.a. Wangde Shense Lhaje and Nyö Nyima Sherab, extracted [the two cycles] from the two places [mentioned above] and translated them from the pure language of the devas into Tibetan, and finalized them in the secret cave of Kebu Naro. He also extracted the *shang* cymbal[80] called Trilo Namdrag and many other objects.
>
> Third, the Bön textual content. The texts extracted from the Karu stupa in China were the *Dharanis in Fifty-Five Chapters* (*Gzungs sde le'u lnga bcu rtsa lnga pa*) and *The Short Sutra* (*Mdo thung*). The texts discovered in Kham at Dori Kangkar and Ragtrom (Rag phrom) were the *Root Sadhana of Namgyal* (*Rnam rgyal rtsa sgrub*), the *Qualities of Auspiciousness* (*Bkra shis yon tan*), *The Averting of Epidemics* (*Nad yams bzlog pa*), *The Accomplishment of Fortune and Prosperity* (*Phywa g.yang gi sgrub pa*), *The Supreme Subjugator for Taming the Za* [Class of Beings] (*Gza' 'dul gtso mchog rnam 'joms*), [and] ten different tantric cycles.
>
> Moreover, from the rock of Yungdrung Sengchong in Northern Tsang he extracted the *Abridged Scripture of the Sadhana*

> *for Accomplishing the Unsurpassable State* (*Bla med go 'phang sgrub thabs kyi mdo rgyud*), *The Immortal Vast Expanse in Twenty-Eight Chapters* (*G.yung drung klong rgyas le'u nyi shu rtsa brgyad pa*), *The All-Knowing* (*Kun rigs* or *Kun rig*), *The Asceticism of the Shen* (*Gshen gyi dka' thub*), and other [texts]. As scriptures of oral transmission he received the Dzogchen cycle of *The Golden Teaching of Trenpa* (*Dran pa gser gdams*) and many others.
>
> Fourth, the transmission. Kode Phagpa transmitted them to Khyungpo Nangchen Tragpa, and to his nephew Pönge. The latter two transmitted them to Khyungpo Sögyal, and thus they became widespread.[81]

In *The History of the Teaching of the Immortal Bön* written by the Bönpo scholar Palden Tsultrim (1902–1973), we read:

> Concerning the cycle of *Namgyal* extracted from the rock of Ragtrom in Kham and from the Karu stupa in China, first of all the *Shang Shung Cycle* was hidden by De Gyimtsa in the place Doti Ragtrom, while the *Chinese Cycle* was hidden by Legtang Mangpo in the Karu stupa. Later, from both these treasure places, Kode Phagpa, also known as Wangden Shense Lhaje and Nyö Nyima Sherab, an individual praised as a supreme emanation of Trenpa Namkha, extracted the *Great Dharanis* (*Gzungs chen*) and the *Short Sutra* (*Mdo thung*) of both terma cycles, the ritual text of *The Accomplishment of Fortune* (*G.yang sgrub*), *The Root Sadhana of Namgyal, The Supreme Subjugator* (*Gtso mchog rnam 'joms*), [and] ten different tantric cycles.
>
> As material termas, he discovered the golden *shang* cymbal [known as] Trilo Namdrag, and from the boulder of Ko he extracted the *Sutra of the Fortunate Kalpa* (*Skal bzang gi mdo*), *Amending Disagreements with the Sadag [Class of Beings]* (*Sa bdag 'khrug bcos*), and other texts. Moreover, from the Chong rock in Northern Tsang he discovered *The Abridged Scripture of the Sadhana for Accomplishing the Unsurpassable State* (*Bla med go 'phang sgrub thabs kyi mdo rgyud*), *The Immortal Vast Expanse in Twenty-Eight Chapters* (*G.yung drung klong rgyas le'u nyi shu rtsa brgyad pa*), *The All-Knowing* (*Kun rig*), *The Asceticism of the*

Shen (*Gshen gyi dka' thub*), and so forth. They were all transmitted to Khyungpo Nangchen Tragpa.⁸²

Concerning the cycle of *Namgyal* we read further in the *Lineage of Transmission of the Kangyur*:

> The lineage of transmission of the *Great Dharani of Namgyal* in fifty-five chapters obtained as a siddhi by the nirmanakaya Wangden Shense is as follows. The victorious and omniscient lord of the teaching [Shenrab] transmitted it to the four qualified students.⁸³ They transmitted it to Mucho Demdrug, Mutsa Trahe, Ghuhu Li Parya, Lhadag Nagdrol, Legtang Mangpo, Serthog Chejam, and De Gyimtsa Machung. Then the teaching was put into terma, and later Kode Phagpa, emanation of De Bön [Gyimtsa Machung], opened the door of the treasure at Ko Ragtrom, and transmitted it to Khyungpo Nangchen Tragpa.⁸⁴

And concerning the *Short Sutra* quoted above:

> The lineage of transmission of the [cycle] known as the *Short Sutra of Praise and Homage to Namgyal*, including the *Series of Dharani of the Precious Necklace* (*Gzungs sde rin chen phreng ba*), offered by Kongtse to the Teacher [Shenrab] is the following. The Buddha, lord of the teaching, transmitted it to the four qualified students in the temple of Karnag Trasal.... They transmitted it to Gyaltheb Mucho Demdrug and others. The latter transmitted it to the scholar from Tagzig Mutsa Trahe, Guhu Lipar Ya, and Trithog Partsa. These three transmitted it to the scholar from India Lhadag Ngagdrol, to the scholar from China Legtsang Mangpo, and to the scholar from Trom Serthog Chejam. These three transmitted it to Gyimtsa Machung, Mupung Saltang, Chetsa Kharbu, and Shari Uchen.... Then when the teaching was declining, the Chinese Legtang Mangpo hid it inside the Karu stupa, and later Kode Phagpa, alias Wangden Shense, alias Nyö Nyima Sherab, extracted it from the treasure, and in the secret cave of Kephu Naro translated it from the pure language of the devas into Tibetan, and transmitted it to Khyungpo Nangchen Tragpa.⁸⁵

Concerning the rediscovery of the *Supreme Subjugator* (*Gtso mchog rnam 'joms*), in the *History of Bön Lineages*, in the section on the transmission of the outer tantras we read:

> *The Tantras of the Wrathful All-Subjugator* (*Kun 'joms khro bo'i rgyud*) were taught by Sangwa Düpa to Taglha Menbar and the rest of the supreme six,[86] who transmitted them to the twelve lineage descendants,[87] who in turn transmitted them to the four scholars. [The four scholars] transmitted them to Lhadag Ngagdro, who transmitted them to Serthog Chejam, who in turn transmitted them to Legtang Mangpo.[88] The latter hid them in the black stupa in China. Wangden Shense, having been prophesied as the owner of the terma, opened the treasure and transmitted it to Khyungpo Tragpa Gyaltsen.[89]

Concerning the discovery of the *Kalzang* or *Fortunate Kalpa* cycle, also known as *Kode Kalzang*, the *Lineage of Transmission of the Kangyur* says:

> The lineage of transmission of the *Sutra of the Fortunate Kalpa for Saving Sentient Beings* (*Bskal bzang 'gro ba 'dren pa'i mdo*) in twenty chapters, a terma rediscovered by Kode [Phagpa], is the following. When the omniscient and all-victorious Shenrab Miwo reached the age of seven thousand, he taught it to a retinue of bodhisattvas[90] at Trimön Gyalzhe and Shampo Lhatse. The compiler of the teaching, Azhang Sangthub, transmitted it to the regent Mucho Demdrug.[91] The latter transmitted it to Mutsa Trahe, Trithog Partsa, and Guhu Li Parya. These three transmitted it to the Indian Lhadag Ngagdro, to the Chinese Legtang Mangpo, and to Serthog Chejam from Trom. These [three] transmitted it to Tongyung Thuchen from Shang Shung, who transmitted it to Shari Uchen, Gyimtsa Machung, and Chetsa Kharbu. When the Teaching was declining, thanks to the aspirations of these [masters] it was entrusted to a guardian of the treasures and hidden. Then, as it says in the prophetic guide of the terma, "One called Kode Phagpa, emanation of Tongyung Thuchen, will open the door of the treasure from the Divine Boulder Similar to a Yak (*lha ri pha 'ong g.yag 'dra*)." When the time became ripe, Kode Phag Gom Yungdrung Yeshe, having been

instructed by the *walmos*[92] of wisdom, extracted it from the treasure and transcribed it without mixing it with human words.[93]

The colophon of the terma also gives a date for this discovery:

This was extracted from treasure by Kode Phag Gom Yungdrung Yeshe on the fourth day of the third Horse month in the Fire-Dragon [year].[94]

The Fire-Dragon likely corresponds to the year 1256, considering that Shense Lhaje entered the spiritual path at the age of twenty-two, that is, in 1236.

The ritual cycle *Amending Disagreements with the Sadag [Class of Beings]* (*Sa bdag 'khrug bcos*) quoted by Palden Tsultrim is generally known as the *Sadag Cycle of Kode* (*Sa bdag go lde ma*). It was obtained as a siddhi from the Yak Boulder of Ko (*go yi pha bong g.yag*).[95]

Concerning the rediscovery of textual treasures in northern Tsang,[96] related by both Shardza Trashi Gyaltsen and Palden Tsultrim, the only text presently contained in the Bönpo canon is *The Asceticism of the Shen* (*Gshen gyi dka' thub*), which we find in the Katen under the title *The Asceticism of Shenrab, the Removal of Emotions* (*gShen rab kyi dka' thub nyon mongs drung byin*).[97] Regarding its transmission we read:

De Gyimtsa Machung hid it in the mountain of Yundrung Senge Chog in northern Tsangpo. Then the bodhisattva Kode Phagpa extracted it from the treasure and spread it in Tibet.[98]

Of the remaining three rediscoveries, the *Abridged Scripture of the Sadhana for Accomplishing the Unsurpassable State* (*Bla med go 'phang sgrub thabs kyi mdo rgyud*) is only found in the Bönpo canon as a ritual cycle belonging to the sutra section of the Kangyur revealed by the tertön Sekun Ratna (tenth century).[99] *The Immortal Vast Expanse in Twenty-Eight Chapters* (*G.yung drung klong rgyas le'u nyi shu rtsa brgyad pa*) could be identified as the *Mdo g.yung drung klong rgyas* rediscovered by Trangje Tsünpa Sermig (eleventh century).[100] Related to *The All-Knowing* (*Kun rig*) cycle, we have only a very short text in the Katen, *The Opening of the Mandala of the Deity of Fire* (*Dkyil 'khor me lha'i sgo dbye*), composed by Shense Lhaje and probably associated with his own terma cycle.[101] We have therefore strong reason to believe that these texts are no longer extant, as there is no trace of them in the Bönpo canon, nor in the historical books dealing with the transmissions of the teachings.

As mentioned above in Kundrol Tragpa's text, Shense Lhaje is considered to have discovered Buddhist termas as well. In the above-mentioned eight-volume biography of Trenpa Namkha, in the chapter dealing with a prophecy of future treasure-discoverers, Shense Lhaje is identified with the Buddhist tertön Nyalpa Nyima Sherab:

> The bodhisattva known as Kode Phagpa and also as Nyalpa Nyima Sherab will obtain from the Keru (*ke ru*) stupa and from the place of Ke Ragtram (*ke rag phram*) the cycles of the *Supreme Subjugator* (*Gtso mchog rnam 'joms*) and *The Taming of the Za* (*Gza' 'dul*), the *Sadhana of the Great Dharani of Shenrab Namgyal* (*Gshen rab rnam rgyal gzungs chen sgrub pa*), and ten different tantric cycles of Bön. As oral transmission he will obtain the Dzogchen upadesha of *The Golden Teaching* (*Gser gdams*) and many extraordinary Bön cycles by Trenpa [Namkha]. As Buddhist termas, from the treasury of Chagöshang he will obtain the [cycle of] the *Most Secret Red Vaishravana Bearing a Red Spear* (*Rnam sras dmar po yang gsang mdung dmar po*) and the *Treasury Gate for Fulfilling All Wishes* (*Dgos 'dod kun 'byung gter sgo*).[102]

This identification is also asserted in a history book by Jamyang Khyentse Wangpo (1820–1892), who writes:

> Concerning Nyalpa Nyima Sherab, in the Bön tradition he is known as the nirmanakaya Kode Phagpa or Wangden Shense Lhaje. He discovered the Chinese cycle of Namgyal from the white rock of Kepu Ragtram in Kham, and other texts.[103]

If we examine the biographical details of this Buddhist tertön as given in the *History of the Hundred Tertöns* by Jamgön Kongtrul Lodrö Thaye (1813–1899) and other histories such as the *History of the Dharma* written by Guru Trashi[104] (eighteenth–nineteenth century), Nyalpa Nyima Sherab was a master active in Nyal, southern Tibet, and mainly involved in the Yogatantra tradition. Jamgön Kongtrul writes:

Nyalpa Nyima Sherab was born in Nyal, and was a student of Phagpa Sherab, the translator from Sangkar. Having trained in Yogatantra, he was extremely learned in this tradition. He established Dharma centers in both upper and lower Nyal, and installed images of Vairochana in many temples. As he turned the wheel of Dharma of the teachings of Yogatantra, and so forth, during his time the cycles of Yogatantra became exceptionally widespread. Thus he was of great benefit and kindness to the Yogatantra teachings. He made Tsangpo Dong his main residence. From the extension wall of the Chagöshong temple he discovered an image hidden there in the past by the great minister Lhazang Lupal, and at the same time a large silk banner with [a figure of] Vaishravana known as Jongyulma, and the sadhana cycles of *Vaishravana Bearing a Red Spear* (*Rnam sras mdung dmar can gyi sku skor*), whose transmission has remained uninterrupted until today.[105]

Now, Shense Lhaje was a Khampa mainly involved with Dzogchen teachings, while Nyalpa Nyima Sherab lived in southern Tibet and was a protagonist of the Yogatantra tradition, one of the lower or outer tantras having little in common with Dzogchen. Therefore, it is difficult to accept this identification, although Kundrol Tragpa himself, who is our earliest source at the moment, gives the same terma cycle as one of the Buddhist discoveries of Shense Lhaje. Probably the identification arose because of the name Nyima Sherab, which is one of the names, preceded by Nyö (Gnyos, a Tibetan clan), of Shense Lhaje, while in the case of the Buddhist tertön, it is preceded by Nyalpa (hailing from Nyal). We would also have a problem in the chronology, since Shense Lhaje is supposed to have lived in the thirteenth century while Nyalpa Nyima Sherab, being a student of the translator Phagpa Sherab (eleventh century), should be considered to have been active in the eleventh and/or twelfth centuries.[106]

Another dubious identification is the one that would consider Shense Lhaje and the tertön Tsenden Trungmu Hara (Mtshan ldan Drung mu ha ra, also known as Wer ya drung mu), to be one and the same person.

One example of this identification is to be found in the volume *Drung mu gcod chen* published in Dolanji in 1973,[107] where the name Shense Lhaje is given as the treasure-revealer instead of Trungmu Hara. The reason might be that Trungmu Hara is the Shang Shung equivalent of Yungdrung Yeshe, a name by which Trungmu Hara sometimes appears in the colophon of some of his rediscoveries, and that Yungdrung Yeshe is also one of the names of Shense Lhaje. However, in the case of Shense Lhaje, it seems to be always preceded by Kode Phagpa (Go lde 'phags pa g.yung drung ye shes, or Go lde 'phags sgom g.yung drung ye shes). This confusion is also evident in the *Lineage of Transmission of the Kangyur*[108] where the author, while discussing the transmission of the *Kode Kalzang* (*Go lde bskal bzang*), writes:

> [Shense Lhaje] had many worthy disciples for this terma, the chief among them being Kyura [Chura] Wözer Gyaltsen, to whom he transmitted it.[109]

Kyura Wözer Gyaltsen was the main student of Trungmu Hara and had no historically acknowledged relation with Shense Lhaje. Moreover, the text continues by quoting a list of masters belonging to the lineage of Trungmu Hara, none of whom are ever listed in the transmission lineage of Shense Lhaje. This is probably due to the fact that in the Bönpo Kangyur there exists another terma cycle of Kalzang known as *Trungmu Kalzang* (*Drung mu bskal bzang*), discovered by Trungmu Hara.[110]

In any case, in Bön histories the two personages are always treated separately, and also their discoveries do not match. For example, Palden Tsultrim writes:

> Tsenden Trungmu Hara was born in Kham from the Shang clan. He followed the Togden Yeshe Sangthal and others, had visions of Tongyung Thuchen and other knowledge-holders and dakinis. He developed many Bön teachings of sutra and tantra such as the oral transmission of the Bön Chöd, and set on the path of maturation and liberation many fortunate [students]. His student was Kyura Wözer Gyaltsen.[111]

Moreover in the *Lamp That Clarifies the Origin of the Chöd Teachings* (*Gcod gdams sngon byung lo rgyus don gsal sgron ma*), a text about the history of the discovery of this cycle of Chöd teachings, Trungmu Hara himself states:

> In this life when I was six I studied writing and calculating, and having desire to follow the Bön of the Great Vehicle, I was kindly accepted as a student by my master and experienced the meaning

of the secret mind. When I was twelve I started a retreat, and I also had many dreams and signs.... Once the Lama Tongyung [Thuchen] arrived in the guise of a yogin and showed me the mirror which gives liberation by sight of the provisional meaning and of the real meaning of the mind.[112]

As we can see, this directly contradicts Shense Lhaje's own statement quoted above that he was immersed in the thoughts of samsara until the age of twenty-one, and that he started his spiritual path at the age of twenty-two, although in both cases it is the siddha Tongyung Thuchen who acts as a doorway for spiritual awakening.

We have no exact record concerning the circumstances and the year in which Shense Lhaje passed away. According to the *Lives of Wangden Shense* (*Dbang ldan gshen gsas kyi skyes tshogs*), Shense Lhaje died on the fourth day of the last month of autumn, the ninth month of the Tibetan calendar of a Dragon year, which could be identified as 1268, taking the year as Earth-Dragon, one year after he wrote his *Visionary Encounters*. In this case, he would have been fifty-three. However, only the animal of the year is given and not the corresponding element, and therefore the same Dragon year could be identified as 1280, 1292, and so forth, following the twelve-year astrological cycle.

Here follows a tentative chronology of Shense Lhaje's life:

1215 born in the Wood-Pig year of the fourth rabjung
1236 entered the spiritual path in the Fire-Monkey year
1242 received *The Lamp of One's Instant Presence* (*Rang rig sgron me*) from Trenpa Namkha in the Water-Tiger year (or 1254, Wood-Tiger)
1245 received the *Trenpa Serdam* from Tsewang Rigdzin in the Wood-Snake year (or 1257, Fire-Snake); received also one section on phowa from *The Lamp That Removes the Darkness from Preliminary Practices* from the dakini Nyima Wöden
1246 received *The Lamp That Illuminates the Bardo* (*Bar do gsal ba'i sgron me*) from Trenpa Namkha in the Fire-Horse year (or 1258, Earth-Horse)
1256 discovered the *Kode Kalzang* in the Fire-Dragon year
1267 composed his autobiographical *Visionary Encounters* in the Fire-Hare year
1268 died in the Earth-Dragon year (or 1280, Iron-Dragon)

The Visionary Dimension

Visionary Encounters with Knowledge-Holders and Dakinis, the first text translated in this book, introduces us to the visionary dimension of a realized being, a fundamental characteristic common to all the ancient spiritual traditions, as it is the origin of the spiritual revelations received by most founders of religions. In particular, it has always been associated with that complex of ecstatic practices and traditions known as shamanism. The dimension in which the shaman lives and acts is a visionary reality, indispensable for his or her qualification as a shaman. Visionary accounts have also been recorded outside the field of religious traditions, and we have an outstanding case of visionary art and literature in the works of the English poet and painter William Blake (1757–1827), a "natural born visionary" whose spontaneous wisdom, in my opinion, has no equal in Western culture.[113]

Tibetan literature is full of visionary elements, but it is essential to distinguish between those magical-religious aspects pervaded by a taste for the supernatural, very typical of Eastern literature in general, from the descriptions of actual visionary experiences that are particularly tied to the terma literature. Termas, as already explained, can be either sacred texts or objects which are hidden by a realized master in a specific place or in the consciousness of a student, and afterward, even centuries later, rediscovered by a tertön, or treasure-discoverer. Termas can also be received through visions or extraordinary states of consciousness. In either case, the tertön needs to open himself or herself to a new dimension of reality that is loaded with symbols and meanings hidden to ordinary human perception. This dimension is also the source of the teachings of Tantra and Dzogchen, but it does not manifest openly because of the obstacles of karma and dualism.

Shense Lhaje in this and other texts of *The Golden Teaching* shares with us his various visionary experiences that give him access to the pure nirmanakaya dimensions in which the knowledge-holders, masters who attained realization by means of the Dzogchen path, and the dakinis, female personifications of primordial energy, live. The message that shines through these pages is that of a dimension of total openness, of a way of being disentangled from all preconceptions created by the limited capacity of our dualistic mind. This dimension is communicated through symbols: visions of superhuman beings endowed with unlimited powers and infinite aspects of manifestation, whose only aim is to help Shense Lhaje to free himself from the shackles of limitations and regain an authentic state of freedom. At times visions take on wrathful features, at times a pleasant guise, but the divine manifestation always reminds him that all the images that he sees are only a reflection of his own energy, a trial to test his capacity to maintain undistracted, pure instant presence.

Sometimes these extraordinary experiences manifest through dreams of clarity, such as this episode from *The Lamp of One's Instant Presence*, another text from *The Golden Teaching*:

> I, a beggar whose karmic traces have reawakened from former lives, one early morning before dawn between the seventh and the eighth month of the Tiger year,[114] while I was lying down with the impression that I had fallen asleep, as a prediction of clarity in what seemed to be a dream, the dakini Logcham Nyiwöma arrived riding a white hawk. By the strength of the blessings of her wisdom mind my instant presence was free of any impediment or covering, and I asked her, "Mother and sister dakini, source of all knowledge-holders, bless this fortunate being who has the deepest faith. Where are you coming from? Through which path did you arrive? Toward which *shen*[115] practitioner are you directed now? Don't keep any secret, please tell me all!"
>
> She replied, "Noble son of good karma, lineage of the shen, listen carefully and attentively, without agitation or drowsiness! From the secret cave of Mula Chingchen I have been sent here by Khöpung Trenpa [Namkha]. I trod the path of miraculous power without any material obstruction, directed toward you, Shense. Come immediately to the treasury house of Bön in the ganachakra[116] rows; there are siddhis there! Come with me, we have a common karma."
>
> After she said this, I involuntarily became an immaterial body and flew like a bird. After a short while I saw a temple entirely made of various precious substances where I had never been before, about one thousand meters in size. The roof and its projecting beams were like a pavilion of rainbow-colored lights. Everywhere various kinds of flowers were blooming. Everything was shining with light and rays in all directions. In this astonishing palace-temple, [so majestic that it was] unbearable to look at, I entered without any control from my side. On various thrones

I saw fifteen shenpos, the foremost of them being the Great Lama [Trenpa Namkha]. The rest, about a hundred male and female shens,[117] were reciting secret mantras and practicing circumambulation.[118] I also started to recite the secret mantra essence of the knowledge-holders that pacifies suffering[119] and to practice circumambulation together with them. The Great Lama, Gyungyar [Mukhö], and the four scholars were sitting in a state of ineffable contemplation. Tsewang Rigdzin, Lhundrub Yeshe, Mula Yungdrung, and Nyiwö Chose were performing all the stages of the ganachakra according to the ritual scriptures. Nyima Sertro and Sukasiti were arranging the preparations for the ganachakra. After a while the wise Tongyung [Thuchen] made a mudra[120] with his hands and gazed in space. Thinking that the time of the distribution of the siddhis of the ganachakra had arrived, I started to dance and run without control.

The Great Khyentse[121] [Tsewang Rigdzin] then said, "Son, don't let your instant presence wander: remain in the immovable condition. Unless control over one's mind has been obtained and an immutable confidence has been gained, however certain one may feel, it is not possible to proceed on the path. Therefore, hold on to stability, and all of you take your place in the rows!"

As soon as he said this, all of us accordingly sat down in the rows one after the other, and we all obtained human flesh[122] and so forth, the six medicinal substances, and offerings of consecrated nectarous *chang*.[123] Then everybody, except the Great Lama and his son [Tsewang Rigdzin], turned into vultures and left. I did not feel like leaving and remained naturally seated, and the Great Lama told me, "Son, don't be distracted and listen to the true Bön!"[124]

After which Shense Lhaje receives a complete Dzogchen instruction. The same happens in the dream through which the complete cycle of the *Trenpa Serdam* was received as "oral transmission" (translated in the next section). In a similar way, in *The Lamp That Illuminates the Bardo*, we read how Shense Lhaje was invited by an unknown yogin to receive *bardo* instructions from Tsewang Rigdzin, although this time Shense Lhaje specifies that he thought he was not asleep when this happened:

> In the early morning of the fifteenth day of the fourth month of the Horse year,[125] while I thought I was not asleep, a naked yogin with long braided hair whom I could not recognize arrived near me and asked, "Will you come to the ganachakra gathering?"
> "What is it and where should we go?" I replied.
> "In the secret cave of the Three Stacked Swastikas[126] the nirmanakaya Khyentse [Tsewang Rigdzin] is turning the wheel of Bön. I am Yungdrung Wösal, and I came to lead you there," he explained.
> Then, unable to control what was happening, I went there as if in a dream. On the top on something similar to many layers of white rocks I saw a tent full of various rainbow lights. There were many male and female knowledge-holders, and I too obtained my share of ganachakra offerings. It was at that time that I received this upadesha.[127]

At other times, as we read in *Questions and Answers for a Fortunate Being, Quintessence of the Mind of Wöden Barma*, the vision appears in the daylight while Shense Lhaje is busy with his activities:

> I, a lunatic yogin who has understood everything in one single point, once was performing a dedication practice for the benefit of a nomad, when a girl with many ornaments told me from the sky, "Son, don't let yourself be distracted by worldly appearances. Wöden Barma and other wisdom dakinis have arrived at your tent; go there quickly, there are siddhis to receive!"
> Then that dakini and I arrived inside the tent at the same time. The tent looked like a [majestic] temple impossible to forget. At its center was Trenpa Namkha with three other knowledge-holders. In the right row there were Wöden Barma and countless other dakinis. After a very short time the compassionate Tsewang [Rigdzin] arrived together with a large number of knowledge-holders. Tsewang sat at the head of the left row. The Great Lama [Trenpa Namkha] told me, "Son, don't have doubts; sit beside Tsewang!" So I sat there. After me, many knowledge-holders sat down too.
> Then I asked Wöden Barma, "Queen of all the mother dakinis, sovereign lady! Please bestow the siddhis upon the fortunate ones!"

"Sons, you all possess the wisdom of instant presence. I don't have any siddhi that can be conceived in terms of ordinary characteristics. The real siddhi beyond characteristics is in you. Search for that siddhi inside and you will find it. If you don't search inside, any outer siddhi can only derive from the karma of an ignorant mind. Enjoy the precious jewel of your own natural siddhi and all wishes will be fulfilled!"[128]

Besides the visionary dimension of Shense Lhaje, it is also his human quality of sincerity in telling his autobiographical episodes that makes his stories special and well worth reading. I remember one day, after we had finished translating one story, Lopön Tenzin Namdak told me, "You see, in these short stories of his life, Shense Lhaje shows himself as he really is: maybe one day he feels happy and elated, but the next day he can be in a different mood, just like us practitioners. Therefore I like this book so much."

The Origins of *The Golden Teaching*

Concerning the origin of the *Trenpa Serdam* or *Golden Teaching* cycle, in the *History of Bön* by Palden Tsultrim we read:

> *The Golden Teaching Upadesha of Dzogpa Chenpo* was taught to the great lama Trenpa Namkha by Samantabhadra himself. The great lama put this crucially direct upadesha similar to precious gold into writing, composing also twenty-one golden teachings as secondary subjects,[129] and gave all to his supreme son Tsewang [Rigdzin], protector of beings. The lord Tsewang and Thugje Kundrol[130] transmitted it to the nirmanakaya Wangden Shense. The latter passed the transmission to Khyungpo Nangchen Tragpa, empowering him as the holder of this teaching.[131]

And from the same text:

> The cycle of teaching of the *Dzogchen Golden Teachings of Trenpa*, and so forth, transmitted orally by Tsewang and his consort to Wangden Shense Lhaje, were then passed to Khyungpo Nangchen Tragpa, and others.[132]

THE ORIGINS OF THE GOLDEN TEACHING — 29

In the *History of Bön Lineages* we read:

> As to the transmission of the *Upadesha of the Golden Teaching*, Samantabhadra transmitted it to Trenpa Namkha, who transmitted it to Tsewang Rigdzin. The latter transmitted it to Thugje Kundrol, who transmitted it to the nirmanakaya Wangden Shense Lhaje. Also, Tsewang Rigdzin transmitted it to Wangden Shense, who transmitted it to Khyungpo Nangchen Tragpa.[133]

The main upadesha cycle of *The Golden Teaching* contains eleven main chapters, from the first, which introduces the teaching and leads the practitioner from calm abiding to the knowledge of contemplation, to the last, which gives instructions on the bardo or intermediate state after death. The actual tantra contains ten chapters, which are numbered at the end of each. Nonetheless, the text immediately following, called *The Upadesha That Instantly Cuts All Doubts about the Bardo*, contains a detailed colophon regarding the origin and transmission of the tantra, and therefore it can be considered an integral part of *The Golden Teaching*.

In the first chapter, *Pointing-Out Instructions on Primordial Wisdom*, Tsewang Rigdzin explains the origin of and the reason for this teaching:

> This tantra that contains instructions for perceiving nakedly one's instant presence is profound and not like ordinary upadeshas. Therefore it was not taught by any shenpo of the past, nor was it transmitted to any meritorious knowledge-holder. Although it has been taught a few times, it has never been possible to write it down. This is also called "The King of the Upadesha Instructions," "The Key for the Authentic and Secret Meaning," "The Condensed Essence of the Dzogchen Bön," "The Quintessential Sphere [*thigle*] of the Great Vehicle," "The Gradual Instructions for the Naked Perception of Instant Presence," and "The Golden Teaching Upadesha." The transmission of such a precious teaching was originally requested from Samantabhadra. Then it was transmitted to Khöpung himself [Trenpa Namkha]. At the end, it was contemplated by myself, Khyentse [Tsewang Rigdzin].[134]

In the chapter on the bardo instructions mentioned above, Shense Lhaje himself gives a detailed explanation about how he received this teaching through a dream, and also gives a Snake year as the time when this happened. This Snake year could be reasonably identified with the Wood-Snake year corresponding to 1245, or with the Fire-Snake year corresponding to 1257. He writes:

> This tantra called *The Golden Teaching*, king of all upadeshas, a teaching that has appeared again and again in the wisdom mind of the lord Samantabhadra and was established after having been continuously pondered, is not similar to other scriptures. Since it is the quintessence of the wisdom mind and concentrates all in one [teaching], it was not transmitted to any sugata, it was not recounted to any knowledge-holder shenpo, and it was not taught to any mother dakinis, but was kept hidden in the center of the wisdom mind. Nowadays that the degeneration of time of the [last period] of five hundred years' [duration of the teaching] has arrived, the kalpa of weaponry with illnesses and famines is spreading, murders of blood relations and fights caused by attachment and hatred are increasing, all Buddhists and Bönpos stir up internal strife, supreme individuals teaching the authentic meaning are rare, ignorant beings degrade because of their actions, and there is no time to practice for attaining enlightenment in one lifetime: these all imply that the last period of time has arrived. Therefore [Samantabhadra], seeing that the time was ripe for this teaching that gives liberation in the same moment that it is seen, thought of transmitting it to Khöpung. Then, in the supreme place of Blissful, Akanishtha, he opened the door of his wisdom mind to the Great Lama Trenpa Namkha and taught the teaching without distortions, gave the transmission of the scripture without flaws, and bestowed its initiation including full authorization for its transmission. Thus Trenpa Namkha obtained its teaching, transmission, and initiation in their entirety.
>
> Then in the great temple of Khyunglung Ngulkhar, the father Great Lama Trenpa [Namkha] thought of transmitting it to his son the Great Khyentse Tsewang Rigdzin. Thus he opened the door of his wisdom mind and taught the teaching of the tantra, gave its scriptural transmission, and bestowed the full initiation. In that supreme place, the great Tsewang Rigdzin obtained at the

same time the teaching of the tantra, its scriptural transmission, and its initiation.

Then I, the fortunate, lunatic Shense Lhaje, on the night of the eleventh day[135] of the second month of autumn of the Snake year, while I was sleeping inside a tent, in the early morning before dawn saw Thugje Kundrol arrive riding a reddish tiger. I sat up straight in position and showed my devotion and respect to her. Thugje Kundrol ordered me, "Meritorious being, mount the tiger! Come immediately to the place of Chari Tsugden![136] The great knowledge-holder Khyentse [Tsewang Rigdzin] is teaching the tantras of Bön. If you desire the quintessential siddhi, come now!"

I, the lunatic, did not have any doubt, and overcoming all considerations, mounted the tiger. Then I flew in space like a bird. After a little while I reached a large and spacious cave, where I had the impression that the sun, the moon, and the stars were all shining. The eight cardinal and intermediate directions were all clearly visible. Inside the cave there were twenty-one knowledge-holders including Khyentse, and twenty-one dakinis including Thugje Kundrol. They were diligently attending to the preparation of the torma[137] initiation and the ganachakra.

Then the Great Khyentse said, "Fortunate beings, present your offering to the teacher!"

I asked Lishu Tagring, "Which offering would be appropriate?"

"I will offer [a set of] the five precious materials which I have," Lishu Tagring replied.

Thus Lishu Tagring, the shenpo from India Ragya Yeshe, the shenpo from Tagzig Urgyen Hringni, the shenpo from Shang Shung Anu Tragthag, and me, the five of us, presented an offering of the five precious materials. Then the Great Khyentse opened the door of his wisdom mind and taught in detail *The Golden Teaching*, king of the upadeshas, citing quotations, and bestowing simultaneously upon the five of us the initiation, including the full authorization for its transmission. Thus also I at that time undoubtedly obtained the teaching, its scriptural transmission, and its initiation on the same occasion.

Then the Great Khyentse gave this command: "Sons, listen! This king of upadeshas called *The Golden Teaching* was displayed by Samantabhadra as the essence of his wisdom mind and then transmitted to Khöpung Trenpa Namkha in the place of Akanishtha, with the order of not teaching it to ordinary individuals. Then Khöpung Trenpa Namkha transmitted it to me in the place of Khyunglung Ngulkhar, with the order of keeping it secret and not proclaiming it to unsuitable individuals. I have taught this to you in the center of Chari Tsugden, and I strictly request that you don't teach it to individuals with wrong views. Apart from meritorious, noble individuals, you cannot bestow it upon those who are great in faith with their lips but who have little faith inside, or upon those who are not generous but are bound by stinginess. Keep this profound seal [of secrecy]. Yet, it is important that you teach this upadesha to individuals who will benefit [other] suitable beings."

Thus he said, and gave this strict command. Then, having obtained the initiations and transmissions, I arrived back in my bed. I [finished] transcribing [the teaching] on the morning of the eighth day of the last month of autumn.[138]

Editions of *The Golden Teaching*

Three different editions of the *Trenpa Serdam* exist today. The first, published in Delhi in 1972 and reproducing a manuscript in *ume* script from the Samling monastery, Dolpo, bears the title *Man ngag rin po che dran pa gser gyi gdams pa*, or *The Precious Upadesha, the Golden Teaching of Trenpa*.[139] It is referred to here as edition A, or the Delhi edition, and contains twenty-seven texts, among which the upadesha of *The Golden Teaching* covers eleven chapters, from the fourth to the fourteenth. Some of the texts, however, seem to be unrelated to the cycle.

In 1998 another edition of the text was found in Tibet and published with the title *Dran pa gser gdams* in volume 39 of the Bönpo Katen.[140] It also contains twenty-seven texts in *ume* script, and the main upadesha also covers chapters four to fourteen. This edition, here marked as B, contains a greater number of spelling mistakes than the edition published in Delhi in 1972. In a catalogue of the Bönpo canon written by Yungdrung Tsultrim Wangdrag (nineteenth century), the *Trenpa Serdam* is described as containing twenty-seven texts that match those of this edition, although the order is different, with the first eleven forming the *Upadesha of the Golden Teaching*.[141]

In other volumes of this Katen, we find a number of texts related to the *Trenpa Serdam*. These are referred to here as edition B2.

More recently, as mentioned before, a different edition has been found in a copy of the Tengyur arranged by Düddul Yungdrung Tragpa, the twenty-third master in succession in the lineage of the Khyungpo Tengchen monastery. Marked as edition C in this book, the *Trenpa Serdam* appears in volume 82 and contains twenty-eight texts in *uchen* script and seems to be the most complete edition so far. It closely follows the Katen edition examined above, the only difference being the inclusion of a text, *Questions and Answers with Knowledge-Holders and Dakinis* (*Rig 'dzin mkha' 'gro'i zhus len*), already found in a different volume of the Katen B edition. A characteristic of this copy is that it contains many variants of spellings in brackets, as if another source has been consulted while it was being written down.

Lastly, in 2013 an edition in Western-style book format was published in Sichuan containing twenty-nine texts that are basically the twenty-eight of the Tengchen edition. However, this edition does not take into consideration the Dolpo manuscript published in Delhi (edition A) and nevertheless presents numerous mistakes. For a complete list of the texts included in the various editions, see appendix 1.

The Translated Texts

Visionary Encounters with Knowledge-Holders and Dakinis, the first text translated here, contains autobiographical episodes of Shense Lhaje's visionary encounters and dreams, and it has been already dealt with in the "Visionary Dimension" section.

The second translation, *Clarifying the Real Nature*, belongs to the *Golden Teaching* cycle. It is a beautiful example of Dzogchen literature in which the essence of this teaching is explained in a language of utmost simplicity and clarity.

Texts 3 and 4, translated here as *The Garland of Nectar, Orally Transmitted Advice from Eighty Knowledge-Holders in the Form of Questions and Answers* and *The Precious Golden Lamp, Advice from Eighty Dakinis*, contain short aphorisms mostly in four-line verses, that were transmitted to the author by many male and female realized beings. Sometimes the verses express the meaning directly and clearly, pointing to the very essence of the natural state of the individual as the core of Dzogchen practice. At other times, especially in the advice from the dakinis, the language becomes cryptic and enigmatic, which reminds us of the use of symbolic language or *deu*[142] as a special characteristic of the ancient Tibetan culture. It is also interesting to notice that the name or part of the name of the knowledge-holder or dakini is often contained in the advice, sometimes as the first syllable, although this is lost in the English translation. The knowledge-holders quoted in the text actually number seventy-eight, while there are eighty-three dakinis, although Yingsalma appears twice. Some of their names appear with spelling variations in the different editions of the text. See appendices 4 and 5 for details.

Note on the Translation

I started my translation in 1982 with the edition of the *Trenpa Serdam* published in Delhi in 1972, which was the only one available at that time. Recently I reviewed it and corrected on the basis of the Katen edition, checking as well the section of scattered texts contained in volume 61 of the Katen. Just prior to sending the manuscript to the editor, I had the chance also to briefly check the edition from the Tengchen Tengyur.

In general, the edition published in India in 1972 is more accurate and contains fewer spelling mistakes than the Katen edition, although sometimes I had to integrate passages from the Katen edition that are missing in the former edition. Due to the large number of discrepancies between the two editions on which I mainly worked, I have only marked in the notes the most remarkable and relevant to the translation. A list of most of these variants is to be found in appendix 6 at the end of this book. One of the most consistent differences between the two texts is the alternative use of *byar med* (nonaction) in the Delhi edition and of *dbyer med* (inseparable) in the Katen edition. In other instances, I have found the same sentence written in two ways, both of which can make sense, but with different meaning. Generally I have preferred to follow the first one, as it was the edition from which Lopön Tenzin Namdak was reading when orally translating the text.

In any case, some passages still remain somewhat obscure. As for the terminology, I have used Sanskrit equivalents for terms nowadays in common usage among readers of Tibetan Buddhism, although I am aware that some scholars may criticize my usage of "dharmakaya" for *bon sku*, when the exact Tibetan equivalent would be *chos sku*. I have adopted this choice also for other expressions where the term *bon* is consistently used instead of *chos*, such as *bon nyid* for *chos nyid*, *bon dbyings* for *chos dbyings*, and so forth. A special mention is needed for the term "vision" to translate the Tibetan *snang ba*, which is used in this book, according to the explanations of Chögyal Namkhai Norbu, in the sense of any perception of the five senses, and not only sight. A short glossary at the end of the volume will allow general readers to understand basic Tibetan Tantra and Dzogchen terminology, while Tibetologists will find there the Tibetan equivalents of many terms that I have used throughout the translation.

Four Texts from *The Golden Teaching*

TSEWANG RIGDZIN. THANGKA FROM DOLPO, ARTIST UNKNOWN.
OWNED BY ADRIANO CLEMENTE. PHOTO COURTESY OF ALEX SIEDLECKI.

I

VISIONARY ENCOUNTERS WITH KNOWLEDGE-HOLDERS AND DAKINIS

||མན་ངག་རྒྱལ་པོ་ལས་རིག་འཛིན་མཁའ་འགྲོའི་མཇལ་སྣང་བཞུགས་སོ||

Marvelous!
I pay homage to Samantabhadra who encompasses all without limitation,
To the liberating, wrathful Khangying deities,
To the five buddhas in union with consorts and to their retinue,
To the shenpo Tseme Wöden,[1] the sambhogakaya,
To Chime Tsugphü, the supreme nirmanakaya,
To Tongyung Thuchen, king of knowledge-holders,
To Trenpa Namkha and his son Tsewang Rigdzin, protectors of all beings,
To Gyermi Nyiwö, seedling of the buddhas, and so forth,
To all the buddhas and knowledge-holders in their peaceful and wrathful manifestations!

I pay homage to Kalzang (Fortunate Kalpa), unique mother, and to Wöden Barma (Flaming Light),
To Nyima Wöden (Light of the Sun) and Chucham Gyalmo (Queen of the Waters),
To Tsogdag Karmo (White Lady of Accumulations) and Göcham Barma (Flaming Dakini),
To Nyima Tongkhyab (Encompassing One Thousand Suns) and Nyima Saltser (Bright Sun),
To Nyiwö Barma (Bright Light of the Sun) and Nyiwö Dangden (Color of Sunlight),
To Yingchug Gyaltsen (Banner of Rich Space) and Wangchug Drönma (Lamp of Power),

To Draké Bumgyur (Speaker of One Hundred Thousand Languages) and
    Wözer Dangden (Color of Sunrays),
To Choza Bönmo[2] and Sukasiti,
To the four Goddesses of Flowers,[3] and so forth,
To all the great mother dakinis!

I pay homage to the empty and immense nature like the sky,
To the clear and unseizable luminosity like the light of the sun and the
    moon,
To the empty and immaterial self-liberation like the energy of the wind,
To the self-perfected essence, the three kayas themselves!

I am an aimless, great liar who talks nonsense.
As a result of my practice in former lives, I obtained the five jewels.
Without searching anywhere, I received great treasures inside me.
I understood the outer and the inner, samsara and nirvana, as the
    fundamental essence.
I swam in the sea of the original and unmodified total state.
I slept in the expanse of all-encompassing space.
I fed on the inexhaustible food of nonthought.
I realized the primordially self-perfected dharmakaya.
Having crossed the perilous passage of the steps of hope and fear,
I caught hold of the immutable final fruit:
Such is the nature of a lying beggar!

All the sugatas, knowledge-holders, and dakinis
Gave me advice, revealed themselves to me, bestowed outer and inner
    initiations,
And prophesied the rediscovery of impartial, profound, secret treasures.
They showed me what ignorant births I had taken in the beginning,
How I should help others after attaining realization myself,
And where the nirmanakayas, hidden or visible, who benefit sentient
    beings, are dwelling.
They showed me the situations of evil beings guilty of crimes with
    immediate karmic retribution,[4]
And taught me how to lead through compassion ignorant beings who
    have committed negative actions.
They also revealed in which ordinary human beings have emanated

The dakinis of wisdom, of miracle, and of action,[5] and where they are
     dwelling,
And told me how, by having contact with them, one's qualities would
     greatly increase.
Thus the supreme masters of the past have shown me
The higher, lower, and middling condition of beings,
But if I had to write it all down, one thing after the other, I would never
     come to the end.
Therefore, in order that beings may have faith and devotion,
I will write down only a little of all that I have seen.
Buddhas of the direct transmission, knowledge-holders of the oral
     transmission, and mother dakinis, I beg your forgiveness!

First Encounters Early in My Life

1

One day, while I was meditating in a state beyond limitations,[6] a man I had never seen before approached me. "Where have you come from?" I asked him.

"I am not coming from anywhere, and I am not going anywhere. I dwell in the emptiness devoid of self-nature, and in a place that has no substance there is no path to tread," he replied.

"Traveler, you are amazing, and your speech is excellent. I would like to talk about spiritual practice with you."

And he spoke: "Hey, son! You are distracted by the illusory vision of the world. Don't you remember how, throughout limitless time, you have been transmigrating in the six classes of beings? And how you have been entering the wombs of ignorant women and taking illusory bodies, grounds for accumulating negative actions? Don't you remember all this now? Don't you remember the unbearable suffering? Still, you are not doing anything for your benefit but just the ordinary work of demons. Give up the illusory worldly deeds now and remain in the state beyond actions and concepts! Don't be attached to the body: it has to be left behind. Don't try to grasp the mind with your thoughts: it is beyond thinking. Understand that all is emptiness! If you know the condition free from limitations, sustain it in the state of dharmakaya. Overcome your clinging to pride and timidity! Tie a knot in your throat and put the seals of secrecy on it. I am known as Tsewang the Hermit[7] and I have come to give you advice and words of upadesha. In general, it is always better to be without attachments and go far away!"

Then he disappeared, I could not tell how.

2

One day while I was riding my donkey on my way to work, I met a Bönpo with a smooth brown beard wearing a blue shawl. He told me: "If you let yourself get distracted by worldly appearances, there is danger of being beguiled by demons."

"What do you mean?" I replied. "Where do you come from?"

"There is no place where I come from, I come from all directions. Now I've just arrived from Nepal. I will give you the common and supreme siddhis," he said, and gave me a yellow-leafed, fresh arura[8] fruit spreading luminous rays in all directions. I started to eat it, but then I thought that I should save a third of it.

"Son, let the common and supreme siddhis be absorbed in you. Do not tell the people of the world about this. Leave the worldly vision and go to the mountains. Give up the ties of attachment; realize they are unreal! Once you go far away without a fixed destination, the practice you have done throughout the previous kalpas will reawaken. My name is Tongyung Thuchen; keep our encounter secret!" And turning into a leper, he disappeared.

3

One day I was lying down near a spring grazing my donkey, when I fell asleep. In that very moment a Bönpo wearing a white cotton shawl came up to me and said, "Intelligent young man, do not sleep! Get up! Keep the wisdom of instant presence clear and without thoughts, beyond grasping! Don't nurture desires and attachments toward appearances that lack any substance! This vision is like a magical illusion or a dream, the nature of emptiness. Until you dwell in the real meaning of 'without substance,' you will not be able to see the ineffable and ultimate essence."

I was wonder-struck and thought, "He must be Tsewang!"

"I am not Tsewang; I am Lishu Tagring. I have just come from India to give you a supreme secret siddhi," he said and in his right hand I saw a crystal swastika[9] that was hollow inside. With this he struck me on the chest, and I felt as if my body had become a transparent body of light, visible but without substance. Thus I had certainty and a feeling of joy arose in me, and I prostrated myself before him. Then he jumped three times and disappeared, walking up through the face of a rock.

4

One day at sunrise I thought, "I want to go!" and went. Then I instantly lost consciousness of what was happening, as if I had fallen asleep, and dreamed of a white and charming woman coming near me. She was so beautiful that I could not bear to part with her.

"Where have you come from, and for what purpose?" I asked her.

"I come from the country of Oddiyana, and I am directed to meet fortunate beings. I travel on miraculous feet and my aim is to accomplish aimless actions. Now I have come to meet you."

Not being able to keep my practice,[10] I felt frightened and happy at the same time. And I thought, "She must be a mother dakini, but who is she?"

"Son, don't let your instant presence slip away; keep the natural state in its place! Recognize your sensation of fear: if you do, you will discover that it is empty and beyond thoughts. Your sensation of pleasure is the ordinary mind and concepts: release your feeling of joy, immaterial, into emptiness! The one who feels fear and the one who feels pleasure are united in the nature of mind that is instant presence. Keep mind-essence, without modifying it, in the all-pervading expanse! Don't have doubts about me. I am Göcham Barma. Don't stop your devotion and invocations, and I will continuously give secret advice and siddhis to you."

Thus she said and blessed me by placing her right hand on the top of my head. I felt a white letter A coming out from the palm of her hand and descending through the fontanel into my chest. Through the power of the luminous rays of the A I became transparent, without a front or back side, and I felt a limpid, unobstructed clarity in all perceptions. In that very moment her white body became as small as a thumb and slowly disappeared into space.

5

One morning I was sitting near the ruins of a house when a stone rolled down from above and hit me right in the center of my head. In that instant I felt my body splitting into four equal parts, but my instant presence was integrated into space beyond meditation and postmeditation, and a pure luminosity manifested vividly clear. I was in a state free from limitations, with no hope and no fear. After a moment, that stone became a very pretty and lustrous young boy, my body was no longer split but unified with my mind again, and I remained in the equanimity of contemplation. I had no thoughts whatsoever concerning the fact that the rolling stone had turned into a boy.

"Son, wonderful, excellent!" he said. "You must surely belong to the lineage of the wondrous knowledge-holders! Noble son, remain in the imperturbable state without fixating on anything! I come from Chari Tsugden, and I am one of the four emanations of the Great Lama Trenpa Namkha. I have come to give you the siddhi of the ultimate meaning. Faith, devotion, and respect on your side are very important," and he spat at me. The spittle turned into the letters A and OM, which then dissolved into me.

Then I asked him, "If you are one of the four emanations of the Great Master Trenpa Namkha, where are the other three? Where are they acting for the benefit of sentient beings? Please tell me."

"I will tell you briefly. One is in the palace of Chari Tsugden explaining all the general Bön teachings of the *Senkhar Shitro* (Mandalas of Peaceful and Wrathful Deities) to innumerable male and female shens. Another is in the palace of the Thirty-Three Devas explaining a Bön commentary to gods and goddesses. The third is pacifying conflicts between the asuras and the nonhuman beings. I have come to give you some advice and instruction. Oh! I will reveal to you the undefiled nature of your mind, your immutable root. Set yourself free, without grasping at anything, in the expanse of the unmodified, clear basic space! Without meditating, remain in the imperturbable state beyond thoughts! Put these words into practice and I will always bestow siddhis on you." Thus he spoke, and turning into a beggar, disappeared along the main road.

6

One day I was lying down on the roof of a house when I saw a woman waving to me from the sky. I felt such joy that, when she disappeared without a trace, I went out and walked until I reached a meadow. There I fainted and fell down. When I recovered my senses and got up, I looked into the sky and saw an assembly of innumerable knowledge-holders and dakinis. At the center between the rows, sitting on a throne of five rainbow colors, was a brown-hued Bönpo with a long beard in brahmin attire. At the head of the right-hand row was a terrifying dark blue man wearing the ornaments of the wrathful deities. At the head of the left-hand row was a dark maroon woman, fierce and majestic. I saw countless other knowledge-holders and dakinis who were offering a ganachakra feast with various flowers and human flesh mingled together.

Helping in the preparation was a light brownish Bönpo who was spreading luminous rays in all directions, his hair hanging down to his waist. He had a white crystal vase in his right hand and a plate made of precious stones in his left. There was also a woman wearing jewel ornaments and radiating rainbow lights, so beautiful and charming that I could not bear to part with her. They were both making preparations for the ganachakra feast. Then the woman took me by my right hand and made me sit in front of the one who was at the center between the rows. "Who is this one at the center?" I asked. "And who are these seated at the head of the right and left rows? Who is the one helping you prepare the ganachakra? And what is your name? Please tell me."

"At the center between the rows is Tongyung Thuchen. Trenpa Namkha is at the head of the right row, and on the left is Sipai Gyalmo,[11] the great mother. My assistant in the ganachakra is the Great Khyentse [Tsewang Rigdzin] and my name is Gyenzangma. You are a fortunate lineage holder. The many others that you see in the rows are knowledge-holders and dakinis assembled for the ganachakra. Don't reveal this to the people of the world now, but when the time is ripe don't remain silent but speak!" she replied, and then started to distribute the offerings.

On a plate made of precious stones containing pieces of human flesh mixed with flowers, she put an arura fruit with moist yellow flowers, and offered it to me. I offered it to the one who was sitting at the center, but he said: "Son, there is no one to whom to offer outside. In the precious divine temple of one's heart dwells Samantabhadra, the immutable mind-essence. This Samantabhadra, immutable mind-essence, is nothing whatsoever, empty by nature. If you understand the meaning of this emptiness, it is the highest recipient of offerings."

"I know that the unborn and empty mind-essence dwells inside me," I said, "nevertheless I am always in company of the conceptual mind that creates thoughts of ignorance. As long as the grasping of conceptual thoughts does not dissolve, one cannot see Samantabhadra, mind-essence. Therefore I have understood that until one sees mind-essence, it is very important not to stop performing virtuous deeds and making offerings also with music."

Then the Great Lama [Trenpa Namkha], who was seated at the head of the right row, said, "Good, good, noble son! Very good! Until the whole universe and all beings are perceived as utterly equal in the condition of emptiness, it is important to strive to practice virtue with body, speech, and mind. But now, let us not talk so much, eat your portion of offerings and receive the siddhi!"

So I ate it, and it was tasty with the fragrance of various medicinal herbs. Then the woman who had distributed the offerings told me, "Son, let the common and supreme siddhis enter you. Remain continuously in the state of the undefiled essence! Do not interrupt your invocations and offerings; they are important!"

Then some of them mounted vultures, others turned into vultures themselves, and all of them, clad in rays of various colors, disappeared into the west.

7

One day I was sitting on a grassy plain writing a letter when suddenly a crow appeared near me, I could not tell from where. I gazed at him once, and for a while I was distracted. Then I recognized the face of the wise Tongyung Thuchen and, standing up, I paid homage to him by prostrating innumerable times. But the Great Scholar said, "Son, do you want to know the meaning of your prostrations?"

I answered, "Because of the obstacles of karmic traces, until now I have been born as a human in barbarian regions.[12] And maybe because I didn't practice enough in my past lives, I haven't been able yet to accomplish the great aim. Therefore, in order to purify obstacles, I prostrated before the Great Scholar. Until one's obstacles are cleared away, it is not possible for the unimpeded condition to manifest. Do you possess a teaching that doesn't require one to purify obscurations? Please give it to this ignorant being!"

The Great Scholar replied, "Hey, son, how doubtful you are! You are so eloquent and clever, but you don't get close to the real meaning. Since the all-ground has always been the totally pervading emptiness, committing oneself with effort to the practice of virtue is an illusion. Since the undefiled luminosity of one's instant presence is itself the state of enlightenment, prostrations and circumambulations[13] to purify obstacles are samsaric actions. I do have a teaching that doesn't require purifying obstacles: don't exert yourself to perform ordinary actions based on effort, and understand the effortless essence of self-perfection once and for all! Don't get involved in so many illusory worldly actions: remain without grasping, beyond all activity and concepts! Don't try so hard to purify obstacles with your thought-creating mind: remain in the state beyond mind and thoughts! Don't bind yourself up with the attachment that creates preconceived ideas: play freely and spontaneously in space!" Thus the Great Scholar said, and, turning into a rainbow as small as a butter lamp, shining brightly, he disappeared into the east.

8

One evening I was sitting in a row of people drinking chang. Not being able to keep my instant presence and distracted by the external vision, I thought I'd better go out. Immediately I got up, crossed the threshold to the outside, and looked. There I saw an extremely tall woman dressed in a tiger skin and with a very fierce expression. In that moment my instant presence woke up strong and clear, and I asked her:

"Black lady, how strange and frightening are you! What is the name of the place you are coming from? By which path did you arrive? Where are the people you came to meet? Don't keep any secret: tell me clearly!"

Then her body became normal in size and her face was fair and lovely, with long falling hair adorned with pearls at the bottom. Having become so beautiful, she answered:

"Son, you who are the holder of the lineage of the shens, you noble son, listen attentively! I came in the beginning and I will come in the future, and in between, without going anywhere, I reached everywhere. At last, in the same way, I arrived in this good place. This is my nature."

Hearing these words I said, "Marvelous, lady; what you said is excellent. The condition of the primordial base that you hinted at, and which you have thus understood, is not something difficult. But now I want to ask you: What is your name? What is the good place you are coming from? What is the purpose of your coming here now, and why did you tell me those things?"

"Son, you don't need to doubt! I am the Mind emanation[14] of Namchi Kungyal.[15] Now I just came from Tagzig, and I will go everywhere in the world. I told you those things because I saw you have a purified karma. I came to show you my face and to give you advice. Tell me, what are the signs of progress in your practice?"

"What do you mean by 'signs of progress'?" I asked.

"Do you see the unborn natural condition?"

"How could I see the unborn essence!" I replied. "Right now I am behaving like an ordinary person performing worldly actions. Without getting close to the real meaning, conditioned by worldly demons, I am not in my natural condition and instead I lose myself after the illusory vision in a normal way. I have no signs of progress of the experiences of bliss and heat!"[16]

"Marvelous, noble and fortunate son! Now you don't need to endure hardship anymore; you have already realized the aim long before. Nevertheless, you have to attain the final fruit beyond all concepts."

> Leave the all-pervading sky in its evenness!
> Leave the all-illuminating and impartial sun and moon in their clarity!
> Leave everything in the clarity of absolute equality!
> Overcome the dualistic considerations of hope and fear!

Thus she said and, turning into a rainbow, disappeared I could not tell where.

9

Once I was sleeping in the lower floor of a house when, at dawn, I heard the sound of drums and *shang* cymbals filling the whole world and making the earth and the sky tremble. I got up and went outdoors, and looked around in every direction. There I saw countless male and female knowledge-holders gathering in space, but that didn't especially alter my mind and I remained without thinking in a normal condition.

Immediately afterward, a Bönpo came near to me. He had long hair, half tied on the top of his head and half loose, a white beard falling down to his waist where he had a belt, and bone ornaments. He looked very frightening, and his body was tall and dignified. As soon as he came, he slapped me on my cheek and immediately told me:

"Son, don't fear! I am Tongyung. If you have any miraculous power, take it out now, we must go quickly!"

"Marvelous, wonderful teacher!" I said. "I am an ordinary being, ignorant and deluded, and I've never had any miraculous power. But tell me, what is the place where we should go? And by which miraculous power could I ever go?"

"Son, even though you don't have any power," the Great Scholar replied, "through my miraculous capacity your body will be absorbed into mine and, having become one, we will be able to go. The place we are going is the Heaven of the Thirty-Three, where gods and goddesses have been inviting us again and again. They are now presenting offerings of various musical instruments. We must hurry up!"

Thus he hit me with his hand, and I had the feeling that I had become a white letter A that went to sit on the top of the head of Tongyung. In this way, together with countless males and females, we started on our way. Then we reached the Heaven of the Thirty-Three and countless gods and goddesses made us offerings of songs and dances with very melodious music, of various precious jewels and flowers, and of medicinal herbs and fragrant incense, all in copious quantity.

Then I found myself in my body again, and I saw many houses made of crystal whose projecting roof beams were ornamented with turquoise. We were invited inside a very large and lofty crystal house whose door was made of various precious jewels. This divine palace, surrounded by five-colored rainbows, was replete with all kinds of foods existing in the world. There I saw a big glittering mandala, and various precious jewels, fresh medicinal herbs, and flowers arranged into heaps. Tongyung, the Great Lama [Trenpa Namkha], and Kalzang the Only Mother were sitting in imperturbable contemplation. Tsewang Rigdzin, Tsogdag Karmo, and the dakinis Gyenzangma and Sukasiti were preparing the ganachakra. To the rest of us, countless males and females sitting naturally in rows, they gave our share of ganachakra one after the other.

"Son, don't waste this secret supreme siddhi!" the Great Scholar told me. "Keep it secret and don't show it to others!" and he snapped his fingers at me. Then my body became a white A and I returned to my place. Once I was back on my bed, I felt as if my body was filling the air with the scent of many fragrances.

10

One morning I got up, fastened my belt, went out and uncontrollably started to run. After a while I arrived at a round-shaped cave, and with a spontaneous feeling of happiness, I sat down in the cross-legged position. Then Khyentse [Tsewang Rigdzin] with his consort, surrounded by twenty-one knowledge-holders and dakinis, arrived. Amazed, I sang invocations while making mudras with my hands. Thugje Kundrol, as if she was spitting, flung from her mouth into mine a sparkling multicolored flower whose rays were spreading in all directions. I ate it and felt as if my body was dissolving into rays of light.

Then they joined in sexual union and gave me a secret initiation. The Great Khyentse then said:

"Son, abandon the actions of the demons of samsara! Don't let your mind be distracted by deceitful appearances. Leave your worldly, impermanent relatives."

> Beyond meditation, free from the mind, impossible to modify,
> The consciousness of one's instant presence has no conceptual fixation.
> In the blissful expanse of equality beyond the mind,
> It is nothing definable, and it is free from everything.[17]
> Let the small robin bird fly:
> Wherever it flies, the little bird will never exist!

And they departed.

11

One afternoon, while I was returning home on a rocky path, suddenly I saw a stray black dog running toward me. I sat down on a stone to rest, and the dog bumped into me and went away. Then it came back again and started to growl at me. I thought, "Who is this dog? Could it be a magical manifestation?" and remained seated in a state of meditation. The dog did not bite me, but disappeared behind a cave above me.

After a while, from the place where the dog had disappeared, I heard a sweet melody and the tinkling sounds of cymbals, and, feeling a joyous sensation, I climbed up the rock to look. There I saw Tongyung Thuchen and the rest of the four scholars, together with a retinue of eight knowledge-holder shens[18] who were presenting musical offerings to them. My instant presence woke up strong and clear, and I prostrated and danced innumerable times.

Tongyung Thuchen rose and came to sit upon the crown of my head, and told me, "Son, don't have doubts. Go beyond your judgments! I will give you the initiation of the wrathful power!"

Then on the center of his head appeared a white A that he placed into the center of my head; in his right hand an OM that he placed into my right hand; and in his left hand a HUM that he placed in my left hand. "I will give you, fortunate being, the five supreme initiations of the Body, Voice, Mind, Qualities, and Activities. Once you have received them, benefit other beings! I will give you the initiations of whatever teachings exist in the world." Thus he said, and departed from my head.

Then a power arose in me such as I had never had before, and I was able to emanate three persons from my body. One was making offerings, prostrations, and circumambulations. Another was requesting from Tongyung Thuchen a pointing-out instruction. The third was comparing spiritual experiences with a knowledge-holder shen.

Then the Great Scholar said, "Son, do away with your pride and conceit! Your miraculous power is as insignificant as child's play. Don't be proud nor timid. Go beyond your judgments and remain spontaneously free without limitations!"

Then one of my emanations requested a pointing-out instruction in this way:

"I bow down to the great shen, glory of all knowledge-holders! Please bestow a pointing-out instruction on the essence of all teachings."

The Great Scholar replied, "Son, the various visions are a magical manifestation of the mind. Keep the unmodified mind-essence without agitation. The eighty-four thousand doors of Bön are all released from the expanse of mind-essence. Therefore, as they are all equally one, don't think of them as separate. Free the nonthought essence from all your thinking, and this is it!"

One of my emanations was engaged in discussion with a shen, who said, "The essential condition is completely beyond thoughts and any concept concerning how it is!"

"The essential condition, beyond the grasping of thoughts, manifests spontaneously as clarity in the basic space," I replied.

"If from the beginning it is empty, without limits and without thoughts, how can the nature of clarity exist?" the shen retorted.

"Unimpeded wisdom manifests in all directions," I explained, "and an emptiness in which nothing exists can become a demon for the view. If you want to maintain the self-arising and uninterrupted condition without limitations, but indulge in heavy states of nonthought and bliss, it will not be possible for you to be liberated. For practicing before this vision, I don't know of any meditation in which one has to focus on emptiness." After that, he did not speak any further.

Shari Uchen[19] spoke, saying, "Good, good, what you both say, noble sons, is right! Nevertheless, what Shense Lhaje said corresponds a little more to the truth. You, shen Nyima Kyechig, have only a partial understanding. It is true, as Nyima Kyechig said, that mind-essence is empty and limitless from the beginning. However, in the primordially empty all-ground, uninterrupted wisdom arises spontaneously and without limitations, while this clarity, impossible to grasp, remains empty in the basic space. Thus, what Shense Lhaje said about practicing before this vision is very true. In any case, both of you noble sons, remain in that condition. In the unmodified and immovable state, wisdom beyond grasping will reveal itself. Play freely and without limitations in the expanse that pervades all directions! Remain in the unique state that knows no duality between samsara and nirvana, vision and mind!"

Then they all turned into vultures and disappeared into space. At that point my three emanations again became one body as before.

12

One day, while I was crossing a bridge on my donkey, I met a beggar with short white hair wearing a worn-out felt. I got off the donkey, and while I was leading it across the bridge, the beggar asked me, "Can you lend me your donkey for a while?"

Boundless compassion arose in me toward him, and I replied, "Hello, poor man! Are you tired?"

"I am exhausted. Since this morning I have not touched a mouthful of thugpa.[20] Do you have something to eat to give me out of pity?"

"I have no food," I replied, "but if you are tired I will let you ride my donkey."

The beggar was very happy and mounted the donkey while I held the stirrups for him. In this way we proceeded together. Then the beggar said:

"Ha ha! Son! Not to let thoughts free, but to lock them up in fetters of woolen ropes, how strange! Not to let the winds that move in empty space self-liberate spontaneously without limitations, but to tie them up with the knots of grasping at rejecting or obtaining, how strange! From the beginning the self-liberating nature of emptiness is unlimited, but one tries to achieve it by meditating with the thinking mind!"

Then I said to the beggar, "Beggar, you said something excellent both in words and meanings. This is amazing! Say something more: I don't know who you really are!"

"What? I, a beggar, muttered something without even knowing it. Where would these amazing words and meanings be? I, the beggar whom you don't know, come from the country of Uddiyana and am going to Shang Shung. My name is Mutsa Gyerme.[21] I came to meet you, thinking that you are worthy of it. For this reason I spoke thus to you. If you know how to travel by means of miraculous feet, come with me, where I and the donkey will go now!" And, riding the donkey, he flew off like a bird and disappeared. In that moment I transcended all mental judgment, and within me also a miraculous power arose, allowing me to fly for about one kilometer. Then, a movement of the thinking mind arose and, unable to fly anymore, I hit the ground. From below I looked up and saw Mutsa Gyerme sitting in the sky in the cross-legged position with his hands in the meditation gesture, while the donkey was coming back to me.

Then he said from the sky, "Son, the ignorant mind is always moving with thoughts. If you don't purify the movement of the thinking mind in the [primordial] base, the signs of realization will not arise. You have not transcended your conceptual mind yet, and are enclosed in the net of solidified thoughts. You were flying in the sky by means of a miraculous power, but the movement of a dualistic thought destroyed the miracle. Unable to fly, you fell down and hit the ground. Therefore, it is important that you achieve the great accomplishment of the unagitated state beyond all concepts. Exhausting everything, cut through illusions once and for all! If illusions are eradicated inside, the signs of realization will manifest outside. Therefore continue to practice until you reach the final and ineffable fruit!"

Then I said, "Marvelous! Glory of all the knowledge-holder shens, I praise and pay homage to you, who have unimpeded miraculous power! Of all that you said, I could grasp only one part. You said that if illusions are eradicated inside, the signs of realization will manifest outside, and that therefore I should continue to practice until I reach the final and ineffable fruit. But what does it actually mean that when illusions are eradicated inside, the signs of realization manifest outside?"

"Noble son, I have already told you. It is said that only a few siddhas have obtained the power of all the three outer, inner, and secret initiations,[22] but many more have obtained the power of the initiation of the inner mind."

"How does one obtain the power of the initiation of the mind," I asked again, "and is there a difference whether the signs manifest outside or not?"

"If the mind has obtained control over itself,[23] is there anything higher than that? In any case, if you have definitely understood the unborn base, that is it!" With that, he disappeared, I could not tell where.

13

One morning I was sitting in a small verandah when I saw some ravens in the forest fighting for a piece of flesh. Immediately I rushed there to look, but those birds were not moving their mouths, so I thought to return. On the way back, upon a shimmering rocky hill I saw a yogin with wide open gaze clad in a blue shawl. I stood and watched him, without going near. Then I saw another yogin wearing a white shawl and playing a *silnyen* cymbal,[24] dancing without letting his feet touch the ground. I felt so happy that I ran there, and saw the Great Lama [Trenpa Namkha], Tsewang Rigdzin, and Gyermi Nyiwö, surrounded by eighteen male and female knowledge-holders: Lishu Tagring at the head of eight shens, and Nyima Saltser at the head of ten dakinis.

When I reached there, I saw a shiny red damaru and a *silnyen* cymbal in the hands of Gyermi Nyiwö. He gave them to me, saying, "Son, the offerings of the body are circumambulations, prostrations, and music. Music and dance are offered according to one's capacity. The offerings of the voice are invocations with melodious singing. The offering of the mind is nonconceptual contemplation. Khöpung [Trenpa Namkha] and his son are around: make prostrations, circumambulations, and offerings with your body, voice, and mind!" And he made a mudra with his hands.

In Nyima Saltser's hands I saw a skull cup [kapala] filled to the brim with a yellowish siddhi substance, which she gave me to drink, saying, "Son, take this common siddhi and let's make offerings, prostrations, and circumambulations together!"

As I had the damaru and the *silnyen* cymbal in my hands, I offered no prostrations or circumambulations, but went instead to sit close to the Great Lama [Trenpa Namkha], Tsewang Rigdzin, and Gyermi Nyiwö. Then I asked the latter, "Knowledge-holder of the past, Gyermi Nyiwö! How does the nature of the three effortless and self-perfected kayas exist at the time of the darkness of ignorance? How does it exist at the time of realizing the wisdom of instant presence? Please explain to me all of this in detail, wise Gyermi!"

Gyermi did not reply, but the Great Lama said, "Noble son, listen! This is how the nature of the three effortless and self-perfected kayas exists at the time of ignorance. The nature of the dharmakaya, which is emptiness, exists as neutral ignorance. The nature of the sambhogakaya, which is clarity, exists in the way that one binds oneself with attachments. The nature of the nirmanakaya exists in the ordinary thoughts of emotions. At the time of realization, the nature of dharmakaya exists as the total state beyond limits and modifications. The nature of the sambhogakaya exists as total clarity without a substance and beyond dualistic grasping. The nature of the nirmanakaya exists as total self-liberation, empty and immaterial. Yet, son, cut through your many doubts, and maintain the unmodified mind-essence, clear and beyond thought!"

Tsewang said, "Son, remain in the state of unobstructed wisdom in the immovable, thought-free dimension! Let the fish swim unceasingly in the unmodified lake of confidence! Don't enchain yourself in a prison inside a pit: cut the rope that binds self-liberation! Don't mount the threshold of dualism, and the unique, immutable nature will reveal itself! Even though these are many words and meanings, realize their same flavor in the condition of the primordially enlightened mind!"[25]

Gyermi said, "Son, don't look anywhere: see everything! Don't wander anywhere: reach every place! Don't meditate on mind-essence: let the dharmakaya arise! Don't try to identify thoughts: let them self-liberate in their own place! Don't try so hard to investigate the movement of thoughts: let it dissolve in the primordial base! Don't let attachment to vision arise: let it dissolve beyond all grasping! Don't mix virtues and negative actions haphazardly: behave according to the scriptures—this is important! Don't take rash decisions based on your ideas: follow mainly the precepts! Yet, view everything without dualism, in the unique condition!"

After he spoke thus, some mounted vultures, others garudas, still others swans, and they all flew to the west.

This concludes a brief description of my first encounters in Meshö.

I bow with respect to all the knowledge-holders and dakinis!

14

One evening in Lag, while I was chanting invocations before a torma, first of all I saw directly in front of me what seemed to be Thugje Kundrol riding a reddish tiger. She was rolling her eyes and waving her hands. I felt faith in her, the mother, but I was afraid of the tiger. Then my instant presence became strong and clear, and I suddenly stood up and ran, when I saw that Thugje Kundrol had arrived with a great number of mother dakinis, and also Trenpa Namkha with many knowledge-holders. Among the knowledge-holders, apart from Trenpa Namkha, I could only recognize Khyentse [Tsewang Rigdzin], Lishu Tagring, and Gyermi Nyiwö. The rest were unknown to me. Among the mother dakinis, Thugje Kundrol was the only one that I recognized. Then the Great Lama, and Tsewang with his consort [Thugje Kundrol], bestowed an initiation upon me, while Lishu Tagring and Gyermi Nyiwö each gave me a pointing-out instruction.

Gyermi Nyiwö told me, "Son, in this big city without an owner and full of soldiers without a powerful chief, be the head of the army, king of your instant presence!"

Lishu Tagring said, "Son, don't engage too much in useless ordinary actions; they are the deeds of demons! Attachment to objects is the illusory mind of dualistic thoughts. Therefore, abandon all actions, and remain without acting! Don't let yourself go astray after the dualistic grasping of thoughts: remain beyond the mind! Concerning the real nature of existence, the totally pervading all-ground, what is the use of making efforts to try to understand it through the intellect?"

Then all of them, one after the other, disappeared, and I gave initiations to a large number of male and female students and benefactors, without discriminating.

15

Once I was sleeping inside a tent that I had pitched on the roof of a house. When the day was starting to dawn, I felt as though my house and I had been struck by a finger-snap. I sat up straight in position refreshing my state of instant presence, when I saw vividly the eight gatekeepers[26] [of the mandala] in sexual union arriving in space in front of me, brandishing weapons and surrounded by mountains of flames spreading luminous rays in the ten directions.

At first I was terrified, and by the strength of fear I took refuge in the wrathful deities. Then from above I heard a voice speak, though I did not know whose it was:

"Son, you are seeing your own natural wrathful deities. Why are you feeling fear, terror, and fright? Fear and terror are a magical illusion of the mind. Don't be doubtful: have faith and devotion to the deities. Visions like these exist naturally self-perfected in you; therefore it is important that you carry on your devotions in a peaceful and loving state of mind!"

Then a state of contemplation of unlimited equanimity arose in me, and I remained with my hands joined in a mudra. I saw that they were all reciting secret mantras, and that from their mouths luminous rays were sparkling with the sound of the mantras. "Will they give me an initiation?" I wondered.

"We will not bestow any initiation for now, but we will give you [the essence of] the common and supreme siddhis. Go and get a container!"

I jumped for joy, but could not find any vessel. So I joined my hands like a bowl and the eight gatekeepers, while engaging in sexual union with their consorts, filled it with white and red essences.[27] I did not drink it, and while I was holding the substance, I burst into laughter. Then one of them said, "Son, you have never received such a quintessential substance of the common and supreme siddhis, therefore you have no experience. This siddhi is very rare to obtain, and cannot be compared with ordinary siddhis. So, don't think we are joking, and don't have doubts. Let this heart's-blood siddhi enter inside you!"

I drank it in one gulp, and thanks to its power, all my practice became clear. Then they all went away, although I could not understand where.

16

One evening before midnight, Tsewang Rigdzin and Gyermi Nyiwö arrived. I did not feel any particular joy, but remained in a state beyond limitations.

Gyermi Nyiwö then said, "Son, tell us which are your signs of realization of the view."

"In Khyentse [Tsewang Rigdzin] and Gyermi Nyiwö, master and student, this ignorant being takes refuge!" I replied. "I have no signs of the view: since basic space and primordial wisdom[28] are integrated, I am beyond conceptual fixation. I have no 'manner of arising of meditation': clarity shines in the original nature beyond conceptual constructs. I have no 'way of self-liberating in the conduct': this very vision arises as the energy display [of my primordial state]. I have no 'achievement of the fruit beyond all concepts': I have taken hold of my original condition beyond limitations. This is my partial understanding of all the signs of the natural state."

At that point Gyermi Nyiwö said, "Son, if yours is not merely clever, empty talk, and you have actually realized this meaning, then [your understanding] is very elevated! Yet, being skilled in intellectual talk is not the real view but the cause and condition for deviating into the views of eternalism and nihilism. Attachment to meditation, which is the dirt of the mind, is the cause and condition for deviating severely into drowsiness and agitation. The way of acting with obstinacy for rejecting or obtaining, and for abandoning or taking, is the cause and condition for deviating into the dualism of attachment and aversion. The fruit of mental aspiration, without having taken hold of one's nature, is the cause and condition for deviating into the dualism of hope and fear. If all these causes and conditions are not purified in their own place, even meditating for a kalpa would not help one transcend the mind. Therefore, unfold yourself in the undefiled basic space beyond the conceptual mind!"

Then the Great Khyentse said, "Gyermi Nyiwö, don't say these things! Authentic signs seem to have arisen in this son, and he does not need a pointing-out instruction on the way of removing obstacles and progressing. Whether he follows what you just said or not, whatever he does, he has already reached the ultimate aim." Turning to me, he continued, "Yet, remain in the unmodified and unlimited, empty nature! Don't forget us shenpos, and pray continuously to us. Even though you have taken hold of the natural state, it is important not to part from the yidam deity."

Thus he said, and placing his right hand and his left foot on the crown of my head, gave me an initiation. Then Tsewang mounted a turquoise cuckoo and flew toward the holy place of Chari Tsugden. Gyermi transformed himself into a raven and flew toward India.

17

One evening, immediately after it got dark, I was lying down on my back when Sipai Gyalmo and Gyermi Nyiwö arrived. I sat up straight in position, and then, playing the damaru and the *silnyen* cymbal, I started to dance and sing invocations.

After a while, I found myself in space and saw a temple made of many precious materials, impossible to forget. It was covered with rainbow colors on all sides, and the smells of various cooked foods emanated from inside. I was so surprised that I became distracted by all this. Sipai Gyalmo and Gyermi Nyiwö were inside the temple, from where the sound of all celestial musical instruments could be heard.

Then a woman who was wearing many ornaments came to me and said, "Son, what's wrong with you? In this supreme temple the unique mother Sipai Gyalmo, Gyermi Nyiwö, and countless other male and female shens are gathered because the outer and inner tantras are being explained and the wheel of Bön is turning. If you don't show devotion toward this, if you are not afraid of birth and death but remain with your thinking mind, then tell me, which are your concrete miraculous powers? What is your great confidence? Hey you! It seems to me that your faith has become stale, and that you are still in the thinking mind. Let's hurry to the big gathering of the ganachakra feast!"

My instant presence woke up strong and clear, and without touching my feet to the ground, with a single step I reached the temple. There, upon a big throne, surrounded by a mass of flames and precious materials, the unique mother Sipai Gyalmo, wearing many bone ornaments, was sitting. Gyermi, holding a damaru made of a human skull in his right hand and a small *shang* cymbal of lapis lazuli in his left, was singing with a melodious voice the demarcation of the outer and inner boundaries.[29] I also saw some dakinis, but I could only recognize Tsogdag Karmo.

Then Tsogdag Karmo told me, "Son, the illusory vision of the world is the work of demons. This large ganachakra gathering of enjoyments is only common to the peaceful and wrathful sugatas. For almost all ordinary persons it is impossible to come here. And even if some did come here, few have obtained the siddhis. But don't be proud: meditate on the primordially enlightened mind and partake of the siddhis! Don't feel timid either, and sit close to Gyermi!"

I made some mudras with my hands and stood up beside Gyermi, who said, "All of you sons, remain in the state of equanimity of contemplation. I will explain the tantra of the immutable Yungdrung Bön."

But Tsogdag Karmo said, "There is no need for you to explain the tantra of Bön; it is already contained in the primordially enlightened mind. The primordially enlightened mind is beyond words and explanations. Instead of giving many explanations about it, relax in the basic space beyond conceptual mind. Even ordinary persons don't make too many explanations for fear of deviating from the real meaning. Therefore, don't give this explanation on Bön this time, Gyermi, but stand up! Help prepare and arrange all that is needed for this feast. We mother dakinis have to go for a while."

Thereupon Gyermi replied, "Most excellent of all dakinis, Tsogdag Karmo, listen! Although your words and meanings are very nice, I am not happy that you stopped my explanation on the tantra of Bön. The foundation of all Bön teachings is mind-essence. But even though mind-essence, the dharmakaya, is innate in all, this is difficult to understand for ignorant beings. I was going to explain for those beings who have no understanding, and I have absolutely no doubts about this. If everybody is able to understand without the need of explanations, I will pay my homages to you! Then, what is it that you [dakinis] have to do in some other place while we perform the ganachakra? Besides, is not interrupting a teaching something against the will of the dakini Sipai Gyalmo?"

Tsogdag Karmo again said, "Shenpo knowledge-holder, Gyermi Nyiwö, listen! I don't know logic and so many doubts! Sipai Gyalmo herself has said:

> Without explaining, without meditating, without intention,
> Relax in the totally authentic condition beyond expression!
> However many explanations are made, the meanings never end.

This is why I spoke in that way. Don't nurture doubts; remain in the real meaning! We have to go soon!" Thus she said, and then all the dakinis, turning into ravens and wild asses, went away.

At that point there was nobody who could help preparing the feast, and Sipai Gyalmo remained seated at her place. Also, there was nobody for making offerings, dancing, and playing. After a while, Gyermi emanated eight men, four of whom started to prepare the ganachakra, while the other four, together with Sipai Gyalmo, made the offerings and played the instruments. Then they distributed the offerings and gave the leftovers to all the beings in the universe. They did not bestow any initiation upon me, and they all disappeared, how or where I could not tell.

18

One evening, as it started to become dark, near the pole of the tent I saw a white and luminous body as small as a butter lamp. Jokingly I called out, "Hey, butter lamp, where are you coming from?" and laughed, teasing him.

"You ask from where I come? I don't come from anywhere; I am simply staying in my original place. You pretend to be in your original place, but you have not taken hold of it yet!"

"He must be the emanation of some buddha," I thought, and in doubt I asked, "What do you mean when you say that I have not taken hold of my place?"

"Like iron dust scattered in the air," he replied.

"How could this happen? In the totally pervading emptiness of the all-ground, instant presence plays unceasingly around."

"Son, don't be too eloquent; understand the real meaning at its root! The essence is one's undefiled mind. Become familiar with this undefiled nature! When practicing meditation, it is important to eliminate obstacles and to progress. There are three kinds of obstacles: outer, inner, and secret. You must know the nature of these three.

The outer obstacle is this very vision. Don't follow what appears, but leave it in emptiness. The inner obstacle is the body made of the four elements. It has to be protected from heat and from cold, and it needs food and clothes. Also, the mat where one sits needs to be soft. Don't meditate lying down, don't be lazy. Be alert and relaxed. The secret obstacles are the various thoughts. From the basic space of the all-ground, let primordial wisdom manifest clearly! Remain in a state beyond limitations in which clarity and emptiness are inseparable. Practice in this way!"

Thus he said, and, joining his palms in a mudra, gave me an initiation. At the end, a white letter A[30] emerged from the side of his thumb and hit my heart. As soon as the A penetrated my chest, other similar A letters emanated from it until the whole upper part of my body was full of As. In that very moment, everything shone unobstructed and vividly clear, and I could know other people's thoughts as well as anything anybody was doing in all directions. I could see the sexual acts between males and females, precisely all what they were doing, and whether the females became pregnant with a boy or a girl, and thus, not being able to control myself, I burst out laughing with much fun.

19

One early morning, before dawn, a woman with a perfectly proportioned body arrived. She was wearing a dress of five rainbow colors and various jewels as ornaments. Her face, white and shining like the full moon, had the power to illuminate all regions with its rays. She was irresistibly beautiful and very difficult to part with. I remained naturally gazing at her beauty and became distracted.

Then that woman said, "Noble son, the beautiful and the ugly are the natural energy display of instant presence. Don't try to grasp what is beautiful; look at the mind that is looking! I am the glory and protectress of all mother dakinis, and my name is Nyima Wöden. As we have a karmic connection, I have come to make love to you. Don't have doubts; enjoy me!" and she came into my bed.

I had the impression that my body had become a body of light, and that my tent was a luminous pavilion. But then no sexual desire arose in me, and I felt both joy and fear. Since neither of us made any erotic move toward the other, for a while we remained as two lights merged one with the other.

Then she said, "Noble son, it seems that you are still in an impermanent and mutable condition. Go beyond everything to achieve the final, immutable state!" And she disappeared.

20

Then, starting in the springtime, I had the following encounters.

Once, while I was staying in the house of some of my students and benefactors, in the middle of the night I saw eleven male and female knowledge-holders arrive, among whom were Tsewang Rigdzin, Wöden Barma, and Nyima Wöden. The Great Khyentse [Tsewang Rigdzin] sat upon the torma and blessed it. Nyima Wöden gave me a secret initiation, while Wöden Barma gave me a pointing-out instruction in this way:

> Son, send the clouds in the sky to the wind.
> Throw the jewel in the vessel behind.
> Kill the otter in the water.
> Strip the child naked in the cold wind.[31]
> Follow this advice precisely!

Thus she said, and then sat naturally in space. Then Nyima Wöden showed me her sexual organ, and the red essence poured out continuously from her vagina. I burst into laughter, but the Great Khyentse from the top of the torma rebuked me, saying, "Son, don't think this is a joke. Place your hands like a bowl to receive this siddhi of the supreme essence!"

So I placed my hands in that way, and Nyima Wöden, with an expression of displeasure, filled them up with the red essence. Then they all went away, and I gave an initiation to some of my students and benefactors.

21

One morning when the sun was already warm, while I was in a threshing floor, Trenpa Namkha and his son Tsewang Rigdzin came and gave me a pointing-out instruction. Then around midday I felt happy and inspired, and sang invocations. After a short while Gyermi Nyiwö arrived, and as my state of instant presence naturally woke up strong and clear, I shook my hands and feet to and fro and jumped. Many of my students, male and female, made prostrations. Then I got up and started to dance. Tsewang Rigdzin, Lishu Tagring, Mutsa Gyerme, Gyermi Nyiwö, Thugje Kundrol, Nyima Tongkhyab, Yingchug Gyaltsen, Wöden Barma—these eight knowledge-holders and dakinis—came to me and gave me initiations, advice, and pointing-out instructions.

22

One afternoon some of my students requested me to give an initiation, so I went there and lay down naturally. At one point, from the sky I heard many different sounds, so I sat up straight in position and started to sing invocations, accompanied by the sound of the damaru and *silnyen* cymbal. Then Tsewang Rigdzin, in sexual union with his consort, arrived from space.

Before sunset, Tongyung Thuchen, Trenpa Namkha, Yongsu Tagpa[32] and innumerable other knowledge-holders also came, together with Wöden Barma and many other dakinis. Countless male and female knowledge-holders also arrived, blessing the tormas and bestowing initiations upon all.

23

The following morning, at sunrise, Tsewang Rigdzin and Nyima Wöden came, surrounded by many dakinis wearing ornaments. I offered a dance and invocations, and the Great Khyentse told me from space, "Son, if your joyful feeling is that strong, it is a sign that you have not yet reached the natural condition beyond limitations. All the infinite deities of the peaceful and wrathful buddhas exist self-perfected inside you. Why do you feel joy when you see them? Let your joyful feeling self-liberate in its own place. Remain in the state of the thought-free essence!"

Thus he said. Then some of them turned into rainbows and disappeared. Others emanated into vultures, and left.

24

One day, while I was sleeping inside a tent, I had the impression that I heard sounds like *trog trog sil sil* coming from somewhere. I arose and looked out, and saw the Great Scholar [Tongyung Thuchen] arrive riding a vulture. Without knowing what I was doing, I stood up and ran to the entrance. There I saw Gyungyar Mukhö and Jegyal Lhagom,[33] both of them sitting on seats made of varicolored lotus flowers.

Then Gyungyar told me, "Son, express the measure of progress of your experience of bliss and heat to the master Tongyung."

"To you, marvelous master, and to the other knowledge-holder shens this ignorant being bows down," I replied. "I, the deluded one, am still an ordinary being, and I have no measure of progress of the experience of bliss and heat. To you, supreme masters of the past, I ask to be introduced to their meaning!"

The wise Tongyung said, "Noble son, you who are continuing your practice from past [lives], listen! The measure of progress of the experiences of bliss and heat is merely a verbal definition. Don't analyze intellectually with artificial definitions: strip naked the wisdom that is beyond thoughts and grasping! Set yourself free beyond action and concepts, without following the objects [of vision]! Make the state of meditation in which there is no thinking and no separation shine clearly!"

Gyungyar said, "Relax in the natural condition, unborn and without a basis! Release yourself from the thoughts and emotions that cause fixation on concreteness! Recognize the movement of latent inclinations! Keep this state empty and without concepts!"

Jegyal Lhagom said:

> How strange that nobody sees the jewel of the garuda[34] on the main road!
> How strange that the dry skin in the ocean never gets soaked!
> How strange that the feather never gets burned in the fire!
> How strange that pieces of wool in empty space are never carried away by the wind![35]

Thus they told me, and without giving any initiation, they all went away.

25

One afternoon, while I was walking reciting invocations, I saw Trenpa Namkha entering my tent. By the strength of joy, with one step I arrived inside my tent, where I saw clearly and without obstructions the five buddhas with their consorts[36] in bright colors in the heart of Trenpa Namkha. They bestowed upon me the inner and outer initiations. Then I gave blessings with my feet to some of my students.

26

One evening, while I was in a ganapuja row, Tongyung Thuchen arrived at the head of many knowledge-holders, and also Nyima Wöden together with numerous dakinis, an incalculable number in all. My instant presence became clear and strong, and I started to run everywhere, outside and inside. Everything shone vividly clear and unobstructed, and I felt that I was inseparable from those ancient masters. I did not write down all the initiations and pointing-out instructions that they gave me. That night I gave a good initiation to many of my spiritual brothers and students, and to some male and female benefactors too. And I was certain that, having received the blessings, they would not fall to the lower states anymore.

27

One afternoon, while it was raining intermittently, I was sitting in my tent in the position of meditation, when all the earth, the stones, and the rocky mountains shook and trembled. My body also moved and shook at the same time. After a short while, I saw Chime Tsugphü[37] together with some other knowledge-holders sitting in space. Uncommon faith arose inside me, and I made invocations to them.

Then I heard a voice from space, though I could not understand who it was:

> If you are present to the natural clarity of your mind, contemplation will arise in you.
> If you understand that the field of vision is empty, whatever you do will be perfect as your energy display.

> If you view samsara and nirvana as one, all will be equal in your mind.
> If you understand that thought itself is the dharmakaya, your meditation will transcend the conceptual mind.
> If the solidified states of drowsiness and agitation dissolve, real knowledge will arise in you.
> If you don't put this into practice, what is the use of meditating?

I was so surprised by this that my instant presence became naturally clear and strong. And that time too I gave many initiations to some of my students.

28

Once, during the second half of the night, the Great Lama Trenpa Namkha and Wöden Barma came, surrounded by seven male and female knowledge-holders as their retinue. One of those shens told me:

> In the totally pervading condition beyond concepts and grasping,
> I saw an infant incapable of thinking, naturally enchanted.
> In the pavilion temple made of the five precious jewels,
> I saw a monkey freeing itself from the chains and playing.
> In the inviolable castle of unchangeable gold,
> I saw the self-originated unique man enter.[38]
> These are the visions that I had.
> Which are yours, noble man?

"I pay homage to Khöpung Trenpa Namkha! Knowledge-holder shen, listen!" I replied. "I admire all that you said about the absolute meaning, and all the visions that you had are truly amazing. This stupid beggar has no visions. Whether I look outside or inside, all is in a condition of emptiness. In the nature of emptiness beyond limitations there is nothing to see. If you become familiar with this 'nothing to see,' the three kayas will spontaneously manifest without any effort. This is the meaning of 'having no visions.'"

Then the Great Lama Trenpa spoke, "Sons of noble lineage, what you both said is marvelous! And your words and meanings correspond to the real sense. But if you merely engage in much empty talk without putting its meaning into practice, all becomes useless like the 'cause and effect' repeated by a parrot. Therefore, the absolute meaning is beyond explanation and conceptual mind. Explaining a lot with eloquence can become an obstacle to one's practice. Hence, relax in the authentic condition beyond limitations. Remain in the thought-free and selfless condition of emptiness. If you transcend words, thoughts, and explanations, that is the fruit itself."

Thus he said and came to sit upon the crown of my head. Then they all went away.

29

Once around midday while I was lying facing downward, a red luminous body as small as a thumb told me from space, "Son, don't lie down, sit in position! I will give you a blessing and an initiation!"

I remained normally distracted and did not sit up.

"Hey you!" he rebuked me. "You are the kind of ordinary being who disobeys the supreme masters! Although I have given you teachings and instructions before, you don't sit in position but remain lying down under the power of drowsiness and dullness. For most of those who meditate lying down it is impossible for the state of knowledge to arise. If you meditate in position, the wisdom of instant presence will arise. Since the body depends on the four elements, it is important to practice [the yogic exercises] of tsalungs [channels and winds] and yantras.[39] Therefore, the position of the body is essential."

To this I replied, "I pay homage to the teaching of the supreme masters of the past! Since I meditate [by abiding] in the primordially enlightened mind, I remain freely relaxed without distinction in going, lying down, and sitting. In the unmodified and authentic condition beyond all grasping, I forgot the corrections of tsalungs and yantras. I don't need to tire myself out meditating with the mind; the wisdom of my instant presence arises naturally. This is why I am lying down."

"Eloquent son, listen!" he said. "If your nice words correspond to the meaning in practice, then it is fine. The real meaning is the primordially enlightened mind beyond concepts and thinking. Remain in this primordially enlightened mind without correcting or modifying anything. Therefore, let wisdom shine clearly in the condition of emptiness! And don't be attached to this clarity!"

Thus he said and came to sit upon the crown of my head. I felt my body and mind inseparable in a dimension of emptiness. And I had the impression that my body and his body of light, without duality, were flying in the space of the sky. Then a movement arose in my mind, but I thought to myself, "I have good control of my body!" That thought itself was a deluded thinking of the mind, so I was no longer able to control my body, and fell down. When I looked in space and around in all directions, everything was shrouded in five rainbow colors. Inside a rainbow the size of a house, I saw the body of light shining vividly bright.

He looked at me, and said, "Son, all that you said to me does not get close to the real meaning and was merely eloquent speech. Since you have not become able yet to let your thoughts dissolve in their natural place, it is not proper to speak so boldly in front of the supreme masters. With your body and mind unified you wished to fly. But the movement of a thought of pride arose in you, and, not knowing how to liberate that same thought, you destroyed the power of miracle and fell down. Therefore it is important that you continue with your practice until you achieve the imperturbable fruit beyond all concepts."

Then the body of light and the rainbow disappeared.

30

One morning I saw clearly all the wrathful deities with their entourage arrive in space, attired in glittering colors: the [ten] Chenpos, the [sixteen] Rigpas, the [eight] Gatekeepers,[40] and so forth, all in sexual union with their consorts. They showed me their faces and gave me siddhis. I had the impression that the whole universe and its beings were naturally fainting, while sounds, lights, and rays spread in the regions of the world. Mountains of flame and the luminous rays of their weapons pervaded all places and directions. The colors of their bodies, the objects in their hands, and the radiance in their faces were so terrifying that I could not bear to give even a sidelong glance. The main deities in union with their consorts and their entourage were filling the sky to overflowing.

Then they gave me an abridged initiation, and when my instant presence became strong and clear, I started to dance without control. I had the feeling that I had perfectly received the initiation and the common and supreme siddhis.

Then I gave many initiations and blessings with my feet and in other ways to a great number of my male and female students.

31

One early morning before dawn I was sleeping, and without knowing what was happening I went out and fell on my back. Scared, I got up immediately and looked in front, and I saw that the kind Tongyung Thuchen and Trenpa Namkha, and Tsewang Rigdzin in sexual union with his consort had arrived. Unaware of what was going on, I started to write a lot of things, but the Great Scholar [Tongyung] told me, "Son, what is the purpose of writing that useless stuff? On the seat of the immutable essence of the final attainment, let the man—instant presence—dwell freely relaxed! There is no need of many words and explanations, but tell me, what is the measure of your progress in the ineffable condition?"

This ignorant being replied, "Marvelous! I respectfully pay homage to the masters Tongyung and Trenpa Namkha, and to Khyentse [Tsewang] with his consort! Words and explanations are many, but they arise spontaneously and freely without interruption. They should not be blocked, because they arise from the birthless condition. If words and explanations are blocked, how can that which is beyond words arise? I have no measure of progress. I am just entering the authentic condition beyond limitations. In this regard, whatever you deem appropriate to enhance my practice and to remove obstacles, I plead you, supreme masters, to teach it to me!"

The Great Lama Trenpa said, "Great master [Tongyung], give him an initiation and a blessing! And you, son Khyentse, bestow a secret initiation on him! I, Khöpung, will give him a pointing-out instruction!" And he spoke:

> Don't let the stray dog wander freely: hand it over to its owner!
> Don't ever be attached to being in the dark: stay in the pure self-originated temple!
> Don't put the self-originated man in chains: let him go free in the empty space that has no owner!

Thus he said, and after giving me an initiation he disappeared.

32

Once I was lying down inside my tent on a plain among rocky mountains, when Gyungyar Mukhö and Gyermi Nyiwö arrived. I made some mudras out of respect, and Gyermi said, "Son, have you perfectly understood the three points of learning, reflecting, and meditating?"

"Without a root or basis is total emptiness, and thus I saw no essence to understand," I replied.

Gyermi retorted, "Hey! Your words are too elevated. I wonder whether you have really understood such nice essence!"

And I replied:

> I bow down to the most excellent of knowledge-holders, Gyermi Nyiwö!
> I sleep in the unmodified dimension of emptiness.
> I abide in the condition of spontaneous freedom of self-originated wisdom.
> I remain in the authentic condition that is empty and thought-free.
> I rest in the clarity that manifests unceasingly, without being attached to it.
> I abide in the dharmakaya, the undefiled essence beyond action.
> Since the one who abides has no limitations, he is in the condition of thought-free space.

Gyungyar Mukhö spoke, "Excellent, son! It seems you have understood the real meaning. There is nothing to add besides what you have said. Yet, you have to carry on until you achieve the final fruit beyond all concepts!" And they went away.

33

One morning on the fifteenth day of the lunar month, while I was drinking tea inside a black yak-hair tent, the wisdom of my instant presence became unobstructedly clear. I was astonished, and with trust I looked in every direction and saw clearly in my pure vision where all the buddhas and the male and female knowledge-holders of the past were abiding. In the impure vision, I saw what all the ignorant beings were experiencing and what they were doing. I saw beings wandering in the bardo without a physical support for their minds, and [understood] the ways to benefit them. I saw everywhere Buddhists, Bönpos, and rulers, and all that every man and every woman was doing. For a while all this appeared to me vividly clear, without obstructions.

I looked back inside my tent, and saw Nyima Wöden riding a tiger above it. Without having the time to finish my tea, I went back to my tent and Nyima Wöden told me, "Son, prepare the worldly material offerings, and purify your body, voice, and mind! Get ready for the musical offerings to the wisdom deities. Today it is possible that the five buddhas will arrive. If you want to receive initiations, blessings, and siddhis, place [all your offerings] in a vessel and don't waste this occasion!" and she disappeared in space.

Then I assigned many of my students and monks the task of preparing the offerings for the ganachakra. I remained seated chanting invocations, when after a while I saw clearly the buddhas and knowledge-holders in the sky.

That time, in the rows of the many monks and other students of mine, I recognized clearly and without obstruction a man who had committed negative actions and who had been defiled with the five evil deeds that cause immediate retribution.[41] Since I could not give him the initiation together with the rest, I told him, "Come here!" and made him sit in front of me.

Then, firstly the five buddhas with their consorts arrived, followed by Tongyung Thuchen, Trenpa Namkha and his son Tsewang Rigdzin, and innumerable others, and they all gave me siddhis and initiations. As my instant presence became strong and clear, I started to run everywhere, and I gave the blessings with my hands to my male and female students. Then I gave the initiations and blessings to about a hundred of them according to the instructions.

34

The evening of that same day, while I was drinking tea in the house of a benefactor, my instant presence became strong and clear, and I started spontaneously to run, and in three steps I reached my tent. It was transparent and filled with light, so that I remained naturally enchanted. Then I saw innumerable knowledge-holders led by Tongyung Thuchen and Trenpa Namkha assembling in my tent from the sky. My body and mind united with the dimension of space, without control, like two lights merging one into the other, and, without knowing what I was doing, I danced and ran. Many of my students surrounded me and offered me dances, music, and prostrations. I blessed them all with my feet and hands, and the pointing-out instructions that I gave and the invocations that I made are indescribable.

35

One evening, while I was preparing a large offering of tormas, some knowledge-holders and dakinis arrived. I did not feel any particular joy but remained naturally as if nothing had happened.

One dakini then told me, "Son, you are bound by pride and conceit as you don't show devotion to us, males and females. Do you think you don't need the supreme and common siddhis? Do you dare give initiations to all without first having the tormas for the initiation blessed? Without having achieved the great natural state in your mind, do you deem yourself capable of acting impartially for the benefit of beings?"

I replied, "Mother dakini, how strange and suspicious you are! I who abide in the unmodified and unlimited mind-essence where the outer and the inner, samsara and nirvana, are perfected, have obtained the initiation in my mind, without receiving it from outside. For me, who am the nature of Samantabhadra, there are no blessings that should descend from somewhere. As the three kayas arise spontaneously in me, I have no siddhi to receive from somewhere else."

While we were engaged in this conversation, sounds, lights, rays, and so forth filled the whole world so intensely that they were hard to bear. I stood up and went to my tent, and after a while I saw Khyentse [Tsewang Rigdzin] arrive. I asked him, "Precious knowledge-holder who works for the benefit of all beings, how many buddhas, knowledge-holders, and dakinis will come tonight to this assembly hall? Which initiations and blessings will they give me? Will I not be allowed to give the initiations to others?"

Khyentse replied, "Concerning the knowledge-holders, a large number of shens, male and female buddhas of the direct transmission, and innumerable knowledge-holders and dakinis who are inseparable and indescribable will soon arrive. They will give you the outer, inner, and secret initiations, and also the authorization for transmission, all complete. You will be allowed to give the initiations to others, but, before doing this, you should distinguish well who is fit to receive them and who is not. You can do whatever is beneficial for all beings."

After I received this information, I saw infinite hosts of peaceful and wrathful deities and buddhas together with innumerable male and female knowledge-holders arrive from space and gather in the sky. My instant presence became strong and clear, and I danced in midair. Then they gave me an outer initiation with the authorization for transmission.

Then I bestowed the initiation on many of my students. That time I had the courage to promise to all of those who came to the initiation row that they would never again fall into the three lower states of existence.

36

The following morning, when the sun was already warm, I saw [the dakinis] Gyenzangma and Kunshe Serden sitting upon the tormas. As I was about to give an initiation to some persons who had committed heavy negative actions, the dakini Gyenzangma told me, "Son, you are going to give the initiation to people who did negative actions. Can you promise that you will lead them up?"

"Marvelous, kind dakini, mother and sister!" I replied. "Bless this son who keeps the samayas [commitments].[42] When the supreme knowledge-holders bestowed the initiations upon me, they gave me the authorization for transmission and enjoined me to give in turn the initiations to others too. Therefore I always give initiations to all beings with negative karmas, without rejecting some and accepting others, and as the supreme masters told me, I don't think that they cannot be led up."

Then Kunshe Serden said, "Excellent, son! Whatever you do can bring benefits. You have achieved the fruit of practice started in previous lives, and since pure vision has arisen in you, you have met all the buddhas and received completely the initiations together with the authorizations for transmission. Don't have any doubt: you can really work for the benefit of beings!"

Thus she said, and then they became two rainbows the size of a spindle, and disappeared.

37

One day, while I was performing the DU TRI SU ritual for eliminating negativities,[43] I heard pleasant sounds in the sky. I got up and walked around a little, and when I looked inside my tent I saw that it was full of light, so I jumped and entered it. The unique mother Sipai Gyalmo had descended from space and was looking at me with a joyful expression. I had a feeling of certainty, happiness arose in me, and I sang invocations while making mudras.

The unique mother Sipai Gyalmo then said, "These invocations with much gladness are not different from the mental attitude of worldly people.

The minds of ignorant beings are normally in the illusory vision. You have not overcome your mind yet; hence, get hold of the undefiled essence beyond the conceptual mind! Worldly people, when they become familiar with each other, start to get worse, and from the original intimacy they end up nurturing bad thoughts one against the other. Therefore it is better if you go to empty mountains and rocky caves, and, away from your students, remain alone."

This beggar replied, "I bow down to the unique mother Sipai Gyalmo, glory of all dakinis, great mother and refuge for all! I was struck by all that you said to this beggar; nevertheless, in the teachings of the supreme buddhas of the past it is said that one should lead the lowest ignorant beings by means of a verbal connection. This is the purpose of this wandering beggar!"

"I can't say that what you just said is not true," she explained, "but if you teach someone who has committed heavy negative actions under the influence of demons when the time is not ripe, interruptions can arise for you."

Thus she said, and gave me an initiation. Then my instant presence became very powerful, and I gave blessings with my feet to all of my faithful students.

38

One night, while it was raining hard and I was chanting invocations, I saw Khyentse [Tsewang Rigdzin] arrive. He gave me an empowerment containing all four initiations, and then advised me and instructed me thus:

> You, noble son, who are able to work for the benefit of beings, since you don't judge whom to accept and whom to reject as a student, worldly people will nurture bad thoughts toward you. But you should not have doubts about this, and regardless of the good or bad things they may say, make a verbal connection to the teaching with all. Don't be partial: look on everyone with impartial, equal compassion. Most individuals are not able to abide with confidence and without limitations in the imperturbable, immutable state. Therefore, regardless of the ups and downs and of the good or bad things that may happen, let everything arise as the energy of the wisdom of mind-essence!

Thus he said, and, after pronouncing three words, he turned into a tiger-striped hornet[44] and disappeared.

39

One early morning before dawn, while I was sleeping normally, I heard these words without seeing any form:

"Son, if today at sunrise you go directly wherever you want without a destination and without doubting, it is possible that you will receive the quintessential siddhi."

After I heard this, I sat up straight in position, but I did not hear or see anything else. Then, at sunrise, I refreshed my instant presence and went, but, seeing nothing, I fell asleep once again. And while I was sleeping, this miraculous event happened.

In a pavilion temple of precious materials, Tongyung Thuchen, Trenpa Namkha and his son [Tsewang], Shari Uchen with the rest of the three scholars,[45] and so forth, were seated, and also Wöden Barma, Nyima Wöden, Thugje Kundrol, and so forth. There were no ganachakra offerings nor siddhi [substances], and no objects of enjoyment, but I entered the row. After a while Gyermi Nyiwö arrived with a small golden vessel filled to the brim with human flesh and other foods, and with the six fresh medicinal herbs. Thus they started to arrange the ganachakra and made all the preparations for the offerings.

At one point the Great Scholar [Tongyung] said, "Gyermi, you possess the capacity of wrathful power! You who are so powerful, show miracles! This temple of ours is a purified place; hence, let's have fun performing miracles!"

Khöpung [Trenpa Namkha] asked me, "Son, what kind of miraculous powers do you have?" "I have no miraculous power," I replied. "I am just a sentient being with a human body. If I had any power, you, supreme master, should have known it!" Thereupon Gyermi said, "Son, the capacity of display of the energy of self-originated wisdom exists [naturally] as the energy of the total realization of mind-essence. Therefore, take out whichever miraculous power is possible for you!"

Then Gyermi performed the following feat. From the trunk of his body he emanated a gigantic wrathful deity; from his arms and legs, the four great kings;[46] from his ten fingers, ten shens; and from his ten toes, ten female deities. The wrathful deity was sitting in space, but the four kings, the shens, and the female deities were displaying many magical feats of wrathful power as an offering. Also I, without control, became five bodies. One of them was sitting in front of Khöpung [Trenpa Namkha], another was assisting

Khyentse [Tsewang Rigdzin], while another still was helping distribute the ganachakra offerings, another was arranging the first ganachakra offerings, and another was holding flowers and offering them.

Then the Great Scholar [Tongyung] told me, "Gyermi has unobstructed power, but what you did is like a small child's game. Don't be either proud or timid about it, but relax in your own nature. If it were not for me, you would not have been able to display such capacity. Anyway, even if you possessed this kind of capacity, if you didn't keep it secret it would create interruptions to your life."

Thus he said, and gave me some initiations. Then everybody went away.

40

One day I was lying down on a hill when I saw the Great Lama [Trenpa Namkha] and others, seven knowledge-holders in all. In front of Khöpung [Trenpa Namkha] was a tall and dark-skinned knowledge-holder, with a brown face and brahmin attire. He was wearing a blue shawl and a collar made of tiger skin, while in his right hand he was holding a yellow bamboo walking stick. As I had never seen him, I did not know his name. So I asked Khöpung, "Who is this shen?" Khöpung did not reply, but he himself said, "Son, you don't need to wonder who I am. I am one who has reached the dimension that never changes. Don't have doubts about me, but tell me something about yourself!"

Then I said, "Wondrous, unknown knowledge-holder! For certain you must already know about me, it is not really necessary that I tell my story. Instead, tell me something about your life."

"Listen to what I say, noble son!" he replied. "I am a son of the immutable and immortal swastika, and my working activity involves what is beyond thoughts, self, and limitations. I play games with the unborn child Unique State. I emulate the vault of the undistracted sky. I sit on the shimmering precious jewel. This is the life-story of me, a shen."

I replied, "Immutable being, knowledge-holder shen! Concerning the absolute, natural state you hinted at, I am also roughly never separated from it. But when I asked about your life-story, what I meant was, which knowledge-holder of the past are you? How are you thinking to benefit sentient beings? What is your name now? Please, reveal to me all these things!"

Thereupon he spoke. "Listen you, son of the clear instant presence! When I was still in the impure, material condition my name was Yelo. At that time

I made connections with all beings and led many of them to the blissful dimension. Also, by means of good connections as well as bad connections[47] I prevented them from falling into samsara, and I accepted many of them as my students. When that time was over I departed, and for the benefit of beings I was reborn in Kashmir, where I led millions of beings to liberation. My name was Yeshe Lama. I looked with compassion upon all those who saw me and heard me. Then, when I had achieved the purified, immaterial condition, my name was Milü Samleg.[48] You are still in the ignorant mind, and since you did not recognize me, it means you have karmic traces. You have yet to transcend the illusory mind and establish yourself in the real nature!"

Thus he said, and, by the power of happiness, I stood up and danced, and also made many prostrations. Then he gave me an initiation containing all four initiations, and a letter A appeared on his neck and chest. From those [two] As, innumerable A letters spread and vanished inside me, and I became a body of light without substance, unobstructed, clear, and transparent, without an inside and an outside.

41

One day in the early afternoon I was lying down on a green meadow when my senses became blurred without control. Then three white vultures came and told me, "Son, what are you doing here? Now is the time to rush to the great ganachakra assembly of seven thousand knowledge-holders."

I replied, "Where are you three coming from? Where is the ganachakra assembly of seven thousand knowledge-holders? I do not know you, who are you? I have a material, illusory body made of flesh and blood, and since I have no miraculous power like you three, will it not be difficult for me to reach the knowledge-holders' rows?"

"Son, you needn't be so doubtful!" they replied. "Without hesitating, take out your miraculous power! As we four have to go quickly, we'll tell you everything once we have reached the great ganachakra assembly."

Then I lost my senses, became naturally drowsy, and fell into a deep sleep. While I was sleeping, the following miracle manifested.

I too had turned into a vulture and the four of us were flying in the sky. After a short while I had the feeling we had reached the town of Sukhavati [Blissful] in the west. At the center of Sukhavati was a citadel built with the five precious materials that was immense, impressive, and amazing. We entered a temple of precious stones that was spreading rainbow lights in all directions. Inside this impressive, supreme temple was Trenpa Namkha at the head of innumerable knowledge-holders. Some of them were explaining the outer, inner, and secret tantras of Bön; some were prostrating themselves out of faith while asking for teachings; some were dancing and playing instruments; some were attending to all the ganachakra preparations; others were sitting in contemplation; and still others were making various mudras with their hands.

As there was no place for me to sit, I remained standing normally, and without showing any devotion I became distracted in an ordinary way. After a while one of the vultures who had previously assisted me came, I could not understand from where, and told me:

"Son, you have not carried to completion your final realization yet, and in this shining, amazing temple, Trenpa and other knowledge-holders have assembled to perform a ganachakra and to explain the tantras of Bön. What sort of person are you that you don't show faith, devotion, and respect for this great, pure accumulation of enjoyments? Do you think such a vision is not worthwhile to see? Or maybe you think that it is not something superior to you? Son, it is not like this! With faith, devotion, and respect, remain in immovable contemplation without separating from it, and continuously sing invocations with a nice melody!"

Thus he said and led me to sit next to Lishu Tagring. In an immovable state, I started to sing invocations without interruption. Sitting in cross-legged position with my hands in the meditation mudra, I joined my palms and sang invocations to all.

Lishu Tagring said, "Son, if you have the confidence of immutable bliss, you don't need the artificiality of words and invocations!"

Then, sitting next to the Great Khyentse [Tsewang], I saw a knowledge-holder shen that I had never met before. He was wearing a cloak of tiger skin ornamented with precious jewels, and was reciting secret mantras with a whispering *si li li* sound. As I had never seen him, I observed him for a short while. But the shen told me, "Son, your senses are distracted by the outside and thus you lose your instant presence. As you don't observe yourself, but instead look at me thinking that I am still in the impure condition, the profound state of contemplation cannot arise in you. You don't need to gaze at me wondering who I am. I am always a helper of beings who holds the transmission lineage of the past."

"You are very envious, shen!" I replied, "I was simply looking at you for a moment since I had never seen you before, and this would not bother anyone. Wherever I look, be it outside or inside, I always maintain the immutable essence. Thus, it makes no difference at all to me. You are still accepting or rejecting, taking or abandoning!"

Thereupon he said, "If your words correspond to the real meaning, listen to this:

> The vase of gold, the tent of coral,
> The white conch-shell stupa, the castle of gold, and sand:
> When the sun strikes upon them, they have beautiful colors,
> But when the moon rises, they become black.

Do you understand thoroughly the meaning of this verse?"

Right away I replied, "You don't need to clarify these examples for me; I understand their meaning. I trust your sayings, but tell me about yourself!"

"Noble son, if you already know it in your mind, it is sufficient. It is not necessary for me to tell what you already know."

Thereupon Lishu Tagring said to me, "He is one of the emanations of Tagla Menbar.[49] When he was not yet purified, his name was Trowo Gyaltsen. He protects all beings with compassion. You don't have to tell this to ordinary people. If you know this in your mind, that is enough!"

Then I received all the siddhis even though they did not distribute the ganachakra offerings nor did they give any initiations, whereupon I thought, "Now I want to go back."

42

One morning when the sun was already warm, I was drinking a cup of yogurt when I saw a red tigress arrive above in front of me. After a short while, this miraculous event happened.

The tiger spoke, saying, "Son, don't stay here, we have to hurry! Don't have doubts, mount me, and we will go to the Great Scholar Tongyung!"

I was terrified by the tigress, and not daring to ride it, replied, "I have nothing urgent to ask the Great Scholar Tongyung at this moment, therefore I am not coming. You go, tigress!"

"Don't be afraid, son!" the tigress reassured me. "There is no viciousness in me. If you don't overcome the mind of fear and find an imperturbable condition, you will not be able to be in the state of contemplation, and you will act like any ordinary person. Hence, do not have doubts. You can ride me!"

"Tigress, you have the body of a beast, but the mind of a buddha. Whose magical emanation are you? Tell me this, and I will mount you!" I replied.

"I am an emanation of the mother Sipai Gyalmo," the tigress explained, "and you are still like any ordinary person. You are suspicious about a deity, and do not have the courage to touch me. You have not yet overcome the mind that creates fright. Hold on to the fundamental condition and maintain the essence without concepts! If you wish to go to the supreme sage, let's go now, I will take you."

I plucked up my courage and mounted the tigress without nurturing doubts, and we rode. After some time in the dimension of empty space I saw the four scholars sitting on big thrones made of rainbows and lotus flowers. I dismounted the tigress, and was led to sit in front of the wise Tongyung. The tigress that I had ridden turned into a radiant white-skinned girl adorned with bone ornaments. She gave me a fresh arura, and I ate that medicinal siddhi. Then I remained normally seated, without saying anything. Thereupon the wise Tongyung told me:

"Hey, son! You are not in the real condition! You have not overcome the demon of fright, and of hope and fear. As long as the demon of this attachment is not pacified, it is essential that you continue to practice hard."

Thus he said, and gave me an initiation. Then, as if waking up from sleep, I returned to where I was before.

43

One day at sunset I was drinking tea in the house of a student when I heard a sweet sound coming from inside my tent. I wondered what it could be, so I got up and went there, and I saw a reddish hound lying down. I did not think that it was a dog, hence I prostrated myself three times and entered the tent. The dog transformed itself and showed me the face of the Great Lama [Trenpa Namkha]. Then he emanated into a white body as small as a thumb which remained suspended in the air in front of me, and I sang many invocations accompanied by the sound of ritual instruments.

That time I recognized a person who in his previous life had committed a crime difficult to purify. He had stolen the offerings of butter which were meant for the lamps in the temple. Compassion arose in me and I gave him initiations and blessings, and a particular strong blessing with my feet. Khöpung [Trenpa Namkha] himself said that his negative action would be purified, and as he promised so, I felt some pride.

44

One night while I was sitting straight in position singing a spiritual song, many beings belonging to the eight classes of deities and demons[50] arrived, offering prostrations and circumambulations. After a while, a woman whose body and face were radiant arrived. She had twelve eyes, and I was so surprised that I burst into laughter.

Then she told me, "You don't consider the miracle that I am showing as something marvelous, you think it is a joke! Son, your mind is twisted. Don't see this as a joke: have deep faith, and I will give you a siddhi!"

I respectfully prostrated in front of her, and in her hands I saw a crystal stupa as small as a thumb and a *mala* [rosary] for reciting the SA LE WÖ[51] mantra. She gave these things to me and said, "Keep all this a secret!"

Then the SA LE WÖ mala and the stupa vanished naturally into my body, whereupon my body became transparent, without an outside and an inside.

45

One early morning before dawn, while I was sleeping, I had the feeling that Pönshig[52] had arrived. I sat up straight in position and gazed in front of me. And I saw a black body of light, a cubit in size, sitting directly in front of me. It was spreading rainbow lights in all directions and apparently reciting secret mantras.

Then the body of light told me, "Son, do you know a way to liberate the prisoner in the dungeon who has no freedom?"

"If he does not set himself free by himself, it is impossible for others to liberate him," I replied.

The body of light continued, "I don't say that it is not like this, yet, understand definitely that all multiplicity is one! Stay inside the immutable castle. Let the unseizable little bird fly! Let the prisoner who has chained himself up be released!"

He said all this, and then added, "This is the siddhi of the dakinis," and gave me a piece of human flesh with glittering white relics[53] upon it, and disappeared.

46

Once around midnight, while I was sitting in a normal way, I saw a dog as small as a bird enter. I raised my head to look at it, and saw a butter lamp vividly shining inside its mouth. Amazed, I remained gazing while the dog became smaller and smaller, and the lamp brighter and brighter. After a while the body of the dog vanished completely, and only a big butter lamp remained. I took it in my hand to observe it, and saw that its cup-shaped container was a yellowish skull full of relic pills. Then the lamp turned into a white, beautiful body of light ornamented with a necklace of jewels, and distinctly reciting the SA LE WÖ mantra with a whispering *si li li* sound.

An uncommon feeling of faith arose in me, and without knowing what I was doing I suddenly got up, but the body of light told me, "Son, there is nowhere to go that you should stand up: keep the essence in its natural place. Don't let yourself become tired of faith. Look at the real nature beyond union and separation. Don't meditate creating something with your thoughts: relax in the primordial emptiness devoid of any substance! Don't be glad to eat the food offered by others: cut definitely your attachment to samsara! If you understand these words of advice, they are in perfect agreement with the teaching of me, Samantabhadra."

Thus he said, and went away. I was astonished, and started to cry without control.

This is the nature of me, a lying beggar. I have reached the land of total bliss and acted greatly for the benefit of beings, and my past lives, both pure and impure, have gradually revealed themselves to my mind. I have recorded these stories with black ink on a white conch paper in the year of the Male Fire-Hare [1267], completing it in the morning of the fifteenth day of the middle month of summer.

These visionary encounters of the holy Horshig Lhaje, as they gradually happened, are marked with the sign of preciousness.[54] For sentient beings covered in pitch darkness, the visions of knowledge-holders have gathered like clouds. Do not forget them: keep them in your mind! May they spread like the sun's rays and benefit all sentient beings!

Virtue! Virtue! May it be auspicious!

2

CLARIFYING THE REAL NATURE

The Upadesha That Reveals Nakedly the Wisdom of Clear Insight

༄༄། །སྣང་མཐོང་ཡེ་ཤེས་གཅེར་བུར་བསྟན་པའི་མན་ངག་དོན་གྱི་ག་དར་བཞུགས་སོ།།

Marvelous!
I pay homage to the light of one's instant presence, total bliss,
Whose condition is the all-pervading, empty dharmakaya.

In this upadesha that reveals nakedly the essence of the dharmakaya, it is said:

In the castle of one's body
Dwells the heart, abode of enlightenment.
Inside this temple
The precious, immutable mind-essence,
Nature of Samantabhadra, the dharmakaya,
Shines immovable and unseizable by concepts.
Although it abides as such and is one's natural possession,
There is a difference whether it is recognized or not.
The wisdom of one's instant presence exists primordially,
But since instant presence is covered by the darkness of ignorance
Wisdom does not manifest
And one becomes slave to the ordinary actions of illusory vision.
The undefiled state of knowledge is one's natural possession,
But since one is polluted by the dirt of the mind
Thoughts cannot dissolve in the original base.

As long as thoughts do not dissolve in the original base,
There is no way to perceive nakedly one's instant presence.

Therefore this is the crucial upadesha that reveals nakedly the wisdom of clear insight.

Pointing out primordial wisdom: Look inside, backward, at the essence of your consciousness.
    If, when you look, you don't see anything and find a condition of emptiness, this is called the dharmakaya.
    In this condition that is empty and beyond thoughts there is a clarity which shines naturally: this is called primordial wisdom.
    Recognizing that instant presence, while manifesting everywhere, has no substance, is the primordially existing enlightenment. Enlightenment is not outside: if you search in yourself, it will be found.
    You don't need a particular method for searching; just look at this essence and set yourself in your natural condition. There is not even something to set in its natural condition, but just be in a condition of pure emptiness. You must not have doubts about this. If you are confident, that is enough!
    An example for one's mind, empty and without any concrete existence, can be found in the sky. In the same way, analogies can be found in the sun and moon, in the wind, in a river or a stream, in the ocean, and in the earth. All these examples that indicate the same meaning have to be understood in the following way.
    Like the sky, it is empty and without any substance, and thus unlimited. In this empty condition without substance, movement arises in any possible way, but whatever manifests remains emptiness.
    Like the sun and the moon, although emptiness is our original condition, there is a clarity that manifests vividly and unhindered. But just as we cannot define the sun and the moon in terms of clarity alone, [the original condition] is empty and has never been something concrete: this is the dharmakaya [or dimension of pure being]. Since [this nature] without substance manifests vividly as clarity, it is also the sambhogakaya [or dimension of perfect enjoyment]. Since the light and rays shine distinctly, it is also the nirmanakaya [or dimension of manifestation]. Thus the sun and the moon are an analogy for the natural condition of self-perfection of the three kayas.
    The wind in space: Since the wind does not have any material substance, it is an analogy for emptiness. Its natural blowing in all directions symbol-

izes the arising of various, distinct thoughts. Its calming down in its own condition of nonduality is an analogy for primordial wisdom.

The ocean, the river, and the stream: The ocean, imperturbable and beyond the limits of surface and depths, is an analogy for the unmodified, naturally relaxed condition of the original all-ground, and thus, an analogy for the empty condition without a substance. The waves arising out of this imperturbable state represent the movement of consciousness.

The river and the stream: Since they continuously flow without stopping, they are an analogy for the nature of one's instant presence that is innate from the beginning and never separate from oneself even for an instant, whether it is recognized or not.

The earth that is totally pervading symbolizes the original all-ground. Since there is nothing of all the existing variety that is not born out of the earth, it is an analogy for the [arising of] thoughts.

Although there are innumerable analogies and definitions for the nature of one's consciousness that is instant presence, they are all contained in the single, absolute meaning. The single, absolute meaning is the essence of enlight-enment: if it is [understood] beyond any mind-made modification, that is it!

This naturally existing wisdom that does not grasp at anything, take it out nakedly without mixing it with the thinking mind. This does not mean that you should reject the thinking mind, but just leave it freely [to dissolve] in the empty condition of the original all-ground. If one binds oneself with one's own thoughts, they cannot self-liberate.

Since the all-ground is primordially empty, what is there to meditate on?
Since instant presence is clear by itself, what is there to look at?
Since thoughts arise spontaneously, what is there to reject?
Since vision is the radiance of one's primordial energy, where is its materiality?
Since everything has the same flavor, where is dualism?

To sum up, since this condition is primordial enlightenment itself, without the need of meditating, relax in your natural state. If you let yourself relax, liberation [of thoughts] will spontaneously occur. If you remain in your natural state, [thoughts] will be purified, and, if you are completely free from doubt, you will slowly achieve realization.

For the undistracted state in which there is nothing to meditate, put instant presence continuously on guard! Meditating with an intention is an illusion; the natural clarity of one's state is wisdom.

The view that fixates on emptiness, instead of liberating, is a view that binds oneself. Such a view does not see the real meaning. If you remain without fixating on anything, that's it!

The meditation in which thoughts bind themselves and one is forcing oneself falls under the power of agitation and drowsiness. Such meditation does not reach the goal. If there is clarity in your natural condition, that's it!

The conduct that conceives the duality of vision and mind, instead of becoming helpful [for one's practice], is the work of the various illusory thoughts. Such conduct will never bring one to liberation. If whatever you do arises as the energy display [of your primordial state], that's it!

The fruit that is a result of conceptual thinking due to not having seen mind-essence, instead of leading to final realization, is the illusory mind of hope and fear. Such a fruit does not reach nirvana. If there is no separation between basic space and primordial wisdom, that's it!

All phenomena explained with many words become truly the same when you reach the primordially enlightened mind.

Clear in its natural condition without meditating, beyond the limitations of concepts, not definable as something existent, the primordially enlightened mind that is your instant presence, primordially empty and without thoughts, makes the stakes of the grasping of thoughts fall apart.

This wisdom that clearly manifests in the condition where there is no grasping by thoughts, separate it from the illusory mind of actions and ideas, and let the attachment of thoughts dissolve in the basic space!

All the visions that we perceive have the nature of dharmakaya. Leave visions empty in the immovable state of dharmakaya!

Don't allow your consciousness to follow the various appearances: remain in the condition of mind-essence beyond the limitations of vision and emptiness. When instant presence is purified in the original base, visions naturally become emptiness.

If you don't have knowledge that visions are emptiness, and practice only with the recognition that instant presence is empty, you will not achieve enlightenment. Therefore, you must know that both vision and mind, nondual, are empty. But it is not enough merely to know: it is necessary that the wisdom of realization arise and that you transcend the conceptual mind.

It is not possible to see enlightenment through concepts and words. Yet, I don't mean that they should be abandoned. In the immovable condition of mind-essence, they have to arise as the energy display of the wisdom of instant presence.

In brief, it is called wisdom of instant presence when the mind is realized as mind-essence. But even though we speak of "mind-essence," it is nothing whatsoever that can be conceived: it [simply] refers to that which is clear and empty, beyond thoughts. This condition of clarity and emptiness beyond thoughts is called enlightenment. If you recognize your own immaculate mind, you will definitely understand the root of the three self-perfected kayas.

If you find that the present movement of various thoughts has no substance, and that it is just emptiness, this is called the wisdom of one's instant presence. This wisdom of instant presence is the innate enlightenment. This unborn essence and empty all-ground, without any substance whatsoever, and which has the nature of space, leave it in its condition of natural relaxation, without agitating it or modifying it!

If you have knowledge, the various thoughts that arise without interruption, empty and immaterial like the wind in space, are the clarity of the self-originated wisdom. In the condition of the original all-ground, which is like a mother, place the child instant presence!

In conclusion, this primordially enlightened mind which is the original all-ground, from the beginning has never been something concrete, and, like the sky, has always remained empty by its own nature. Therefore, there is no need to meditate on it: emptiness is one's natural possession.

This instant presence of yours that is Samantabhadra, primordially empty and primordially clear, leave it without modifying it with your mind and concepts, without any intention toward it.

The sudden arising of the movement of thoughts like a flash is itself the dharmakaya. If there were no thoughts, the dharmakaya could not exist. Why is it so? Because if one knows the very essence of thought, the wisdom that is clear and beyond thoughts arises. If one recognizes the nature of thought, that itself is the dharmakaya essence which is clear and beyond thoughts.

How could the emptiness nature of the outer space, without the wisdom of instant presence, ever be the dharmakaya? If the unceasing wisdom of instant presence is not revealed, the real meaning of the view cannot be perceived through a mere blank emptiness. Wisdom cannot be achieved by abandoning emptiness. Emptiness cannot be obtained by abandoning wisdom. To show it nakedly, emptiness itself is wisdom, wisdom is emptiness. They cannot be separated; therefore, remain in clarity and emptiness beyond thoughts! Emptiness is the essence, the basic space; primordial wisdom is the wisdom of instant presence. If one sees the nonduality of basic space and primordial wisdom, there is no other final realization.

In brief, leave the empty essence without agitating it, and leave the wisdom of instant presence without modifying or defiling it. All artificial modifications are the mind. What is called "the mind" must disappear in its own place and become primordial wisdom. If thoughts do not become the thought-free wisdom, and ordinary illusion remains the same, how can enlightenment be achieved?

For this reason, look backward at your essence! There is nothing to see, but the wisdom of your instant presence is clear. This clarity and lack of substance are nothing other than the naturally clear and impossible-to-grasp dharmakaya.

> From the condition of space, empty and without a self,
> A wisdom child, clear and without the grasping of thoughts, is born.
> The child disappears into that which has no substance.

The meaning is clarified in the following way.

"Space, empty and without a self" refers to the dharmakaya essence, empty and without thoughts, and completely beyond all.

"A wisdom child, clear and without the grasping of thoughts, is born," refers to the vividly clear nature of instant presence of this very moment, when the various thoughts that unceasingly arise dissolve in the original base.

"Disappears into that which has no substance" means that the clarity of primordial wisdom exhausts itself in the expanse of emptiness, inseparable and beyond limitations. In reality, this refers to the single sphere [of the primordial state], and all the distinct explanations are the delusion of ignorance.

In conclusion, the essence of enlightenment is one's own mind, and as long as one does not recognize it, it must be shown. But to show one meaning, it is necessary to search for a hundred examples. If this is not done, the meaning cannot be discovered. Therefore, one has to show the single essence by explaining the examples and the meanings separately. They have to be explained until one understands. Until real knowledge arises, one has to meditate. Until final realization is achieved, one has to persevere.

Although I explain separately all the doubtful points with many explanations, I have never taught anything except that one's mind is the state of enlightenment. I have never taught anything other than that which is birthless. Birthless means empty, that which clearly manifests in the natural condition without any substance. This wisdom of instant presence is naturally clear in its condition. Remain in the state of its recognition!

In the freely relaxed condition that is naturally clear, impossible to grasp, and unmodified, the energy display of undefiled wisdom beyond any attachment has the nature of the dharmakaya as inseparable clarity and emptiness, free from all and beyond the domain of the mind. When realization beyond the conceptual mind is finally attained, the immutable, immortal fruit is established in one's condition. Once it is established in one's condition, there is nothing to hold on to, because instant presence is established in the state of the empty essence.

In the ineffable final realization beyond thoughts, one's instant presence shines clearly in the authentic condition without distraction. The essence of this clarity is without substance, like moonlight reflected upon water, spontaneously shining in oneself but impossible to identify. This naturally shining clarity is Samantabhadra, one's instant presence. This is what is meant by "dharmakaya." Apart from that, there exists no enlightenment.

You don't believe it? Then, look again and again at the essence of your consciousness. If you see a material substance or color, that is not the dharmakaya. If there is nothing to see and you find pure emptiness, recognize this to be [the state of] enlightenment! Play with this nothing to see, and you will become familiar with this nature. It is one's natural possession, but when the impurities of the mind manifest due to karmic traces, it is impossible for the state of knowledge to arise.

Therefore, don't be distracted from the wisdom of instant presence that naturally shines, without grasping, in the condition of emptiness beyond thoughts. Don't let thoughts create attachment inside: take out wisdom directly and nakedly! Let all thoughts dissolve immaculately in their own condition. Let all grasping by the thoughts subside gently in the natural condition. Let wisdom manifest vividly clear. Leave the all-ground quietly, in its original condition of free relaxation.

In the words of Samantabhadra:

> If there is no viewer in the view, it is a sign of being beyond
>   conceptual fixation:
> This is the view that encompasses all.
> If there nothing to meditate in the meditation, it is a sign of being
>   purified in one's own condition:

> This is the meditation that has the absolute certainty of the authentic state.
> If there is no accepting and rejecting in conduct, it is a sign that it is perfected as the energy display [of one's primordial state]:
> This is the conduct of total self-liberation.
> If the fruit dissolves into the basic space, it is a sign of having carried one's practice to conclusion:
> This is the fruit of the real manifestation of the three kayas.
> The view, meditation, conduct, and fruit, these four, are the single sphere,
> And since the single, primordially enlightened mind has no substance,
> Understand once and for all that it is the fundamental essence!

This is said. Therefore, since the primordially enlightened mind is inexpressible, it has always transcended the realm of speech, thought, explanations, and words.

Since the primordially enlightened mind cannot be killed, the essence of hate is emptiness, beyond any object. This is what is called love.

Since in the primordially enlightened mind there is no wrath, there is [also] no pride because its nature is emptiness. This is what is called peacefulness.

Since in the primordially enlightened mind there is no malice, there is [also] no jealousy, because it transcends the domain of characteristics. This is what is called open-mindedness.

Since in the primordially enlightened mind there is no beautiful or ugly, the essence of attachment is nonattachment, beyond any object. This is what is called generosity.

Since the primordially enlightened mind cannot be obscured, the essence of ignorance is one's instant presence that is clear to itself. This is what is called primordial wisdom.

The nature of the five poisons does not exist in the primordially enlightened mind: the thoughts of emotions dissolve in the expanse beyond conceptual constructs.

Notwithstanding all the many words that are used, this ultimate essence is nothing concretely existing: thus, keep it in its nature of emptiness! "To keep" is not just for words and designations: there is nothing to keep but to remain in one's natural condition.

Being birthless and uncompounded, it is not material. Since one's instant presence shines clearly everywhere, it is not emptiness. Being immaterial and transcending limitations, it is not clarity. It is not "something." It is beyond thought, just that! It is nothing whatsoever; the mind has no concrete existence.

Since it cannot be modified, it is the great unmovable state. Being beyond hope and fear, one's mind is the dimension [kaya] of enlightenment. All the words and meanings refer to the condition of this fundamental essence. Do not examine it: transcend your thoughts!

Unborn and without substance is the dharmakaya. The clarity of the wisdom of one's instant presence is the sambhogakaya. The unceasing arising of manifestation in all possible ways is the nirmanakaya. The essence of these three designations is the empty nature. This essence is beyond thoughts: it is the very state in which the basic space and primordial wisdom are united.

The outer basic space is the sky; wisdom is the sun. Yet their absolute essence is emptiness.

The inner basic space is the original all-ground; the manifestation of variety is wisdom. Yet their essence is emptiness and clarity devoid of a substance.

The secret basic space is the nature of existence [dharmata]; the manifestation of the three kayas is wisdom. Their essence is actually the same, indivisible.

Basic space and primordial wisdom are indissolubly integrated, clarity and emptiness beyond thought like a cloudless sky. It is this limitless condition that has to be concretely realized!

Some practitioners, not letting the mind abide in a naturally relaxed condition, bind and imprison themselves with their fixations. Obscured by themselves, they are always accompanied by thoughts due to karmic traces. When thoughts arise, they try to block them. When thoughts do not arise and they find a calm state, they try to arouse something. With their presence distracted by the outside, they are unable to conquer the unruly flow of thoughts and remain in an ordinary way. Continuing in such a manner, even if they meditated for a kalpa they could not possibly transcend the domain of illusion. As long as the domain of illusion is not transcended, the total bliss of nirvana cannot be reached.

Therefore a meditator, when practicing, should naturally and loosely relax in one's original state. Also, when abiding in the naturally relaxed condition, one should not try to arouse on purpose the clarity aspect of wisdom.

By remaining in the original all-ground as it naturally is, wisdom will spontaneously arise with its own clarity. If wisdom arises with its natural clarity, thoughts will subside by themselves. If thoughts subside by themselves, the karmic traces will purify themselves. If karmic traces become purified by themselves, the domain of the mind and thoughts will be transcended. If the domain of the mind and thoughts is transcended, that itself is enlightenment free from impurities!

In conclusion, if self-originated wisdom manifests spontaneously, the karmic traces of illusion will become naturally purified. If one abides in the authentic condition, thoughts will become purified in the original base. If the subduer watchman [of presence] conquers [the mind], the movement of thoughts will be transcended. If one knows that everything is empty, whatever one does is the energy display of the view. If one definitely understands that both samsara and nirvana are the mind, this is the bliss of nirvana.

Therefore, strip this vividly clear consciousness of yours naked: that is wisdom!

Look inside without a reference point: that is the view!

Play a game with what spontaneously arises: that is meditation!

Understand samsara and nirvana to be one and the same: that is conduct!

Take hold of your authentic, natural place: that is the fruit!

Leave the variety [of manifestation] in its original base: that is the beyond conceptual mind!

To sum up, if one abides in the condition devoid of any substance, that itself is the great aim!

For the original all-ground that from the beginning is the nature of enlightenment, you don't need a way of looking [to discover how it is], but simply relax in your own condition.

In the spontaneously free and unceasing wisdom of instant presence, whatever arises is never outside the natural state. Since the various phenomena that spontaneously arise are primordially empty and self-perfected, they should be allowed to flow freely without trying to identify them. This is not something to meditate upon, but to become familiar with. All meditations are the conceptual mind. The real essence is not seen through the effort of illusory thoughts. It is this fundamental essence that the wisdom of instant presence has to become familiar with.

Without meditating, [this wisdom of instant presence] is naturally free to wander in the fundamental essence. Without being modified, it remains naturally in the fundamental essence. Without practicing, it reaches the state of the fruit. Since everything is this condition of this fundamental essence, one has to become familiar with it.

It is said:

> In the castle of five precious jewels
> Is a coral stupa with a conch-shell dome.
> Inside there is a man sitting at his own place.
> Five savages arise at his sides and don't let him stay,
> Lifting him up and dropping him down.
> Then a self-originated child arises who has a method for reconciling them.

The meaning is clarified in the following way: "The castle of five precious jewels" symbolizes one's body made of the five elements. "The coral stupa" is the heart. "The conch-shell dome" refers to the white collar-like upper part of the heart. "The man" is the precious mind-essence. "Sitting at his own place" means abiding in one's natural condition, unmodified and unmovable. "Five savages arise and don't let him stay" symbolizes the illusory mind of emotions lost in the castle of the five poisons. "A self-originated child arises who reconciles them" refers to the wisdom of instant presence arising in clear insight.

Then, although there are countless words and meanings, their conclusion is the essence of one's mind that, although empty and without substance, abides vividly clear. This self-originated wisdom that is clear beyond the grasping of thoughts is the essence of the dharmakaya. Unobscured, all-illumining, and without material obstructions, in this moment it abides inside one's heart. The empty mind-essence has no outer or inner, no front or back, but now it is wrapped inside the net of our body.

What is seen outside, manifesting clearly and unobscured from the eyes, is the light that arises from within the heart and simply passes through the channels of the eyes. As the eyes and the heart are directly connected by a channel, when [the light] is projected to its door which is the eyes, it manifests visibly outside, clearly and without interruption. Do you see any materiality in the condition of instant presence? Look backward at the nature of all that appears outside! If you find it is empty and devoid of a substance, that is it!

In the words of Khöpung [Trenpa Namkha]:

> If one knows the nature of the mind, that is enlightenment!
> If thoughts are liberated in clear insight, that is the dharmakaya!
> If instant presence abides in its natural clarity, that is wisdom!
> If the movement of consciousness dissolves in the basic space, that is freedom from the conceptual mind.

Now, some practitioners claim that they see the essence of the mind, but the majority affirm that this is due to their meditating with the mind and concepts, and do not agree. To know the nature of the mind one has to discover that it is empty, inconceivable, and beyond all limitations. This is not an external understanding based on mental analysis. To see the essence of the mind means to abide in its very condition, without any change. Therefore, if one knows the nature of the mind, this is what is called enlightenment.

"If thoughts are liberated in the clear insight, that is the dharmakaya" means that the thoughts become instantly the empty essence beyond the conceptual mind.

"If instant presence abides in its natural clarity, that is wisdom" means that the vividly clear consciousness of instant presence of this very moment is unspoiled by illusion.

"If the movement of consciousness dissolves in the basic space, that is freedom from the conceptual mind" means that the basic space is not outside, but it is one's empty essence from within which the movement of all gross and subtle thoughts arises and then dissolves, purified in its own condition. Thoughts arise by themselves and subside in their own place. You don't need to follow after them: leave them in their emptiness devoid of any materiality.

Since wisdom is one's natural possession, it manifests from the empty, original base. Do not bind it with grasping by thoughts: leave it vividly clear beyond thoughts!

Since the mind is the Buddha, you have to know your own nature. Do not wrap it up with the conceptual mind obscured by the darkness of illusory thoughts: strip the dharmakaya essence naked and remain in it.

Do not follow the various visions, but [knowing that they are] your own manifestation, let them become a help for [the arising of] wisdom.

Do not accept what is good and beautiful, and reject what is bad and ugly: experience all as equal in the nondual primordially enlightened mind.

Do not engage with your concepts in elevated, empty talk about the view, and wisdom will reveal itself in the condition beyond thoughts.

Do not look after the visions [projected] outside by the eyes: put the watchman of undistracted, vividly clear awareness on guard over the mind!

Do not let the thoughts and mind go wild: let the subduer primordial wisdom eclipse them!

Do not let your mind-essence fall under the power of drowsiness and torpor: overcome them with the lamp of the wisdom of your instant presence!

The immaculate, clear luminosity is the nature of the dharmakaya. This instant presence of yours, whose essence is empty and without a self, abides in you without having ever been produced by anyone.

This essence that is your natural possession without having to be searched out anywhere, unmodified and empty, is endowed with the core of wisdom. Without grasping, practice that which is clear and beyond thoughts!

The essence of instant presence is the emptiness that has no root or basis. The core of thoughts is the clarity of wisdom. The precious mind-essence in which clarity and emptiness are inseparable is Samantabhadra, the state which has no causes and conditions. It is your very instant presence, clear and empty, and without a self.

Primordially empty and all-pervading, it has the nature of space. When the primordially clear instant presence is recognized as being empty, this is called "primordial wisdom" (*ye shes*).

"Conceptual mind" means the unruly proliferation of various thoughts; "beyond" means their passing into the empty condition of the original all-ground. This is the meaning of "beyond conceptual mind" (*blo 'das*).

"Mind" means the ordinary mind of illusory, worldly actions; "essence" means the wisdom of emptiness in the real condition of existence. This is the meaning of "mind-essence" (*sems nyid*).

As for what is called emptiness, "empty" means that even this essence has no substance; "-ness," that the core of emptiness manifests clearly as instant presence. This is the meaning of "emptiness" (*stong nyid*).

Although these terms are explained separately, their conclusion is one and the same in the absolute condition. However many explanations are given, hundreds or thousands, the ultimate source of the teaching of Bön, its basis or root, is nothing other than the empty mind-essence. For this reason, although there are many explanations, take hold of the single ultimate condition! Keep the essence of this ultimate condition in emptiness, without modifying it.

Thus ends the fourth chapter from the *Upadesha of the Golden Teaching*, which shows the way of practicing the real condition.

U YA [Keep it secret!]

May all be auspicious!

A A A

3

THE GARLAND OF NECTAR

Orally Transmitted Advice from Eighty Knowledge-Holders in the Form of Questions and Answers

༄༅། །རིག་འཛིན་བརྒྱ་བཅུའི་ཞུ་ལེན་སྨན་རྒྱུད་ཞལ་གདམས་བདུད་རྩིའི་ཕྲེང་བ་བཞུགས་སོ།།

Marvelous!
The supreme state of Samantabhadra beyond all limitations,
Without moving from the unsearchable, all-pervading dimension of the nature of existence, the space where everything is liberated,
[Manifests] effortlessly as the energy display of the wisdom of one's instant presence:
With my body, my voice, and the intention of my mind, I respectfully salute and praise
Samantabhadra in whom the three kayas are spontaneously perfected.

To Tseme Wöden, whose essence is Samantabhadra,
To the supreme knowledge-holder Tongyung Thuchen,
To Trenpa [Namkha] and his son [Tsewang Rigdzin], protectors of all beings,
To Gyermi Nyiwö, sprout of the sugatas, and so forth,
To the hosts of sugatas, knowledge-holders, and bodhisattvas,
All beings of the six lokas pay homage!

I, a faithful beggar whose knowledge has reawakened from the practice done in former lives, feeling compassion for all beings, noticing the meditative experiences of some individuals, and knowing also that some small degree of knowledge has arisen in me, thought I should ask all the sugatas and knowledge-holders of the past for an essential and profound teaching as the innermost siddhi of the quintessence of their Mind, an advice concentrating the meaning in a few words, and easy to understand.

Thus I went alone on a mountain and made invocations, but I was not able to invite any of the sugatas and knowledge-holders. All of a sudden, my instant presence became strong and clear, and I started to dance without my body touching the ground. Then, rainbows filled the space all around, while infinite sounds, lights, and rays manifested in the sky.

After a short while, the divine forms of twelve enlightened beings suddenly arrived near me. I had never seen them before. The chief of them had a red body and a luminous face spreading rays in all directions, and was ornamented with a necklace of jewels. He was staring at me, and said, "I am Tseme Wöden," then gave me a supreme secret siddhi and told me many secret things that I did not write down.

"Who are the others?" I asked, and he told me their names. So I welcomed them.

1

I asked Tseme Wöden for advice from the treasury of his Mind, and he said:

> Son, don't fall under the power of the agitated mind
> And practice luminous clarity without the spreading of thoughts.
> The limitless condition of basic space and primordial wisdom
> Is my state of knowledge. Know it!

2

I asked Lishag Wönam, and he said:

> In the base, you have to find bliss.
> In the path, you have to find clarity.
> You have to experience nonduality,
> Without separation, beyond limitations.

3

I asked Hripa Chosé, and he said:

> Son, don't make elaborate explanations: it is ineffable!
> Don't reflect too much: it is unthinkable!
> Don't get involved in many actions: it is beyond acting!
> Don't try so hard to examine: it is beyond concepts!

4

I asked Pungnam Chergyung, and he said:

> If you look outside instead of looking inside,
> You will fall in the mistake of becoming fixated on something.
> If you don't cut the fetters of clinging inside,
> There is danger of being suddenly carried away by the demon of attachment!

5

I asked Mula Barwa, and he said:

> Mind-essence is empty and limitless from the beginning,
> And clinging to it as something with material characteristics is an illusion.
> Self-originated wisdom knows no interruption:
> Keep it vividly clear, unspoiled by the attachment of the mind!

6

I asked Yetong Shangsal, and he said:

> In the totally pervading all-ground, devoid of a self,
> The unseizable wisdom of instant presence leaps forth
> Clear and empty, unblemished by defects:
> It is your consciousness in this very moment!

7

I asked Yeshe Lhungyal, and he said:

> Son, emptiness needs the ornament of compassion.
> Clarity needs the ornament of wisdom.
> Without separation, you have to go beyond the conceptual mind,
> And go still further beyond this very limitation!

8

I asked Nyisal Wötse, and he said:

> The essence of enlightenment is your mind itself.
> You don't need to perform the worldly practice of virtue.
> You may train your mind over and over,
> But until you see mind-essence, you will not discover enlightenment.

9

I asked Lungnön Wangdrub, and he said:

> Don't look at the base:
> Know the one who is looking!
> Don't tread the path:
> Leave in his natural place the one who is treading!

10

I asked Wangchug Hringwö, and he said:

> Unless you look at the base,
> How can you know the one who is looking?
> Unless you tread the path,
> There is no way to reach its destination.

11

I asked Wönam Mupung, and he said:

> If you recognize the base,
> That itself is the training of the path.
> If there is no treading on the path,
> That is the perfect ripening of the fruit.
> Yet, look upon everything as unreal, and that is it!

12

I asked Nyila Shelwö, and he said:

> Unborn from the beginning is the empty base.
> That which arises unceasingly from it is the path.
> The inseparability where all is perfected as one is the fruit.
> Yet, you have to get rid of the considerations "it is this" and "it is not this"!

One day, while I was dancing, three divine shens arrived. I asked them [for advice], and they replied, "Since this is our heart's blood, don't put it into writing: understand it orally!"

13

I asked Tsugshen Wönbar, and he said:

> Without a base, a path, and a fruit to achieve,
> Clinging to the various definitions is the cause of illusion.
> All is included in this essence.
> Don't nurture the dualism of hope and fear: remain in the unique state!

14

I asked Mingyur Tönsal, and he said:

> There is none who understands the natural condition beyond limitations.
> There is none who can guide on the path of the authentic nature.
> There is none who abides in the meditation of the self-liberation of clinging:
> The yogin who acts discriminating virtues from negativities is the cause of samsara.

15

I asked Salwa Wöden, and he said:

> Son, abandon the actions of the body,
> And nonaction will naturally arise.
> Leave instant presence without a reference point,
> And the state beyond limitations will be spontaneously perfected.
> Relax your body and mind, and desire will cease.
> Leave everything in the great condition beyond conceptual mind!

One day, while I was sleeping on a mountain, I saw the knowledge-holder Tongyung Thuchen arrive near my pillow. By the strength of devotion, I briefly praised and saluted him thus:

> Marvelous!
> Essence of all sugatas,
> King of all knowledge-holders,
> Lord of all beings of the six lokas,
> Sun and moon illuminating the darkness,
> Master of the meritorious ones,
> Leader of all, I praise you, Lord Tongyung!
> Bestow upon me, the fortunate one, the supreme and common siddhis!
> In order to illuminate the darkness of ignorant beings,

And to enhance the practice and remove obstacles for those who are progressing along the path,
I beg you to grant a pointing-out instruction in four written lines.

This I asked, and made a mudra with my hands.

16

Tongyung [Thuchen] said:

In the all-pervading base of emptiness, impossible to locate,
A traveler goes without an aim, unaware of the route.
Until he reaches the supreme place, whose direction is unknown,
Carefully be on the watch for the bandits: nobody knows where they run!

17

I asked the Great Lama [Trenpa Namkha], and he said:

Son, in the empty essence impossible to grasp,
Wisdom beyond illusion arises in all directions.[1]
Clear and empty, immaculate, beyond conceptual mind is the dharmakaya:
Abide continuously in it, without indifference!

18

I asked Tsewang [Rigdzin], and he said:

Since one's mind is primordially free from the impurities of thoughts,
Samsara and nirvana, without dualism, are pure in the base.
Hope and fear, beyond rejecting or accepting, self-liberate in their own place.
Don't be distracted from the view of the single flavor of multiplicity!

One day at sunrise five of the six great lamas[2] arrived, as Tagla Menbar was missing. I asked the five of them for advice.

19

I asked Malo Tarchang,[3] and he said:

> Son, samsara and nirvana, without duality, are contained in the unique state.
> Realize once and for all the self-liberation of pleasure and suffering in your mind!
> The great meditator who is bound by the dualism of hope and fear
> Will not discover the real essence but fall again in samsara.

20

I asked Yongsu Tagpa, and he said:

> Son, don't create attachment to samsara.
> With absolute certainty, pursue the aim of nirvana!
> There is no spare time, like the sun at the top of a mountain pass.
> Don't remain indifferent: be strong-willed!

21

I asked Milü Samleg, and he said:

> All human beings are distracted by what is meaningless,
> And there is danger that they neglect the preparation of permanent benefit.
> Worldly success leads to the lower states of rebirth.
> The one who is determined is a child of the sugatas.

22

I asked Ludrub Yeshe Nyingpo,[4] and he said:

> Son, since vision is the natural radiance of the mind,
> Cut the fetters of attachment!
> Since mind-essence is the dharmakaya,
> Be always in it, beyond the idea of being united or separated from it!

23

I asked Nangwa Dogchen,[5] and he said:

> In the birthless and primordially pure all-ground
> The sun of self-originated wisdom arises
> Clear and empty, beyond concepts, without limitations.
> If you don't abide continuously in it,
> It will be difficult to reach the supreme place of total bliss!

24

I asked Mutri Tsenpo,[6] and he said:

> The empty, infinite mind-essence
> Is like the pure vault of the sky.
> Meditating on something is the impurity of the conceptual mind.
> Practice the single nonmeditation!

25

I asked Hara Chipar,[7] and he said:

> If there is no duality of samsara and nirvana, that is the view.
> If there is no clinging to the concept of self and other, that is meditation.
> If whatever appears manifests as a help, that is conduct.
> If the essential condition has no border or center, that is the fruit.

26

I asked Anu Tragthag,[8] and he said:

> The empty essence of the mind is free from clinging to a self.
> The naturally clear instant presence is free from attachment.
> The self-liberation of thoughts is free from emotions.
> Experience in your mind the condition of the three kayas!

27

I asked Sene Gau,[9] and he said:

> If you have no clinging to a self, that is the view.
> If you abide in your natural condition, that is meditation.
> If [everything] manifests as a help, that is conduct.
> If you are free from any consideration, that is the fruit.

28

I asked Thami Theke,[10] and he said:

> The mind of sentient beings is enlightened from the beginning,
> But it binds itself with the movement of the thoughts that cling to a self.
> Look at the mind that binds itself and let it liberate in its own place:
> It has to self-liberate in its natural condition of emptiness.

29

I asked Hringni Muting,[11] and he said:

> If one is too intent upon the wisdom of mind-essence
> Or dwells only in a pleasure devoid of thoughts, enlightenment will not be attained.
> From the beginning vision and mind are self-perfected without duality:
> Considering vision a defect is a mistake.

30

I asked Langchen Muwer,[12] and he said:

> Son, to be born in this world is like a star at dawn.
> To accomplish the great aim is like the wish-fulfilling jewel.
> All is impermanent like a rainbow in the sky.
> Therefore, son, look at your mind again and again!

31

I asked Shepu Rakhug,[13] and he said:

> People of this world, instead of abandoning samsara, deliberately produce suffering.
> Clinging does not self-liberate, but their efforts are aimed at amassing and storing.
> Instead of accomplishing the real condition, they are carried away by useless distractions.
> Son, as there is no escape from birth and aging, it is essential to achieve enlightenment!

32

I asked Singpa Thuchen,[14] and he said:

> Son, don't be attached to food and wealth:
> There is danger of being carried away by the demon of your karmic traces.
> Don't long for women and relatives:
> They are the rope that binds one to samsara: know it!

33

I asked Pebön Thogtrul,[15] and he said:

> Son, don't cling to the idea of a self and others.
> All dualities are illusion.
> Don't reject or accept, negate or affirm:
> Let everything self-liberate in your mind!

34

I asked Pebön Thogtse,[16] and he said:

> Son, don't be attached to acting for things created by causes and conditions:
> As they are impermanent, they will perish in one moment.
> Acquaint yourself with what is not created by causes and conditions
> And it will always accompany you, without separating.

One evening, while I was inside the cleft of a rock, the three scholars came, and I asked them for advice.

35

Shari Uchen said:

> Until you enter the castle of no birth,
> You may get lost in the courtyard of the uninterrupted.
> Until you understand the ineffable nature of existence,
> You may stray in the wrong path of words and objects of explanation.

36

I asked Gyimtsa Machung, and he said:

> Since the nature of existence is beyond words and explanations,
> Don't talk too much with eloquent assumptions: it is a mistake!
> Since the ultimate view is beyond thoughts and limitations,
> Don't spoil the real meaning with ideas conditioned by the conceptual mind.

37

I asked Chetsa Kharbu,[17] and he said:

> If the all-ground is free from limitations, that is the nature of existence.[18]
> If variety is purified in its natural place, that is mind-essence.
> If one has the capacity of omniscience, that is the final accomplishment.
> If everything dissolves into the basic space, that is the state without limitations!

One early morning before dawn, while I was sitting straight in position, three knowledge-holders came, and I asked them for advice.

38

Jegyal Lhagom said:

> Son, if you look at your mind, you will see the Buddha.
> If you meditate alone, experiences and knowledge will arise.
> If you abandon samsara, happiness will be found.
> If you know that all is a magical illusion, you will be free from attachments.

39

I asked Rasang Khöram,[19] and he said:

> The essence of samsara and nirvana is empty from the beginning,
> But sentient beings are deluded because they cling to them as something concrete.
> Thoughts, without the need of meditating, are one's natural dharmakaya:
> Considering them a defect, one is deluded by the foolishness of ignorance.

40

I asked Lönchen [the great minister] Muthur,[20] and he said:

> If you succeed in leaving naked and vividly clear
> This thought-free self-originated wisdom,
> Total bliss will naturally arise.
> Therefore, practice naked clarity!

One day, with a feeling of happiness, I went to a mountain. There a large number of knowledge-holders arrived, many of whom I already knew.

41

I asked Gyungyar Mukhö, and he said:

> Samsara and nirvana are equal in the mind:
> They are not a duality but in a condition of same flavor.
> Don't be indifferent: look at your mind.
> If you do, the one who looks will self-liberate in its own place.

42

I asked Lishu Tagring, and he said:

> Since mind is without a self, empty and limitless,
> Clinging to it as a self is an illusion.
> Remain in the empty condition devoid of a self.
> If you abide in it, that is the real state of knowledge.

43

I asked Ngampa Chering,[21] and he said:

> From the birthless dimension, the unceasing leaps forth:
> Practice with the certainty that they are nondual.
> Vividly, without drowsiness or dullness,
> Practice the immaculate luminous clarity.

44

I asked Sarang Menbar,[22] and he said:

> Carrying to exhaustion basic space and primordial wisdom
> Is like empty, limitless space.
> Establishing instant presence in its natural place
> Is like a lamp in the darkness.
> Abiding in the state beyond conceptual constructs
> Is like a sea without waves.
> The self-perfection of the three kayas
> Is like the cloudless vault of the sky.

45

I asked Mupung Saltang,[23] and he said:

> How black is this small, dark house.
> How afflicted is the man of ignorance.
> How feeble the lamp that should make light.
> The sun of wisdom never shines there.

One evening while I was drinking tea, a woman wearing bone ornaments told me, "Son, don't remain there! The sugatas, knowledge-holders, and dakinis, they are all turning the wheel of the outer, inner, and secret Bön teachings.[24] Hurry up!"

"Who are you?" I asked.

"I am Sukasiti," she replied.

Then I unified my body and mind with the dimension of space and went. Thus I arrived in front of Chime Tsugphü and innumerable sugatas and knowledge-holders, and I also saw all the siddhas of the past who had reached the level of knowledge-holders. They gave me countless initiations, and then, for the benefit of all beings, I remember that I requested from each of them a four-line verse of advice.

46

I asked Chime Tsugphü, and he said:

> Son, make the birthless your abode.
> Train with the unceasing.
> Set yourself free in the space of nonaction.
> Remain in the real essence beyond limitations.

47

I asked Tagla Menbar, and he said:

> Son, this mind of yours, empty and devoid of a self,
> Is covered by the darkness of illusory thoughts that cling to a self.
> With the immaculate wisdom of your instant presence
> Remove the darkness of the illusory thoughts!

48

I asked Lhaje Pargom,[25] and he said:

> Son, deities and evil spirits, without duality, are equal in the mind.
> Mind is empty and devoid of a self, like space.
> Become familiar with the nature of limitless, total bliss
> And carry on with this familiarity until you reach perfect mastery!

49

I asked Kurgom Tare,[26] and he said:

> Son, the clear presence of this very moment
> Is the dharmakaya: recognize it!
> The variety of appearances of the outer world
> Is the radiance of one's [primordial] energy: recognize it!
> Look at visions and mind as the single state of nonduality.
> Remain in a state of nonduality beyond the conceptual mind.

50

I asked Kurgom Drepo,[27] and he said:

> Son, hated enemies are part of mind's clarity:
> Let viciousness naturally subside!
> Friends and relatives are the fetter that chains one to samsara:
> Don't have attachment: let it dissolve in its own place!

51

I asked Lhaje Tönme, and he said:

> Son, all the deities and evil spirits are this very mind of yours.
> Don't let your mind be distracted: keep it in its natural place!
> Don't impose hardships upon yourself: be spontaneously free!
> Don't remain in an ordinary way: be naturally relaxed!

52

I asked Partang Shangtön, and he said:

> Son, if basic space and instant presence are integrated, that is the real nature of existence.
> If everything self-liberates in its own place, that is mind-essence.
> If bliss is unceasing, that is the dharmakaya.
> If one is free from the considerations of hope and fear, that is the fruit.

53

I asked Sumpa Ukar,[28] and he said:

> Son, if one doesn't know that one's instant presence is the
>   dharmakaya,
> The various fruits of worldly virtuous practice will be the only result.
> Therefore, know the natural state of the mind!
> If you understand mind-essence, that itself is Dzogchen!

54

I asked Trotsang Druglha,[29] and he said:

> Son, unify the instant presence of the all-ground with the basic space.
> Let visions and mind, nondual, be unified in the expanse of the real
>   nature.
> Let samsara and nirvana be perfected in the single state of nonaction.
> Remain in the condition of the same flavor, without the separation
>   of self and other!

55

I asked Milarepa,[30] and he said:

> Son, directly discard vision that has nothing to cling to.[31]
> Proceed aimlessly on the path that has no direction.
> Without attachment, flee like a fox from appearances.
> Understand that your mind is the dharmakaya!

56

I asked Lingje Repa,[32] and he said:

> In this place, if you don't work for your benefit
> You will never be released from the abode of samsara.
> At this time, if you don't practice for enlightenment
> You will never reach the land of total bliss.

57

I asked Shugom Trulzhig,[33] and he said:

> In the dimension of the all-ground, thoughts disappear.
> In the dimension of space, the wind and clouds vanish.
> In the dimension beyond concepts, karmic traces dissolve.
> In the dimension of the nature of existence, one's instant presence is integrated.
> Therefore, enlightenment is one's state.

58

I asked Megom Shigpo,[34] and he said:

> Son, for dwelling, there are slate mountains and snowy rocks.
> For fleeing from, one's paternal village and maternal relatives.
> For going to, any human country without partiality.
> For looking at, one's enlightened mind.

59

Kunga Shigpo[35] said:

> If you understand that mind-essence is the dharmakaya, wherever you are there is bliss.
> If you are free from attachment, your homeland and any other country are the same.
> If real knowledge does not arise in your mind, what is the use of staying in a retreat place?
> If ultimate understanding of the mind is not achieved, however fine your view may be, you will not reach the goal.

60

Pönzhig[36] said:

> For one's mind, immaterial and empty,
> Refreshing undistracted presence is crucial.
> For the deceiver through various appearances,
> Keeping the view of self-liberation without attachment is crucial.[37]

61

I asked Trulzhig Dombu,[38] and he said:

> Purified in the emptiness that has no birth and cessation,
> Liberated in the basic space free from attachment and clinging,
> Self-perfected beyond thoughts and the conceptual mind,
> The kayas and wisdoms expand in all directions.

62

I asked Tampa Yuzhig,[39] and he said:

> The all-ground is birthless and empty;
> The uninterrupted movement dissolves in this base.
> Keep this nonduality of birth and interruption
> In a condition beyond limitations, without clinging!

63

I asked Pöbar Shigpo, and he said:

> Mind-essence, primordially empty and undefiled, is the dharmakaya.
> The disappearance in the base of whatever one does is self-liberation.
> The nonduality of vision and mind is primordial wisdom.
> Since everything passes into the basic space, there is no border and center.
> Self-originated wisdom cannot be conceptually identified.
> In the self-liberation of clinging there is nothing to accept or reject.
> In the mind-essence Samantabhadra there is no hope nor fear.

64

I asked Nyö Tsultrim Gyaltsen,[40] and he said:

> Son, all the outer, inner, and secret Bön teachings,
> If you look at your mind continuously, will be perfected in you.
> The state of profound experiences and knowledge,
> If you meditate alone, will arise in you.

65

I asked Tretön Kocha,[41] and he said:

> The eighty-four thousand treasuries of Bön are one's mind.
> Open the door to the treasury of your mind, and clear up all doubts inside!
> Understand once and for all that the authentic teacher is in your mind.
> In the birthless and empty divine temple of the mind
> Dwells the master, the wisdom of one's instant presence.

66

I asked the two, Chodung and Choyung.[42] The first [Chodung] said:

> Reach a definitive understanding of the birthless base.
> In the basic space, train in the path of noninterruption.
> For the fruit, carry to conclusion the nonduality of basic space and instant presence.
> There is nothing anywhere superior to this.

67

The other one [Choyung] said:

> Leave instant presence in the unmodified base.
> Maintain the path continuously, without too much effort.
> Let the unalterable fruit release itself in the basic space.
> Free from center and border, remain like the sky!

68

I asked Guru Notse,[43] and he said:

> There is no base and no path, and there is no fruit in the basic space.
> View, meditation, conduct, and fruit, these four, are self-liberated in one's natural condition.
> The three effortless kayas are self-perfected from the beginning.
> Free from the considerations of hope and fear, the essence is not created by causes and conditions.

69

I asked Matön Soldzin,[44] and he said:

> Son, understand definitely in your mind that there is no self and others.
> Look at your mind and transcend hope and fear.
> Let the various illusory thoughts be purified in the basic space.
> Don't be distracted from the limitless state of total bliss.

70

I asked Dütsi Gyaltsen,[45] and he said:

> In the vast, gray plain of the primordially empty base
> Let the self-arising instant presence of the path play around.
> Understand definitely inside you that the fruit is nonduality.
> Get rid of the outer and inner layers that cover you, and set yourself free in the primordial expanse.

71

I asked Gongdzö Ritrö Chenpo,[46] and he said:

> If the state of knowledge is like the sky, there is no hope or fear.
> If wisdom is like the sun, one is free from the defects of illusory thoughts.
> If one is unshakable like the ocean, self-perfection is steadily attained.
> If you understand these three points as the great aim, that is the state of Samantabhadra.

72

I asked Mutsa Gyerme, and he said:

> The various outer appearances arise in yourself,
> Their manifoldness is your own vision.
> Without abandoning or trying to obtain them, apply them as the path.
> Without attachment or clinging, remain in your natural condition.

73

I asked Shuye Legpo,[47] and he said:

> Open the door to the treasury of your mind
> And the inexhaustible great goal will spring forth.
> Get rid of the idea of amassing and storing
> And all wishes will be fulfilled in you.

74

Someone said to be the nirmanakaya Luga[48] emanated into a magpie and came to me. I requested advice from him, and he said:

> Son, until you feel revulsion toward samsara,
> It will be impossible for impermanence to arise in you.
> Until you understand that enlightenment is your own mind,
> There will be no way to reach the land of total bliss.

75

I asked Nagpo Ralpachen, and he said:

> Since mind is spontaneously perfected with bliss-emptiness, clarity, and absence of thoughts,
> That itself is the self-liberation of the conceptual characteristics of permanence and annihilation.
> Don't fall under the power of the illusion of ignorance:
> Take out naked the wisdom of instant presence!

76

Pönzhig[49] came in the form of a body of light. I asked him [for advice], and he said:

> In the kingdom of no directions or partitions
> A child who has no conceptual fixation
> Has ended up wandering everywhere.
> Don't allow him to roam: restore him to his original place!

77

I asked Wangden Shense,[50] and he said:

> Don't tie yourself up by focusing upon a target.
> Be spontaneously free, without a goal: this is crucial.
> Don't be distracted from the birthless condition.
> Seal yourself with "nothing to cling to."

78

Kyangphag[51] emanated himself into a raven and came to me. I asked him for advice, and he said:

> Remain evenly without a target.
> Leave everything freely without clinging.
> Relax directly in the state of nonaction.
> Look at the essence where there is no separation!

This is the quintessence of the Mind of Samantabhadra, the pith of the state of knowledge of the sugatas, the profound treasure of the knowledge-holders, a siddhi for meritorious beings, a blessing for faithful ones, a lamp for illuminating the darkness, a staircase for those who are progressing along the path, a hook for saving the beings of the six lokas, and the ultimate essence of the eighty-four thousand teachings of Bön.

I, a confident man who has faith, requested these words of advice from the supreme masters for the benefit of all beings, and in order to arouse faith and devotion, I put them into writing. To receive their blessings, I asked the supreme masters to consecrate them.

This garland of nectar of advice should be kept by meritorious beings. It should be taught to people whom one knows and who have faith, but kept hidden from those who have violated their samayas or who nurture contrary views. Since the seal of secrecy has been repeatedly affixed to it, it should not be propagated anywhere if the time is not ripe. If it is spread indiscriminately, the punishment of the supreme knowledge-holders will be received and the *walmo* dakinis will draw out one's heart's blood.

May all those who have seen these teachings with their eyes or heard them with their ears be sustained by the compassionate energy of the supreme sugatas! May they reach the land of the heroic knowledge-holders! May they become nondual with all meritorious beings! May they abide in the limitless state of total bliss, and when they have reached the supreme land of total bliss, may they lead the beings of the six lokas to liberation!

I am an aimless, lunatic, follower of the basic precepts,[52] [like] a small insect. May all those who have had the connection of seeing and hearing me in this life, in the future practice the Bön of Dzogpa Chenpo teachings! May all those with whom I established a connection in this life based on the authentic nature, in the future realize concretely their state of instant presence. May all those connected with me in this way, in the future abide in the authentic nature. After establishing in happiness and without any hindrances all the faithful, fortunate ones whom I have taught, may I also reach the land of nirvana!

All the merits accumulated with this writing I dedicate to the benefit of all beings of the three worlds.

May this be auspicious!

U YA

AGA THAM

GYA GYA GYA[53]

4

THE PRECIOUS GOLDEN LAMP

Advice from Eighty Dakinis

||མཁའ་འགྲོ་བརྒྱ་བརྒྱད་ཀྱི་ཞལ་གདམས་རིན་ཆེན་གསེར་གྱི་སྒྲོན་མ་བཞུགས་སོ།།

Marvelous!
Precious queen of the *walmo* dakinis,
Precious protectress of all beings of the six lokas,
Your body, like the sky, has no color;
The rays of your blessings fall like rain from space.
Like the sun and moon in the sky, you illuminate all directions:
To you, Kalpa Zangmo,[1] refuge for all,
I respectfully pay homage with my body, my voice, and my devotion.
Please, sustain me and all beings with your compassion.
Please, bless my body, voice, and mind.

Marvelous!
Kalzangma, you are the queen of all dakinis:
Of the wisdom dakinis, of the dakinis of miraculous power,
Of the dakinis of action, of the dakinis of samaya, and so forth.
Kalzangma, unique mother of all the knowledge-holders,
Unique mother and treasury of all supreme and common [siddhis],
Unique mother who is the source of meritorious beings,
Compassionate guide of the beings of the six lokas,
You, mistress and great mother of all, I praise!
Bestow the siddhis on me, the meritorious one!

Remove ignorance, the darkness of samsara!
I bow down to you Kalzang, queen of all!

Inseparable from her are you, Wöden Barma:
You are dark red with a majestic brilliance,
You spread rays of light impartially to all sentient beings
And bestow the supreme and common siddhis on the meritorious ones.
You, great mother, who are the secret consort of the knowledge-holders,
    I praise!

Nyima Wöden, sovereign lady of all dakinis,
From you, compassionate rays spread in all regions,
Your face is white and luminous like the full moon,
Your head is adorned with precious ornaments,
Your well-proportioned body captivates the minds of men,
You expand the storehouse of great treasuries of the supreme and common
    siddhis.
In your right hand you hold a vase of precious jewels;
In your left hand, a golden mandala.
Your body has no specific form, and you can manifest in any miraculous
    transformation.
By virtue of past karmic connections, you have been my secret consort.
You, kind sovereign lady Nyima Wöden, I praise!

I, an aimless and unconcerned beggar from Ling,
Seeing individuals making progress worried about taking a wrong path,
Being aware of the beings of the six lokas obscured by ignorance
And of how difficult it is to reach the supreme land of total bliss,
Thought to provide those who are progressing
With something that encapsulates the essence of the swift path
And eliminates the darkness of those who are confused.
Therefore I requested the multitude of mother dakinis
To give some advice as their heart-essence,
A lamp for the mind of instant presence,
The heart-essence of the outer, inner, and secret instructions,
A path that is quick if practiced,
An upadesha that grants enlightenment if one meditates alone.

For putting them into writing, one after the other,
I ask forgiveness of the mind lineage of the sugatas,
Of the oral lineage of the knowledge-holders,
Of the lineage of the dakinis,
And of the siddhas who have achieved the final attainment.

1

I asked the unique mother Kalzang, and she said:

> In a vast gray plain without directions and partitions
> There is a man who doesn't come and doesn't go anywhere.
> Without doing anything, he is surrounded by soldiers on all sides.
> Son, if you have no material obstruction, be their witness![2]

2

I asked Wöden Barma, and she said:

> A traveler who does not depend on a cause and has no concrete existence,
> With nothing to accomplish, goes around the world.
> His actions never end, like churning water in a bag.[3]
> Don't be attached to useless actions: remain in the condition of space.

3

I asked Nyima Wöden, and she said:

> Don't cultivate the four elements:
> Accomplish the great aim inside you!
> Don't search for enlightenment elsewhere:
> The dharmakaya is your very self!

4

I asked Sipai Gyalmo, and she said:

> In the unmodified and imperturbable nature of your mind
> Keep instant presence fresh and naked.
> Remain vividly clear without acting and beyond limitations.
> Be freely relaxed without rejecting or trying to accomplish.

5

I asked Thugje Kundrol, and she said:

> Son, what is not to meditate upon is one's mind.
> What is beyond being illumined or obscured is one's instant presence.
> The self-liberation of everything is wisdom.
> Free from the considerations of being this and not that is the fruit.

6

I asked Göcham Barma, and she said:

> Son, don't try to view anything: rest in the condition that has no target.
> Don't meditate on anything: rest in the condition of emptiness.
> Don't put effort into anything: rest in the condition of nonaction.
> In general, transcend the considerations of hope and fear!

7

I asked Tsogdag Karmo, and she said:

> Son, the vision of the six sense-consciousnesses is empty and immaterial:
> Overcome your attachment and let it self-liberate in its own place.
> This world is like last night's dream:
> Keep the presence of impermanence in your mind.

8

I asked Nyima Tongkhyab, and she said:

> Son, wear on your head the hat of primordial pervasion.
> Wrap over your shoulders the coat of primordial emptiness.
> Spread at your feet the mat of primordial omnipresence.
> Put the three unborn children under your armpits.

9

Nyiwö Barma said:

> In the daytime, merge with the empty instant presence.
> In the night, merge with the luminous clarity.
> Remain in this state without distinction of day and night.
> Overcome the limits of clarity and emptiness!

10

I asked Nyiwö Dangden, and she said:

> In the empty sky of the primordially empty mind,
> Emotions, not abandoned, are like thunderbolts, hail, and strong wind
> That dissolve without duality in the condition of emptiness.
> If you understand the meaning, just that is enlightenment!

11

I asked Bumgyurma, and she said:

> If you are carried away by the five poisons of emotions,[4] you will not find enlightenment.
> If you are involved in hope and fear, and rejecting and accepting, you will never attain liberation.
> If you abide in the ineffable condition, that itself is the dharmakaya.
> If you understand that samsara and nirvana are nondual, that is nirvana!

12

I asked Wözer Dangden, and she said:

> The emptiness of luminous clarity beyond conceptual mind is the dharmakaya.
> Clarity manifesting impartially in all directions is the sambhogakaya.
> Self-liberation with nothing to achieve and no distraction is the nirmanakaya.
> Self-perfection free from hope and fear is the fruit.

13

I asked the four Goddesses of Flowers,[5] and Saldrön Gyenchigma said:

> This mind which is the empty essence of enlightenment
> From the beginning abides inside you, unmodified,
> In a condition of primordial self-perfection that does not need to be accomplished.
> Remain without distraction with nothing to achieve or modify!

14

Salden Wöntroma said:

> In a dark nine-layered house that nobody has built
> Is a restless man who does not go anywhere.
> Then he goes out through the nine doors:
> Poor man who suffers without either dying or recovering.

15

Longtenma said:

> Keep instant presence in its own place, and practice without spreading thoughts.
> Let appearances be liberated in their own place, and practice without attachment.
> Integrate vision and mind without duality, and practice free from the conceptual mind.
> Practice free from limitations exactly like space!

16

I asked Göcham Yuthingma, who said:

> If the mind, which is clear and empty beyond concepts,
> Definitely abides in a condition of nondistraction,
> The three kayas will arise in you.
> Practice self-perfection beyond limitations!

17

I asked Gyendenma, and she said:

> Son, how vast is the empty space that has no self!
> How skillful in flying is the small bird that has no direction!
> Does this bird have the idea of a self, or does it not?
> Go ask the king who is the source of all existence and nonexistence!

18

I asked Gyenchigma, and she said:

> In the empty ruins of a house that does not depend on a cause,
> A small child who has no judgment and does not rely on food and wealth
> Has been left in the middle of four rivers.
> Go ask the sky how to carry him to dry ground!

19

I asked Gyendrugma, and she said:

> An unmarried woman who has no parents
> Is leaving for a place that has no direction or entrance.
> Her body is fully attired in clothes and jewels.
> Now is the time for the man of no attachment to escort her.

Then innumerable wisdom dakinis surrounded me and sat down. I had never met them, and I could not recognize anyone's face or name. The one said to be their chief had a luminous bluish green body decorated with bone ornaments intertwined with precious jewels. In her right hand she held a victory banner of precious stones; in her left, a vase of nectar. She came to sit upon the crown of my head and told me, "I am Chucham Gyalmo,[6] and these are wisdom dakinis endowed with wrathful power. Since they transcend names and expressions, it is not possible for me to name them."

I asked, "As I care for the beings of the six lokas, I would like to request an essential teaching that they may understand and put into practice," and my face glowed with joy.

20

Chucham Gyalmo said:

> A lamp that doesn't depend on causes and conditions
> For kalpas has continuously remained inside
> A hollow jar made of the four elements:
> Break the jar and make the lamp shine!

21

Chucham Wöntroma said:

> Son, remain in the unmodified and unspoiled expanse of the real nature.
> Without distraction and beyond thoughts is the dharmakaya.
> Prolong your abiding in the real condition without spreading thoughts.
> If you are integrated into the expanse of nonmeditation, that itself is the fruit.

22

Nyiwö Saldenma said:

> Let your mind be freely relaxed, and the dharmakaya will be spontaneously perfected.
> Keep instant presence fresh, and wisdom will arise in you.
> Relax your body completely, and actions and effort will be naturally forgotten.
> Abandon the distraction of your mind, and diligence will be inside you.

23

Serden Singchigma said:

> Son, understand that the view and the viewer are one.
> Don't separate meditation from the meditator.
> Let conduct and the one who acts self-liberate in their own place.
> Let the fruit be free from the dualism of hope and fear!

24

Trime Wödenma said:

> Son, life is as brief as a flash of lightning in the sky.
> The body is impermanent like the calf of a dzomo.[7]
> Mind is immaterial like the wind in space.
> It is therefore crucial to practice to attain enlightenment!

25

Sengdongma said:

> Keep a clear, undistracted presence of mind that is nothing to achieve,
> And abide in the state beyond limitations that is not to be meditated upon.
> If you remain spontaneously in your natural state, that is Dzogchen!
> If hope for nirvana and fear of samsara are eradicated, that is enlightenment!

26

Logcham Nyiwöma said:

> Son, in the all-pervading, blissful emptiness
> Keep limpidly, nakedly, and vividly
> The clear and unceasing instant presence.
> Pass into the nondual expanse of total bliss!

27

Göcham Tsugtorma said:

> This Samantabhadra that is one's enlightened mind,
> Even if one tries to scrutinize it, cannot be seen.
> Beyond thoughts, without separation, impossible to be distracted:
> The one who understands this has achieved the goal.

28

Dütsi Charbebma said:

> Once you have passed into the expanse of the primordially arising and primordially clear condition,
> The conceptual characteristics of permanence and annihilation, without being abandoned, self-liberate in their own place.
> That which is liberated manifests clearly in the condition of self-originated wisdom.
> When this is concretely realized, it is the state of knowledge of Samantabhadra.

29

Gyenden Sertroma said:

> Beyond the conceptual mind and without limitations, blissful, clear, and thought-free,
> Self-originated wisdom never ceases and has no illusion,
> Transcending the limits of the dualistic considerations of hope and fear.
> Since everything is contained in the same essence, overcome duality!

30

Then a woman came who said her name was Salwai Drönmachen, so beautiful that it was difficult to part from her. Her body was straight and sinuous, and her face was like the disk of the sun. She sat down at my right, and told me:

> Son, since mind is the blissful, limitless dharmakaya,
> Considerations of good and bad, and positive and negative, are the cause of illusion.
> Since everything manifests as the natural radiance of the mind,
> Differentiating vision from mind is a wrong teaching.

31

Logcham Wöngyuma said:

> The consciousness of this moment that perceives everything clearly without obstacles,
> Undistracted, without thoughts, and beyond the conceptual mind,
> Is the dharmakaya, the state of knowledge of Samantabhadra.
> Therefore, son, let basic space and primordial wisdom expand without duality!

32

Natsog Gyendenma said:

> Son, don't impose hardship on your mind; know how to leave it spontaneously free.
> Don't abandon it to distraction; keep it in its natural place.
> Don't think highly of yourself; transcend partiality.
> In general, if your view of "knowing one, all unfolds" is like space, it is fine!

33

Tönbarma said:

> Son, if you don't abide in that which is beyond conceptual constructs,
> The state of knowledge without limitations will never arise.
> Therefore, remain in the immaculate condition beyond the conceptual mind.
> If you carry everything to its exhaustion, that is nirvana!

34

Nyiwö Saltserma said:

> The vividly shining wisdom of impartial luminous clarity,
> The blissful expanse of the ultimate and ineffable nature of existence,
> The condition of bliss and emptiness which is primordially clear and immaculate:
> Let these three unfold inseparably in your mind!

35

Kunbumma said:

> If you leave your instant presence naked, that is the state beyond impurities.
> If variety dissolves in the base, that is the state beyond conceptual mind.
> If you understand impartial, total bliss, that is the state beyond limitations.
> If there is no base, no path, and no fruit, that is nirvana!

36

Kunkhyen Serdenma said:

> Son, not meditating on anything must be like space.
> Not being distracted by anything, like a starving man who has received food in his hands.
> Not being attached to anything, like a coward chased by his sworn enemy seeking revenge.
> To be free from everything, like the wind in space.

37

I asked Karsal Dangdenma, and she said:

> Son, unless you know the natural arising and self-liberation of your mind,
> Birthless bliss cannot possibly arise.
> Through bliss, emptiness, clarity, and nonthought, illusion collapses.
> Practice self-liberation, the essence of total bliss!

38

Thugje Chagkyuma said:

> The all-illuminating instant presence is empty in the condition of bliss.
> All relative phenomena dissolve in the dimension of the nature of existence.
> Free from apathy, hope and fear are overcome.
> The wisdom of omniscience is without a self-nature from the beginning.

39

A dakini wearing a black silk dress ornamented with dangling tassels of tiger skin told me:

> For the primordially empty, self-perfected luminous clarity,
> Of what benefit will be a few intentional meditations?
> Leave in its own place the energy that unfolds and arises unceasingly in oneself,
> Without spoiling it with the mind of illusory thoughts.

40

Longkhyabma said:

> Son, until you abandon the actions of the practice of virtue,
> You will not get close to the real state of nonaction.
> Until you abandon the worldly vision,
> You will not achieve the authentic, great aim.
> Until the five poisons are liberated in their own condition,
> Wisdom will not abide inside you.
> Until you are free from the thinking mind,
> You will not gain real knowledge of the essence beyond the conceptual mind.

41

Champa Kunsalma said:

> If you know that everything is unreal, attachment will dissolve by itself.
> If you know that the outside has no materiality, that itself is emptiness.
> If you know that mind-essence is the dharmakaya, that itself is enlightenment.
> If the clinging of thoughts self-liberates in its own place, that itself is the supreme aim!

42

Yongkhyabma said:

> If you watch your mind without distraction, that is the ultimate understanding of the view.
> If you abide continuously in the real condition, that is the ultimate understanding of meditation.
> If what spontaneously arises self-liberates in your mind, that is the ultimate understanding of conduct.
> If it is beyond limitations like the sky, that is the ultimate understanding of the fruit.

43

Yongkhyab Chenmo said:

> If the clinging of thoughts collapses inside, that is self-liberation.
> If certainty is inside you, that is the ultimate understanding.
> If the single flavor of nonduality is understood, that is the dharmakaya.
> If actions and effort are spontaneously forgotten, that is the state beyond conceptual constructs.

44

I asked Kunshe Serdenma, and she said:

> If basic space and instant presence are unified, the view is beyond limitations.
> If one remains freely relaxed without meditating, one naturally abides in meditation.
> If whatever one does self-liberates in its own condition, the one who acts disappears.
> If basic space and primordial wisdom are free from conceptual fixation, the fruit is accomplished.

45

I asked Kuntu Nangma, and she said:

> Wise omniscience without impurities
> Is the state of knowledge of the supreme sugatas.
> The recognition of self and other and of defects and qualities
> Is the experience of those who progress along the path.

46

I asked Thogme Wödenma, and she said:

> Son, if there is no material obstruction, that is the view.
> If the clinging of thoughts dissolves, that is meditation.
> If there is no self and other, that is conduct.
> Inconceivable and inexpressible self-liberation is the fruit.

47

I asked Thogme Mingyurma, and she said:

> In a kingdom without an owner,
> A child not born from parents
> Suffers for lack of food and clothes.
> An inexhaustible treasure is there, but he does not know how to enjoy it.

48

I asked Drönme Dangdenma, and she said:

> In a pitch-dark treasure-house nobody knows where,
> An encampment of soldiers that has naturally formed
> Never sees the time to be released from the dark.
> Search inside you for the lamp to illuminate the darkness!

49

I asked Yingchug Gyaltsenma, and she said:

> The vulture in the sky is skillful in flying,
> Without impediments he soars everywhere.
> How quiet is the country without an owner!
> How happy are the deer[8] without an enemy!

50

I asked Wangchug Drönma, and she said:

> Son, the valley without an owner has been seized by enemies.
> The deer, without doing anything, are confounded
> And strongly attached to rocks that give no shelter.
> They are not able to enter the safe forest.

51

I asked Kunjungma, and she said:

> The all-pervading space is boundless
> But familiarity with the wisdom of instant presence is scarce
> And the provisions of diligence are lost to enemies.
> How afflicted is the man of ignorance!

52

I asked Kunshema, and she said:

> A male and a female who consider as two what is one
> Enjoy sexual pleasure without any causes and conditions
> And five children not generated by flesh and bones are born.
> These five children manifest as their parents' demons.

53

I asked Wöntroma, and she said:

> A man who comes from nowhere and does not go anywhere
> Appears in a place that he has no knowledge about.
> Without protection or refuge, he falls into the grip of the enemy's army.
> Not knowing his real state, he is tortured in various ways.

54

I asked Salbarma, and she said:

> Son, let bliss, clarity, and absence of thoughts expand in the basic space.
> Leave instant presence and emptiness inseparably unified.
> Let vision and mind, without duality, transcend the conceptual mind.
> Let samsara and nirvana, without duality, be purified in the base.

55

I asked Kundüma, and she said:

> Son, don't examine the all-ground: remain in a condition beyond thoughts.
> Don't block movement: leave it in a state of spontaneous freedom.
> Let thoughts pass into the condition of the real nature of existence.
> Let movement dissolve in the expanse of emptiness.

56

I asked Kungama, and she said:

> Son, though one may try to go in any direction, there's no hope of reaching anywhere.
> Everywhere is surrounded by soldiers, and there is no place to escape.
> The weapons to destroy the soldiers are in oneself, but there is none to oppose them.
> The armor is in oneself, but there is none who knows how to wear it.

57

I asked Kunkhyenma, and she said:

> In the empty space without an owner
> Two unseizable birds, male and female,
> Fly and soar inseparably.
> Let them disappear in the condition of nonmateriality!

58

I asked Yingsalma, and she said:

> Son, if basic space and primordial wisdom are unified, the dharmakaya will be attained.
> If your cultivation of things produced by causes and conditions is forgotten, the supreme aim will be achieved.
> If the mind that becomes attached is cut off, the great treasure will be found.
> If you recognize as space whatever you do, that is self-liberation!

59

I asked Yingdrolma, and she said:

> Son, the body is an old pigsty:
> Don't cherish it or be attached to it!
> Instant presence is like a small bird on a tree branch:
> As soon as it rests, it flies away: know it!

60

I asked Sukasiti, and she said:

> Son, don't regard anything as lasting:
> Being immaterial, in one instant it will vanish.
> Don't arouse desire and attachment toward anybody:
> Being impermanent, in one instant you will have to part.

61

I asked Thayema, and she said:

> Son, if you are beyond limitations like the sky, total bliss is spontaneously accomplished.
> If you are beyond being illumined or obscured like the sun and the moon, luminous clarity is spontaneously perfected.
> If you are beyond rejecting and obtaining like the wind, self-liberation is spontaneously accomplished.
> If you are like the jewel that is the source of all, that itself is the great aim!

62

I asked Wönbarma, and she said:

> Son, the wide-awake consciousness of this moment
> Is the dharmakaya, the wisdom of your instant presence.
> Keep it immaculate, vividly clear, and naked!
> Leave it evenly, free from thinking and beyond the conceptual mind!

63

I asked Serdenma, and she said:

> All human beings are bound by the illusion of clinging to a self
> And the one that binds is one's empty mind.
> Thus it is crucial to practice self-liberation into emptiness.
> Be free from the mind that holds anything dear!

64

I asked Dedenma, and she said:

> Son, bliss, emptiness, and clarity,
> If you understand mind-essence, are just that.
> Mind-essence is empty like the vault of the sky.
> Wisdom is clear like the luminosity of the sun and moon.

65

I asked Lodenma, and she said:

> Son, if you don't overcome the conceptual mind and verbal definitions,
> You will not be able to see with utmost clarity the nature of total bliss.
> If you don't free yourself from the limitations of clarity and emptiness in [your] mind-essence,
> The essence of the three kayas will not arise in you.

66

I asked Thogmema, and she said:

> In the sky without beginning or end
> The sun and moon shine without attachment to clarity.
> Don't obscure them with the clouds of illusory thoughts:
> Leave them in their immaculate condition of clarity and emptiness.

67

I asked Dangdenma, and she said:

> Son, from the unreal land of mutability
> Go into the expanse of immutable bliss.
> Stay inside the castle of the birthless.
> Keep unceasing instant presence in the basic space!

68

I asked Yesalma, and she said:

> Son, let primordial wisdom expand in the basic space.
> Recognize that samsara and nirvana are the mind.
> Defeat the army of hope and fear.
> Understand definitely mind-essence!

69

I asked Yejungma, and she said:

> Son, in the dimension of the all-ground one's instant presence shines
> [Just like] in the dimension of the sky the sun and moon shine.
> In the dimension of the birthless the unceasing self-liberates
> [Just like] in the dimension of the surrounding space the wind subsides.

70

I asked Yekhyabma, and she said:

> Son, being expert in words and definitions without seeing the fundamental essence
> Is like the song of a blind man.
> Giving superficial explanations without having definitely resolved all doubts inside
> Is as useless as the "cause and effect" repeated by a parrot.

71

I asked Yekhyenma, and she said:

> On a gray, grassy hill with no humans and no villages
> A gazelle moves quickly here and there without restrictions.
> As there are no enemies, how happy is she!
> As the skill of running quickly is perfected in her body, how carefree is she!

72

I asked Yedagma, and she said:

> Son, everything appears everywhere, but it has no materiality.
> Manifold phenomena manifest, but they cannot be identified with concepts.
> Clarity expands in all directions, but it is beyond the clinging of thoughts.
> The essence free from border and center is boundless.

73

I asked Yingsalma, and she said:

> Son, integrate indissolubly basic space and instant presence.
> Look at yourself and others as one without duality.
> Leave vision and mind, nondual, in the basic space.
> Nondual self-liberation is enlightenment.

74

I asked Yingzhugma, and she said:

> Son, watch continuously the spectacle in your mind.
> Keep the watcher in the condition of the sky.
> The clarity that arises in the basic space without meditating
> Is the actual realization of meditation.

75

I asked Töndenma, and she said:

> Son, if mind-essence is realized, the goal is achieved.
> If the land beyond thoughts is reached, nirvana is reached.
> If illusory vision is dissipated, the dharmakaya is found.
> If there is no grasping at self and others, mental judgments are overcome.

76

I asked Töndrubma, and she said:

> On the birthless path, go without stopping.
> In the abode of nonaction, stay free from conceptual constructs.
> In the place of no direction, there is happiness without limitations.
> In the dimension of nirvana, the result dissolves.

77

Once I was sitting in a green meadow singing invocations to the dakinis, when inside a five-colored pavilion of rainbow lights appeared a dakini whose body was red and luminous. The crown of her head was ornamented with three letters A, one atop the other; her ears were radiating five-colored rays; and her tongue was flaming and sparkling with red light. In her right hand she held the skull of a woman with a braid of hair that produced a jingling sound; in her left, the wish-fulfilling jewel; and she was reciting secret mantras with a whispering *si li li* sound.

She came to sit on the crown of my head and said, "My name is Töntönma, and I will give you siddhis!" and she bestowed upon me the outer, inner, and secret initiations. Then I asked her, "Please, give me a pointing-out instruction that concentrates the fundamental essence!"

She said:

> Son, in the unconquerable fortress of the all-ground
> Let the man who is none but yourself wear the armor.
> The enemy army of the emotions is setting forth:
> Destroy it at once!

78

Wösal Dedenma said:

> Son, in the field of the great unmovable
> Sow the seed of the self-liberation of the unceasing.
> Farming it with the diligence of nondistraction,
> And determined on effortlessness,
> See if it will yield the fruit of the three kayas!

79

I asked Rinchen Tönsalma, and she said:

> In the unplowed field of the all-pervading
> A sprout germinates without having been sown,
> Then the enemy army of thunderbolts and hail sets forth:
> Son, drive back the enemy army and make the fruit ripen!

80

I asked Serden Nyima Wö, and she said:

> Two twin children without parents,
> Although there's no reason to quarrel, end up fighting.
> If they search for a witness in themselves
> And are reconciled without further fighting, that is best!

81

I asked Marmo Tragkam, and she said:

> A bitch that has just given birth has nobody to feed her,
> And her puppies, not generated from her body, scratch and suck her teats.
> The puppies are not surviving, and also the mother suffers hell.
> It is better to separate the mother from her puppies!

82

I asked Yungdrung Tsugtorma, and she said:

> A child not generated by a father and not nourished by a mother,
> Without the need of months or years, has a fully grown, strong body.
> Without searching anywhere, the precious jewel arrives in his hand.
> Without being taught by a master, he is a scholar!

83

I asked Rinchen Norjungma, and she said:

> On the roof of a small inhabited house
> A small child incapable of thinking is distracted by play.
> He does not notice that the sun is setting, and it becomes completely dark.
> His parents, impossible to identify, are waiting for him to come back.

These answers by eighty dakinis, with pure intention, I dedicate to the benefit of all sentient beings!

I, a beggar who has found the dharmakaya within himself, have been practicing the authentic nature since infinite births. I touched the feet of qualified teachers, and by remaining continuously in isolated retreat, the view of the authentic nature arose in me. Having purified my obscurations and completed the accumulations [of merit and wisdom], I encountered the knowledge-holders, and all doubts about the outer, inner, and secret teachings of Bön were cleared up in my mind, while the mother and sister dakinis gave me supreme and common siddhis.

My realization was naturally accomplished countless births ago, and then, without searching intentionally [for students], I gradually started to teach beings. Having left incomplete the benefit for others, I had to enter again and again the womb of a mother endowed with material senses, and I took the body of a beggar in this life, like a nonhuman being. Until I was twenty-one my thoughts were only for samsaric things. When I was twenty-two I was introduced to the supreme vehicle, and as a result the practice I had done in the past reawakened. When I reached twenty-three years of age I concretely realized my state of instant presence, and bliss became continuous. Having naturally accomplished the three kayas, I had no dualism of hope and fear any longer. As everything was perfected in me, I had nothing left to search for outside.

When I met Tongyung, king of the knowledge-holders, doors opened in every direction through his kindness and all the sugatas of the mind lineage, the knowledge-holders, the deities, and the mother dakinis gave me advice, showed me their faces, and bestowed upon me the supreme and common siddhis, and the outer, inner, and secret initiations of Bön. This was a brief story about myself.

This teaching, *The Precious Golden Lamp*, is the quintessence of the state of knowledge of Kalzang, the ultimate essence of Wöden Barma, the heart-advice of Nyima Wöden, the siddhi of mother Sipai Gyalmo, the blessing of the wisdom dakinis, the precious jewel for the fortunate ones, the wind that separates samsara and nirvana and the pure from the impure, the guide for the faithful who progress along the path, the key that shows immaterial, great treasures, and the jewel that fulfills all wishes.

For the benefit of beings, I put it into writing: may fortunate beings hold it in their mind! May worthy and faithful beings practice it! May it be kept secret from the unvirtuous who hold contrary views!

As this is the heart-blood of the mother dakinis, if it is proclaimed in an unsuitable place and to unworthy recipients, the punishment of the *walmo* dakinis will be received.

May those who have read or heard this teaching, or received its empowering transmission, and all those who in this life have established even a slight karmic connection with me be always sustained by the compassionate energy of the supreme sugatas, knowledge-holders, and dakinis, and of myself.

May they attain real knowledge of the natural state of the primordially enlightened mind! May they concretely realize the wisdom of their instant presence! May their illusory vision be purified in its own place! May they abide in the state of nonaction beyond conceptual constructs! May they reach the land of the supreme knowledge-holders of the past! May they be liberated in the dimension of total bliss of nirvana! May all this be auspicious!

U YA GYA GYA GYA![9]

Appendix 1: The *Dran pa gser gdams* in the Various Editions

Here follows a list of the texts in the three editions mentioned in the introduction with a brief explanation of their origin and contents. All editions contain spelling mistakes in the titles, which are corrected here in brackets.

Edition A, the Delhi Edition

In the edition published in Delhi with the title *Man ngag rin po che dran pa gser gyi gdams pa'i gsung pod bzhugs so* in 1972, marked as A, we have:

1. *From the King of Upadeśas, Homage to the Lineage of Knowledge-Holders and Ḍākinīs* (*Man ngag rgyal po las rig 'dzin mkha' 'gro'i tshogs kyi brgyud phyag*), pp. 7–23. Transmitted by Tshe dbang rig 'dzin to Gshen sras lha rje as *snyan brgyud*. Contains invocations to various deities, masters, and ḍākinīs, including iconographical details.[1]
2. *From the King of Upadeśas, Visionary Encounters with Knowledge-Holders and Ḍākinīs* (*Man ngag rgyal po las rig 'dzin mkha' 'gro'i mjal snang*), pp. 25–78. Composed by Gshen sras lha rje in the Female Fire-Hare year (1267). Contains autobiographical details of his visionary encounters and dreams and is translated in its entirety here in chapter 1.
3. *From the King of Upadeśas, the Lamp That Removes the Darkness from Preliminary Practices* (*Man ngag rgyal po las sngon 'gro mun sel sgron ma*), pp. 79–84. Contains three different small texts of preliminary practices, the first (pp. 80–81) on purification and composed by Tshe dbang rig 'dzin; the second (pp. 81–82) on 'pho ba, or transference of consciousness, also composed by Tshe dbang

rig 'dzin and transmitted by the latter to Gshen sras lha rje; the third (pp. 82–84) also on 'pho ba, originally taught by the ḍākinī Bskal bzang ma to 'Od ldan 'bar ma, then from 'Od ldan 'bar ma to Nyi ma 'od ldan, and from the latter to Gshen sras lha rje on the fourth day of the second month of autumn of a Snake year (1245 or 1257).

4. *Pointing-Out Instructions on Primordial Wisdom* (*Ngo sprod ye shes mdzub tshugs*), pp. 85–101. This is the first chapter of the *Dran pa gser gdams* or *Golden Teaching* upadeśa cycle originally transmitted by Dran pa nam mkha'*,* which contains specific instructions on the practice of Rdzogs chen contemplation. I will give only the names of the remaining chapters of this cycle.

5. *The Upadeśa of the Naked Perception of the Dharmakaya* (*Men [man] ngag bon sku gcer mthong*), pp. 103–117. Second chapter of *The Golden Teaching*.

6. *The Upadeśa That Concentrates the Essence of Instant Presence* (*Men [man] ngag rig pa don 'dus*), pp. 119–134. Third chapter of *The Golden Teaching*.

7. *The Upadeśa for Clarifying the Real Nature* (*Men [man] ngag don gyi ga dar*), pp. 135–150. Fourth chapter of *The Golden Teaching*. Translated in its entirety in chapter 2 of this book.

8. *The Upadeśa That Liberates upon Seeing the Unified Essence of All Teachings* (*Men [man] ngag kun 'dus mthong grol*), pp. 151–168. Fifth chapter of *The Golden Teaching*.

9. *The Upadeśa That Draws a Line for Pointing Out [the Real Nature]* (*Men [man] ngag ngo sprod thig 'debs*), pp. 169–188. Sixth chapter of *The Golden Teaching*.

10. *The Upadeśa on the Ultimate Essence of the Real Nature* (*Men [man] ngag don gyis yang tig*), pp. 189–208. Seventh chapter of *The Golden Teaching*.

11. *The Upadeśa of the Most Crucial Points* (*Men [man] ngag gnad kyi gzer bu*), pp. 209–230. Eighth chapter of *The Golden Teaching*.

12. *The Upadeśa That Shows the Result of the Final Signs* (*Men [man] ngag drod tshad tha ma'i 'bras bu*), pp. 231–251. Ninth chapter of *The Golden Teaching*.

13. *The Upadeśa of the Crucial Key for Ultimate Realization* (*Men [man] ngag mthar thug gnad kyi lde mig*), pp. 253–276. Tenth chapter of *The Golden Teaching*. At the end of the chapter it says that

"the crucial upadeśa is completed," but we have what seems to be an extra chapter in the following title.

14. *The Upadeśa That Instantly Cuts All Doubts about the Bardo* (*Men [man] ngag bar do gcig chod*), pp. 277–307. In the detailed colophon at the end, the transmission lineage is given: from Samantabhadra in the pure Akaniṣṭha dimension it was transmitted to Dran pa nam mkha'; Dran pa nam mkha' transmitted it to Tshe dbang rig 'dzin in Khyung lung dngul dkar; Tshe dbang rig 'dzin transmitted it to Gshen sras lha rje in Bya ri gtsug ldan.
15. *The Upadeśa of the Lamp of One's Instant Presence* (*Men [man] ngag rgyal po las men ngag rang rig sgron me*), pp. 309–332. Transmitted by Dran pa nam mkha' to Tshe dbang rig 'dzin, and from the latter to Gshen sras lha rje.
16. *Abridged Advice on the Crucial Points of the King of Upadeśas* (*Man ngag rgyal po gnad kyis [kyi] zer [gzer] zhal gdams pa bsdus pa*), pp. 333–359. Composed by Gshen sras lha rje as the essence of *The Golden Teaching*.
17. *The Garland of Nectar, Orally Received Advice from Eighty Knowledge-Holders in the Form of Questions and Answers* (*Rig 'dzin brgya bcu'i zhu len snyan rgyud zhal gdams bdud rtsi'i 'phreng ba*), pp. 361–374. Short poetical instructions, usually in four-line verses, received from various realized masters of the past. Translated in its entirety in chapter 3 of this book.
18. *The Precious Golden Lamp, Advice from Eighty Ḍākinīs* (*Mkha' 'gro brgya bcu'i zhal gdams rin chen gser gyis [gyi] sgron ma*), pp. 375–390. Short poetical instructions, usually in four-line verses, received from various ḍākinīs. Translated in its entirety in chapter 4 of this book.
19. *Questions and Answers with the Great Lama and Tshe dbang rig 'dzin* (*Bla chen tshe dbang rig 'dzin gyis [gi] zhu len*), pp. 391–408. Contains two texts, the first (pp. 392–402) transmitted by Dran pa nam mkha' to Gshen sras lha rje, and the second (pp. 402–408) transmitted by Tshe dbang rig 'dzin to Gshen sras lha rje. Both the first and the second texts are quoted by Shar rdza bkra shis rgyal mtshan in his *Ocean of Scriptural Quotations* (*Bka' lung rgya mtsho*).[2]
20. *The Upadeśa of the Golden Teaching* (*Man ngag gser gdams*), pp. 409–421. Contains two texts, the first of which (pp. 409–412) omits mention of the author, and the second, called *The Heart-*

Essence *Upadeśa* (*Man ngag snying thig*, pp. 412–420), was transmitted by Dran pa nam mkha' to Gshen sras lha rje. Apparently not included in the other editions.

21. *The Upadeśa of the Drop of Nectar* (*Men [man] ngag bdud rtsi'i thig [thigs] pa*), pp. 423–425. Probably composed by Gshen sras lha rje. Not included in the other editions.

22. *Collected Instructions on the Distinction between Virtue and Negative Actions, and between Faults and Qualities* (*Dge sdig shan 'byed skyon yon 'bru thus*), pp. 427–439. The title appears only in the colophon, where it says that it was transmitted by Dran pa nam mkha' and Tshe dbang rig 'dzin to Gshen sras lha rje. The title could be a displacement, as the text contains a visionary description of the pains and tortures of hell akin to the *'das log* literature.[3] Not included in the other editions.

23. *Teachings Given by Dran pa nam mkha' and His Son to the Nirmāṇakāya Gshen sras lha rje for Distinguishing Virtue from Negative Actions* (*Dran pa yab sras kyis sprul sku gshen sras lha rje la dge sdig shan 'byed gsung pa*), pp. 441–463. Transmitted by Dran pa nam mkha' and Tshe dbang rig 'dzin to Gshen sras lha rje. Quoted several times by Shar rdza bkra shis rgyal mtshan in his *Ocean of Scriptural Quotations*.[4]

24. *The Precious Lamp That Clarifies the Levels of Realization and the Paths* (*Sa lam don gsal rin chen sgron me*), pp. 465–493. Transmitted by Dran pa nam mkha'. Contains questions and answers on the fundamental principles of Bön teachings.

25. *The Upadeśa That Summarizes the Essence, Lamp of the Most Secret Mind, Wish-Fulfilling Jewel Instructions on the Nature of Mind* (*Men [man] ngag don 'dus yang gsang sems kyi sgron ma sems khrid yid bzhin nor bu*), pp. 495–510. This is the same text as number 16, with a different colophon.

26. *The Illuminating Lamp of Pointing-Out Instruction* (*Ngo sprod gsal ba'i sgron ma*), pp. 511–514. Unrelated to the cycle. The colophon does not clearly identify the author, as it says only that the text was transmitted by Bkra shis rgyal mtshan, the lazy one from Gling rig, to G.yung drung khri 'od, the monk of the Zhu g.yas lineage, and others.

27. *The Oral Instructions of the Master* (*Bla ma'i gsung rgyun*). Unrelated to the cycle, it contains three short sections, the first (p. 515) com-

posed by one Rig'dzin gshen sgom, the second (pp. 515–516) with no mention of the author, and the third (pp. 516–518) by one Bya bral dpal 'byor lhun grub. I have not been able to identify these names.

At the end, we find two indexes of the texts of the collection, with a lineage of the masters through whom the *Dran pa gser gdams* has been transmitted. The first index (pp. 519–520) has twenty-seven titles that do not correspond to the ones contained in the same edition.[5] The lineage of transmission is given as:

> From Samantabhadra it was transmitted to Dran pa nam mkha', from the latter to Tshe dbang rig 'dzin, from the latter to Thugs rje kun grol, from the latter to the nirmāṇakāya Dbang ldan gshen sras. Otherwise, from Tshe dbang rig 'dzin [directly] to Dbang ldan gshen sras, and from the latter to Khyung po snang chen grags pa.[6]

The second index (p. 521) gives only the titles of the ten chapters of *The Golden Teaching* tantra, excluding thus the *Bar do gcig chod*.[7]

Edition B, the Bka' brten Edition

In the edition published in volume 39 of the Bka' brten in 1998, marked as B in this book, we have the following twenty-seven texts:

1. *From the King of Upadeśas, Appeasing the Host of the Lineage (of Knowledge-Holders and Ḍākinīs)* (*Man ngag gis [gi] rgyal po las rgyud kyi tshogs skong*), pp. 3–31. Same as text 1 in edition A, the Delhi edition.
2. *From the King of Upadeśas, Visionary Encounters with Knowledge-Holders and Ḍākinīs* (*Man ngag gis [gi] rgyal po las rig 'dzin mkha' 'gro'i mjal snang*), pp. 33–123. Same as text 2 in edition A.
3. *From the King of Upadeśas, The Lamp That Removes the Darkness from Preliminary Practices* (*Man ngag rgyal po sngon 'gro mun sel sgron ma*), pp. 125–129. Same as text 3 in edition A but containing only the first of the three texts or sections.
4. *From the Tantra of the Teachings on the Naked Perception of Instant Presence, Pointing-Out Instructions on Primordial Wisdom* (*Khrid*

rim rig pa gcer mthong gis [gi] rgyud las ngo sprod ye shes 'dzug [mdzub] tshugs), pp. 131–179. Same as text 4 in edition A according to the title; however, from page 133 it seems to contain a different text.

5. *The Naked Perception of the Instant Presence of the Dharmakaya, Upadeśa of the Golden Teaching* (*Man ngag gser gyis [gi] gdams pa bon sku rigs [rig] pa gcer mthong*), pp. 181–205. Same as text 5 in edition A.

6. *The Upadeśa That Concentrates the Essence, Naked Pointing-Out Instructions, also Known as The Essence of One's Instant Presence* (*Man ngag don 'dus ngo sprod rjen par gcer bur zhugs/ rang rig don 'dus yang zer ba*), pp. 207–233. Same as text 6 in edition A.

7. *Clarifying the Real Nature, the Upadeśa That Shows Nakedly the Wisdom of Clear Insight* (*Lhag mthong ye shes gcer bur bstan pa'i man ngag don gyi ga dar*), pp. 235–259. Fourth chapter of *The Golden Teaching*. Same as text 7 in edition A.

8. *From the Tantra of the Golden Teaching Upadeśa, Liberation upon Seeing the Unified Essence of All* (*Man ngag gser gyi gdams pa'i rgyud las kun 'dus mthong grol*), pp. 261–285. Same as text 8 in edition A.

9. *From the Tantra of the Golden Teaching Upadeśa, Drawing a Line for Pointing Out [the Real Nature]* (*Man ngag gser gyi gdams pa'i rgyud las ngo sprod thig 'debs*), pp. 287–316. Same as text 9 in edition A.

10. *From the Tantra of the Golden Teaching Upadeśa, the Upadeśa on the Ultimate Essence of the Real Nature* (*Man ngag gser gyi gdams pa'i rgyud las man ngag don gyi yang thugs*), pp. 317–346. Same as text 10 in edition A.

11. *The Upadeśa of the Most Crucial Points* (*Man ngag gnad kyi gzer bu*), pp. 347–381. Same as text 11 in edition A.

12. *From the Tantra of the Golden Teaching Upadeśa, the Result of the Final Signs* (*Man ngag gser gyi gdams pa'i rgyud las drod tshad mtha'i rgyud las 'brus bskur*), pp. 383–416. Same as text 12 in edition A.

13. *The Upadeśa of the Crucial Key for Ultimate Realization* (*Man ngag mthar thugs gnad kyi lde mig*), pp. 417–457. Same as text 13 in edition A.

14. *The Upadeśa That Instantly Cuts All Doubts about the Bardo* (*Man ngag bar do gcig chod*), pp. 459–505. Same as text 14 in edition A.

15. *The Lamp That Clarifies the Upadeśas on All the Great Vehicles, Also Known as the Lamp of One's Instant Presence* (*Thig [theg] chen kun gyis [gyi] man ngag gsal ba'i sgron me las rang rigs [rig] sgron me yang zer*), pp. 507–553. Same as text 15 in edition A.
16. *Abridged Advice on the Crucial Points of the King of Upadeśas* (*Man ngag rgyal po gnad kyi zhal gdam bsdus pa*), pp. 555–583. Same as text 16 in edition A.
17. *The Garland of Nectar, Orally Received Advice from Eighty Knowledge-Holders in the Form of Questions and Answers* (*Rig 'dzin brgya bcu'i zhu len snyan rgyud bdud rtsi'i gdams pa bdud rtsi phreng ba*), pp. 585–610. Same as text 17 in edition A.
18. *The Precious Golden Lamp, Advice from Eighty Ḍākinīs* (*Khro rgyal*[8] *brgya bcu'i zhal gdams rin chen gser gyi sgron me*), pp. 611–639. Same as text 18 in edition A.
19. *Questions and Answers with the Great Lama Dran pa nam mkha'*[9] (*Bla chen dran pa mu la'i zhu len*), pp. 641–659. Transmitted by Dran pa nam mkha' to Gshen sras lha rje. Same as the first part of text 19 of edition A.
20. *Questions and Answers with Tshe dbang the Great Hermit* (*Tshe dbang ri khrod chen po'i zhu len*), pp. 663–671.[10] Transmitted by Tshe dbang rig 'dzin to Gshen sras lha rje. Same as the second part of text 19 of edition A.
21. *Collected Instructions on Virtue and Negative Actions Given by the Great Lama Dran pa [Nam mkha'] and His Son to [Gshen sras] Lha rje* (*Bla chen dran pa yab sras lha rje'i dge sdig 'bru thus*), pp. 673–713. Same as text 23 of edition A.
22. *The Precious Lamp That Clarifies the Levels of Realization and the Paths, Teaching of Dran pa [Nam mkha']* (*Dran pa'i gdams pa sa lam don gsal rin chen sgron ma*), pp. 716–739. In the colophon it says, "Chapter of Direct Introduction, the First." Same as text 24 of edition A but considerably abridged.
23. *Questions and Answers with the Only Mother Bskal pa bzang mo* (*Ma gcig bskal pa bzang mo'i zhu len*), pp. 741–759. Transmitted by the ḍākinī Bskal pa bzang mo to Gshen sras lha rje. Not contained in edition A.
24. *Questions and Answers for a Fortunate Being, Quintessence of the Mind of 'Od ldan 'bar ma* (*'Od ldan 'bar ma thugs kyi yang snying skal ldan skyes bu'i zhu len*), pp. 761–789. Transmitted by

the ḍākinī 'Od ldan 'bar ma to Gshen sras lha rje. Not contained in edition A.

25. *Questions and Answers with the Precious Lord Stong rgyung mthu chen* (*Rje stong rgyung mthu chen rin po che'i zhu len*), pp. 791–806. Transmitted by Stong rgyung mthu chen to Gshen sras lha rje. Not contained in edition A.

26. *Questions and Answers with the Only Mother Srid pa rgyal mo* (*Ma gcig srid pa rgyal mo'i zhu len*), pp. 807–839. Transmitted by the ḍākinī Srid pa'i rgyal mo to Gshen sras lha rje. Not contained in edition A.

27. *The Lamp That Illuminates the Bardo* (*Bar do gsal ba'i sgron me*), pp. 841–864. Transmitted by Dran pa nam mkha' to Tshe dbang rig 'dzin, and by the latter to Gshen sras lha rje on the fifteenth day of the fourth month of a Horse year (1246 or 1258). Not contained in edition A.

Edition B2, Other Bka' brten Texts

In volume 61 of the Bka' brten, marked as B2 here, we find the following titles:

1. *Questions and Answers with Knowledge-Holders and Ḍākinīs* (*Rig 'dzin mkha' 'gro'i zhus len*), pp. 1–22. Written by Gshen sras lha rje, it includes advice from a number of knowledge-holders and ḍākinīs. It is the only visionary account originally part of the *Dran pa gser gdams* that is not included in the A and B editions. It is, however, mentioned in the list given at the end of the A edition as no. 16, *Questions and Answers from Three Scholars and Three Ḍākinīs* (*Rig 'dzin mkhas pa mi gsum dang mkha' 'gro gsum gyi zhu len*), and it is contained in both the Steng chen (C) edition and the Sichuan (D) edition of 2013.

2. *Questions and Answers with the Only Mother Skal bzang* (*Ma gcig skal bzang gis [gi] zhus len*), pp. 23–37. Same as text 23 in edition B.

3. *Questions and Answers with the Great Bla ma* (*Bla chen yi [gyi] zhus len*), pp. 39–53. Same as text 19 in edition B.

4. *Questions and Answers with the Great Hermit* (*Ri khrod chen po'i zhus len*), pp. 55–64. Same as text 20 in edition B.

5. *Questions and Answers with 'Od ldan 'bar ma* (*'Od ldan 'bar ma'i zhus len*), pp. 65–85, same as text 24 in edition B until page 78; the rest, from page 79, contains the concluding part of text 18 of both the A and B editions, the *Mkha' 'gro brgya bcu'i zhal gdams*, starting from the ḍākinī Gser ldan ma and corresponding to p. 385 in A and p. 631 in B.
6. *The Garland of Nectar, Orally Received Advice from Eighty Knowledge-Holders in the Form of Questions and Answers* (*Rig 'dzin brgya cu'i zhu lan snyan rgyud zhal gdams bdud rtsi'i 'phreng ba gdams pa*), pp. 87–108. Same as text 17 in edition B.

In volume 86, we find a *Man ngag gser gdams*, pp. 61–102. This is the same text, with a different colophon, as the *Man ngag rgyal po gnad kyi zhal gdams bsdus pa*, text 16 of both the A and B editions.

In volume 191 we find another *Man ngag gser gdams*, pp. 287–319, but in this case the *Man ngag rgyal po gnad kyi zhal gdams bsdus pa* covers only pages 287–305, while pages 305–319 contain the *Man ngag gser gdams*, thus corresponding to text 20 of the A edition.

Edition C, the Tengchen Edition

The third available edition is found in volume 82 of the Steng chen Brten 'gyur. It contains twenty-eight texts; it is marked as edition C in this book. As it is very close to the previous Bka' brten edition in the texts included, I will give only the Tibetan titles with the spelling variants that appear in brackets in the original copy:

1. *Man ngag gi rgyal po las rgyud kyi tshogs skor*, pp. 1–33. Same as text 1 in editions A and B.
2. *Man ngag rgyal po las rig 'dzin mkha' 'gro'i mjal snang*, pp. 35–138. Same as text 2 in A and B.
3. *Man ngag rgyal po sngon 'gro mun sel sgron ma*, pp. 139–152. Same as text 3 in A and B. The latter edition, as explained above, contains only the first section of the text.
4. *Khrid rim rig pa gcer mthong gi rgyud las ngo sprod ye shes mdzub tshugs*, pp. 153–179. Same as text 4 in A and B.
5. *Man ngag gser gyi gdams pa bon sku rig pa gcer mthong*, pp. 181–206. Same as text 5 in A and B.

6. *Man ngag don 'dus ngo sprod rjen par gcer bu bzhugs / Rang rig don 'dus yang zer ba*, pp. 207–233. Same as text 6 in A and B.
7. *Lhag mthong ye shes gcer bur bstan pa'i man ngag don gyi ga dar*, pp. 235–261. Same as text 7 in A and B.
8. *Man ngag gser gyi gdams pa'i rgyud las kun 'dus mthong grol*, pp. 263–291. Same as text 8 in A and B.
9. *Man ngag gser gyi gdams pa'i rgyud las ngo sprod thig 'debs*, pp. 293–325. Same as text 9 in A and B.
10. *Man ngag gser gyi gdams pa'i rgyud las man ngag don gyi yang thus*, pp. 327–359. Same as text 10 in A and B.
11. *Man ngag gnad kyi gzer bu*, pp. 361–398. Same as text 11 in A and B.
12. *Man ngag gser gyi gdams pa'i rgyud las drod tshad mtha'i 'bras bu*, pp. 399–434. Same as text 12 in A and B.
13. *Man ngag mthar thug gnad kyi lde mig*, pp. 435–477. Same as text 13 in A and B.
14. *Man ngag bar do gcig chod*, pp. 479–529. Same as text 14 in A and B.
15. *Theg chen kun gyi man ngag gsal ba'i sgron me las rang rigs [rig] sgron me yang zer*, pp. 531–579. Same as text 15 in A and B.
16. *Man ngag rgyal po gnad kyi zhal gdam bsdus pa*, pp. 581–610. Same as text 16 in A and B.
17. *Rig 'dzin brgya cu'i zhu len snyan rgyud zhal gdam bdud rtsi'i 'phring (phreng) gdam pa*, pp. 611–638. Same as text 17 in A and B.
18. *Khro rgyal [mkha' 'gro] brgya cu'i zhal gdam rin chen gser gyi sgron me*, pp. 639–670. Same as text 18 in A and B.
19. *Bla chen yi zhus len*, pp. 671–690. Same as the first part of text 19 in A, and as text 19 in B.
20. *Ri khrod chen po'i zhus len*, pp. 691–702. Same as the second part of text 19 in A, and as text 20 in B.
21. *Bla chen yab sras lha rje'i dge sdig 'bras bu thus*, pp. 703–747. Same as text 23 in A, and as text 21 in B.
22. *Dran pa'i gdams pa sa lam don gsal rin chen sgron ma*, pp. 749–802. Same as text 24 in A, and as text 22 in B.
23. *Ma gcig skal bzang gi zhus len*, pp. 803–823. Same as text 23 in B.
24. *'Od ldan 'bar ma'i zhus len*, pp. 825–856. Same as text 24 in B.
25. *Rje stong rgyung mthu chen rin po che'i zhu len*, pp. 857–873. Same as text 25 in B.

THE DRAN PA GSER GDAMS IN THE VARIOUS EDITIONS — 161

26. *Ma gcig srid pa rgyal mo'i zhu len*, pp. 875–910. Same as text 26 in B.
27. *Bar do gsal ba'i sgron me*, pp. 911–937. Same as text 27 in B.
28. *Rig 'dzin mkha' 'gro'i zhus len*, pp. 939–971. Same as text 1 in B2.

Edition D, the Sichuan Edition

The twenty-nine texts of the edition published in 2013 as *Dran pa gser gdams*, volume 21 of the Sangs rgyas g.yung drung bon gyi dpe tshogs series (Si kron mi rigs dpe skrun khang), correspond to the twenty-eight texts of the C (Steng chen) edition, except that the small 'pho ba text in number 3 of both the A and C editions has been taken as a separate text and printed at the end of the volume. The texts are listed as follows:

1. *Man ngag gi rgyal po las rgyud kyi tshogs skor*, pp. 3–20.
2. *Man ngag rgyal po las rig 'dzin mkha' 'gro'i mjal snang*, pp. 21–76.
3. *Man ngag rgyal po sngon 'gro mun sel sgron ma*, pp. 77–79.
4. *Khrid rim rig pa gcer mthong gi rgyud las ngo sprod ye shes mdzub tshugs*, pp. 80–93.
5. *Man ngag gser gyi gdams pa bon sku rig pa gcer mthong*, pp. 94–107.
6. *Man ngag don 'dus ngo sprod rjen par gcer bur bzhugs / Rang rig don 'dus yang zer ba 'dug*, pp. 108–122.
7. *Lhag mthong ye shes gcer bur bstan pa'i man ngag don gyi ga dar*, pp. 123–136.
8. *Man ngag gser gyi gdams pa'i rgyud las kun 'dus mthong la*, pp. 137–151.
9. *Man ngag gser gyi gdams pa'i rgyud las ngo sprod thig 'debs*, pp. 152–168.
10. *Man ngag gser gyi gdams pa'i rgyud las man ngag don gyi yang thugs* [thus], pp. 169–185.
11. *Man ngag gnad kyi gzer bu*, pp. 186–205.
12. *Man ngag gser gyi gdams pa'i rgyud las drod tshad 'bras bu bon sku*, pp. 206–224.
13. *Man ngag mthar thug gnad kyi lde mig*, pp. 225–246.
14. *Man ngag bar do gcig chod*, pp. 247–273.
15. *Theg chen kun gyi man ngag gsal ba'i sgron me las rang rig sgron me yang zer*, pp. 274–300.

16. *Man ngag rgyal po gnad kyi zhal gdams bsdus pa*, pp. 301–316.
17. *Rig 'dzin brgya bcu'i zhu len snyan rgyud rtsi'i gdams pa bdud rtsi phreng ba*, pp. 317–331.
18. *Khro rgyal [mkha' gro] brgya bcu'i zhal gdams rin chen gser gyi sgron me*, pp. 332–348.
19. *Bla chen dran pa mu la'i zhu len*, pp. 349–358.
20. *Tshe dbang ri khrod chen po'i zhu len*, pp. 359–364.
21. *Bla chen yab sras lha rje'i dge sdig 'bru thus*, pp. 365–388.
22. *Dran pa'i gdams pa sa lam don gsal rin chen sgron ma*, pp. 389–417.
23. *Ma gcig bskal pa bzang mo'i zhu len*, pp. 418–428.
24. *'Od ldan 'bar ma thugs kyi yang snying skal ldan skyes bu'i zhu len*, pp. 429–445.
25. *Rje stong rgyung mthu chen rin po che'i zhu len*, pp. 446–454.
26. *Ma gcig srid pa rgyal mo'i zhu len*, pp. 455–473.
27. *Bar do gsal ba'i sgron me*, pp. 474–487.
28. *Rig 'dzin mkha' gro'i zhu len*, pp. 488–502.
29. *Tshe dbang rig 'dzin gyis mdzad pa'i 'pho ba gcig*, pp. 503–505.

Appendix 2: The Previous Lives of Gshen sras lha rje

The following is a translation of *The Lives of Dbang ldan gshen gsas* (*Dbang ldan gshen gsas kyi skyes tshogs*). See bibliography, op. 32.

I bow down to you who, after attaining enlightenment,
Although not falling back into samsara, in order to guide sentient beings
Took birth one more time and through many form manifestations
Untiringly led to liberation countless beings.

After showing my devoted homage and respect, I will write down briefly the forty-three lives[1] of Go sde 'phags pa Dbang ldan gshen gsas, the supreme sage who has the capacity to save beings from the chains of the lower state when they merely hear his name, and in particular who realized the state of the supreme, unsurpassable vehicle.

In the year of the Dragon, on the fourth day of the last month of autumn, Gshen gsas passed away. On the evening of the fifth day he showed his face to his student 'Brug ris Shes rab grags pa, and told him his previous births:

I was blessed by the supreme *gshen* of the past, and for the benefit of beings I went everywhere without partiality.

Long ago, in Snang dang g.yu rtse in the country of Phya, I was blessed by Gshen rab himself. I was Gto gshen drangs dkar. Together with Gshen gyi dpyi bu I turned the wheel of the outer tantras of Bön.

After that I had two manifestations. One was born at G.yung drung gling in Stag gzig and was blessed by Gshen rab. He had a pure household life, and his name was Drang srong blo gros seng ge. Together with Gtsang ma gtsug phud he turned the wheel of the inner tantras of Bön. The other one was in the presence of Buddha Śākyamuni. He was called Btsun chung lo lo, and also Shes rab snying po. Together with Śāriputra he turned the wheel of the sacred Dharma.

After that, after the passing of Gshen rab, the supreme gshen Mu cho ldem drug appeared. He turned the wheel of Bön of the Great Vehicle, and led all beings to liberation. At that time I had two manifestations. One was in the presence of Ye gshen gstug phud and was called Khye'u 'od gsal. Together with G.yung drung 'od 'bar ma he turned the wheel of the Rdzogs chen of Bön. The other one was in the presence of Mu cho and was called Don la 'gyur med g.yung drung. He listened to all the existing Bön teachings.

After that I had two manifestations. One was in the presence of Ye sangs dkar po in the upper part of Dwang ma'i ding in the country of Phya, and was called Don la g.yung drung 'od gsal. Together with Phywa rje Keng tse len med, he explained the Rdzogs chen *Nam mkha' klong chen*. The other one was born in the country of Drang ma and was called Rigs drung 'od nam gstug phud. Together with the six taming gshen (*'dul ba gshen drug*) he established fourteen thousand Bön teachings.

After that the supreme gshen 'Chi med gstug phud appeared, who turned the wheel of the Immortal Bön (*g.yung drung bon*) and led all beings to liberation. At that time I had two manifestations. One in the presence of Gsang ba 'dus pa was Dbang gi gar ma byed. He was also called Gar gshen sras. The other, in the presence of 'Chi med gtsug phud, listened to the teachings of Bön. He was called Legs grub rin chen 'bar ba.

After that, the six great masters (*slob dpon che drug*) appeared, who turned the wheel of the Immortal Bön (*g.yung drung bon*) and led to liberation all beings in samsara. At that time I had two manifestations. One was Gyim tsha rma chung, who turned the wheel of Bön of grammar and logic. The other, in the presence of Gtso mchog, received all the initiations in the form of light.

At that time Bön underwent a decline and all the scriptures of the sugatas were controlled. Guru Padmasambhava appeared. At that time I had two manifestations. One was Vairocana, who had the language skill of Mañjuśrī. The other was Rgyal ba blo gros, who was appointed as supervisor for the construction of Bsam yas. Together with Li shu stag ring and Co za bon mo, he put into gter ma important Bön teachings from Stag gzig.

Then I had two manifestations. One was in the presence of Dran pa nam mkha' and was called Grub thob Ko long lha gsas. For the sake of future generations he expressed aspirations for the teaching. The other was in the presence of Tshe dbang [rig 'dzin] and was called Rig 'dzin G.yung drung 'od gsal. Together with Tshe dbang rig 'dzin he received the initiations of Samantabhadra.

After that I had three manifestations. One was Khro tshang 'brug lha, who removed all doubts about the primordially enlightened mind. The second obtained realization in India and trained in his capacities in the country of Tibet. He was called Pha dam pa the Indian. The third was a descendant of the lo tsa va Sha kya srid 'khor.

After that I had three manifestations. One was born in the country of Zhang zhung and was called Li mun gtsug phud. The second was in the presence of Mañjuśrī and was called Lo tsa mchog sred. The third abided among the ranks of the vidyādharas.

After that I had three manifestations. One was called Sangs rgyas tshab and [at that time] the teaching of the gshen reappeared. The second was Gshen chen re thul, also called the adept yogin Mtha' yas 'phags. The third practiced the Bön of Li tsa, and was called A nu rong tsa. For some years he benefited beings in the country of the nonhumans by means of light.

After that I had three manifestations. One was called Sas jo 'bum me. The second, a hidden hermit, was together with Tshe dbang [rig 'dzin]. He was called Nyong ri khrod pa. The third was born on the banks of the Gnam mtsho lake and was an adept yogin called Ban ma bon ["neither Buddhist nor Bönpo"]. He was also called Shes rab seng ge and spread both Bön and Dharma without partiality.

After that I had three manifestations. One was called Kyu ra rin chen and extracted important gter ma from Rma gnyan pom ra. The second was a minor king in Bha ta hor. He was called Rgyal bu rin chen. The third abided among the ranks of the vidyādharas.

After that I had three manifestations. One practiced the Dharma of Mañjuśrī in Ri bo rtse lnga in China. He was called Dbang phyug shes rab seng ge. The second was the chief at the gaṇacakras of the ḍākinīs in the country of Uḍḍiyāna. He was called Ye grol dam pa bi ti. The third abided among the ranks of the vidyādharas.

After that I had three manifestations. One benefited beings in the dimension of the nāgas. He was called Klu bon gsang ba g.yung drung gtsug phud. The second was born as a minor king in India. He was called Rgyal bu grol ldan. The third abided among the ranks of the vidyādharas.

After that I had three manifestations. One was a hidden yogin, called

Zhig po a rgod. The second was called Skyi rong zhig po. The third was an adept yogin who bound the dbal mo into servitude. He was called Sman rgyal rang grol.

After that I had three manifestations. One was called 'Or phug btsun chung and received the siddhis of the Bön of 'Ol phug. The second was Khro phu lo tsa ba and practiced the Dharma of Guru Padmasambhava. I am Gshen gsas lha rje and extracted important gter ma in Eastern Tibet. Together with one called Khyung po grags pa, blessed by great scholars and translators, I guided beings through compassionate energy and turned the wheel of Bön of the Great Vehicle.

In other texts it is said: After that [he was] Rgyal 'phel slob dpon, then the great scholar and siddha Bsod nams ye shes, then Zhu g.yas rgyal mtshan mchog legs, then 'Gro mgon bsod nams lhun grub. Then, after seven lives, he extracted gter ma in Eastern Tibet and benefited beings. In the future, when the life span will be ten years, he will be born as Thang ma ye sgron and reverse samsara for all the beings of that time[2] and establish them in the dimension of the real nature of existence. May all be auspicious!

Appendix 3: Iconographical Details of Knowlege-Holders and Ḍākinīs

Here follows a list of the vidyādharas and ḍākinīs invoked in the first text of the *Dran pa gser gdams*, the *Rig 'dzin mkha' 'gro'i tshogs kyi rgyud phyag* (op. 41, A: 7–23) or *Rgyud kyi tshogs skong* (op. 41, B: 3–31).

Kun tu bzang po: peaceful, white and luminous, with a necklace of various colors, a wish-fulfilling jewel in the right hand, a white A in the left.

Gshen lha 'od dkar: saṃbhogakāya, crystal white, with a topknot of jewels, spreading five rainbow lights, ornamented with multicolored lotus flowers, sitting on a throne of five jewels, with a crystal swastika in the right hand and an uḍumbara flower in the left.

Rigs lnga yab yum: saṃbhogakāya, peaceful, not described specifically.

Khro rgyal gtso mchog mkha' 'gying: wrathful, with green hair radiating sparks of luminous rays, their roaring voice transforming into hundreds of thousands of languages.

Tshad med 'od ldan: red, wearing jewel ornaments and a crown, with a ritual vase in the right hand, a jewel in the left, sitting on a seat of five-colored rainbows, reciting secret mantras.

'Chi med gtsug phud: white, wearing ornaments of crystal and sapphire and a crown, with a conch shell stupa in the right hand and a small gshang of gold in the left.

Stag la me 'bar: red, wrathful, and surrounded by flames, wearing a crown of garuḍa, holding a sharp sword in the right hand and a wheel of fire in the left.

Dmu khri btsan po: unspecified color, manifesting according to necessities.

Stong rgyung mthu chen: brown, in brahmin attire, wearing bone ornaments.

Lo paṇ gshen brgyad: not described.

Dran pa nam mkha': blue, ornamented with the letter A, sitting on a seat of rainbow colors.

Mkhyen brtse rig 'dzin chen po (Tshe dbang rig 'dzin): white, wearing a crown of jewels.

Ra rgyal ye shes, Li shu stag ring, U rgyan hring ni, A nu 'phrag thag, "the four *gshen po*s that benefit beings" (*'gro ba'i don mdzad gshen po bzhi*): not described.

Bskal pa bzang mo: white, with a conch shell plaited tuft of hair, sitting in meditation on a throne of sun, moon, and lotus, surrounded by goddesses of wisdom.

'Od ldan 'bar ma: peaceful, dark red, surrounded by goddesses wearing ornaments.

Nyi ma 'od ldan: white with a hue of colored rays, surrounded by hundreds of thousands of active goddesses.

Srid rgyal yum (Srid pa'i rgyal mo): wrathful and powerful, coral red, hair braided with jewels, sitting on a throne of fresh and dry skulls, surrounded by *ma mos*.

Thugs rje kun sgrol: red and colorful, with three eyes at the chest.

Chu lcam rgyal mo: bluish green, with a tiara of gold, holding a small cup in the right hand and a *ha lo* flower in the left, surrounded by goddesses wearing ornaments.

Klong brten rin chen gsal sgron (Tshogs bdag dkar mo): white, with wrathful eyes, wearing a patchwork garment of corals, holding a vase in the right hand and a conch shell vessel in the left, reciting mantras, surrounded by ḍākinī assistants in the gaṇacakra.

Rgod lcam 'bar ma: wrathful and powerful, conch white, wearing a cloak of vulture and a skirt of peacock, holding a conch shell stick in the right hand and a crystal cup in the left, surrounded by manifestations similar to her.

Nyi ma stong khyab: yellow, wearing a crown of conch shell, holding a heap of turquoises in the right hand and a mandala of gold in the left, surrounded by oath-bound ḍākinīs.

Nyi ma gsal 'tsher: yellowish green, wearing a tiara of copper and iron twisted together, naked in the upper part, with bone ornaments in the lower part, one leg stretched and one curved in dancing posture, with the fingers pointing to the sky, surrounded by goddesses adorned with fine ornaments.

Nyi 'od 'bar ma: dark blue emanating a turquoise light, dancing sinuously, holding a white crystal vase in the right hand and a small offering bowl of precious materials in the left, singing melodious tunes, surrounded by dancing goddesses.

Nyi 'od mdangs ldan: white and made of silver, wearing head ornaments of three stacked swastikas and a colored dress, spreading the five medicinal substances, holding a vase for burning incense in the right hand and an arura in the left, surrounded by the goddesses of incense.

Dbyings phyug rgyal mtshan: subduer of demons (*bdud*), dark brown and wrathful, with a crest spreading luminous rays, wearing a black cloak of silk, holding a sandalwood dagger in the right hand and a skull cup full of blood in the left, surrounded by wrathful goddesses.

Dbang phyug sgron ma: terrifying, with the hair ornamented with pearls, wearing a white armor of conch shell, holding a silver hook in the right hand, surrounded by flesh-eating ḍākinīs.

Sgra skad 'bum bsgyur: the color of crystal, wearing a crown of sapphire and an animal fur, holding a turquoise swastika in the right hand and a maṇḍala of conch shell in the left, surrounded by the goddesses of melodious sounds.

'Od zer mi 'gyur mdangs ldan: green, wearing a crown and a patchwork cloth of pearls, smiling, with the palm of the right hand toward the sky, holding a vase of nectar in the left, surrounded by beautiful goddesses.

Su ka si ti, ḍākinī from India: yellow, beautiful, wearing a crown of jewels, inside a pavilion of precious stones, hands in the meditation mudra at the heart, surrounded by ḍākinīs that collect the essence.

Kun shes zer ldan, ḍākinī from Stag gzig: wearing various costumes, holding a mala of various jewels in the right hand and a vase with consecrated medicinal *chang* in the left, surrounded by ḍākinīs of activities.

Yongs khyab chen mo, ḍākinī from Oḍḍiyāna: subduer of obstructing forces (*bgegs*), reddish green and terrifying, wearing a diadem of bones and a human skin, holding weapons for cutting, surrounded by fierce goddesses.

Kun gsal lcam gcig, ḍākinī from Zhang zhung: body made of precious materials, with red changeable eyes, terrifying hair, wearing a skin garment with golden ornaments, holding a vessel full of nutritious substances, surrounded by ḍākinīs who feed on corpses (*ro len mkha' 'gro*).

Kun snyoms 'od ldan, ḍākinī from Bru sha: beautiful, with a melodious voice, surrounded by terrifying oath-bound ḍākinīs.

Rdo rje'i rigs kyi mkha' 'gro ma in the east, white.

Rin chen rigs kyi mkha' 'gro ma in the south, blue.

Pad ma rigs kyi mkha' 'gro ma in the west, red.

Las kyi rigs kyi mkha' 'gro ma in the north, green.

Appendix 4: Names of Knowledge-Holders with Spelling Variants

Here follows a list of the names of the *rig 'dzin*, or knowledge-holders, quoted in *The Garland of Nectar, Orally Received Advice from Eighty Knowledge-Holders in the Form of Questions and Answers* (*Rig 'dzin brgya bcu'i zhu len snyan rgyud bdud rtsi'i gdams pa bdud rtsi phreng ba*), with the spelling variations presented in the different editions of the text. See appendix 1 or the bibliography for explanations of the letters indicating the various editions of the *Dran pa gser gdams*.

1. Tshad med 'od ldan
2. A, B2, C: Li shag 'od nam; B: Li shu 'od nam
3. Hris pa jo sras
4. A, B2, C: Spungs nam gyer rgyung; B: Spung nam gyer gyung
5. A, B: Mu la 'bar ba; B2, C: Mu la 'bar nam
6. A, B: Ye stong zhang gsal; B2, C: Ye ston zhang gsal
7. Ye shes lhung rgyal
8. Nyi gsal 'od rtse
9. A, B2: Lung non dbang grub; B: Lung nod dbang grub; C: Lung don dbang grub
10. A: Dbang phyug hring 'od; B: Dbang phyugs hri 'od; C: Dbang rgyug hring 'od
11. 'Od nam mu spungs
12. A, B: Nyid la shel 'od; C: Nyi ma shes 'od
13. Gtsug gshen 'od 'bar
14. A: Mi 'gyur don gsal; B: Sangs rgyas mi 'gyur don gsal; B2, C: Mi 'gyur 'od gsal
15. Gsal ba 'od ldan
16. Stong rgyung mthu chen

17. Bla chen [dran pa nam mkha']
18. Tshe dbang rig 'dzin
19. A: Rma lo dar phyar; B: Rma lo dar spyang; B2, C: Rma lo dar dpyang
20. Yongs su dag pa
21. Mi lus bsam legs
22. A, B2, C: Klu grub snying po; B: Klu grub ye shes snying po
23. Snang ba mdog can
24. A, B: Mu khri btsan po; C: Mu khri btsad po
25. Ha ra ci par
26. A nu 'phrag thag
27. Sad ne ga'u
28. A: Da mi ded ge; B: Tha mi tha ki; B2: Dad mi thad dge; C: Da mi thad ke
29. A, B, C: Hring ni mu ting; B2: Hring ni dmu ting
30. A: Gling chen mu wer; B, C: Glang chen mu wer; B2: Gleng chen mu wer
31. A, C: Shad pu ra khug; B: Shad pu ra gug; B2: Shad bu ra khug
32. Zing pa mthu chen
33. Spe bon thog 'phrul
34. A: Spe thog rtse; B, B2, C: Spe bon thog rtse
35. Sha ri dbu chen
36. Gyim tsha rma chung
37. Lce tsa mkhar bu
38. Rje rgyal lha sgom
39. A, B: Ra sangs khod ram; B2, C: Ra sangs khod rum
40. A: Bla chen mu thur; B: Blon chen mu tur; B2, C: Blon chen mu thur
41. Rgyung yar mu khod
42. Li shu stag ring
43. Ngam pa lce ring
44. Za rang me 'bar
45. A, C: Mu spungs gsal tang; B: Sangs rgyas mu spungs gsal stong; B2: Mu spungs gsal tang
46. 'Chi med gstug phud
47. A, B: Stag la me 'bar; B2, C: Stag lha me 'bar
48. Lha rje bar sgom
49. A, B2, C: Gur sgom da re; B: Gur bsgom da ris

50. A, B: Gur bsgom sgras po; B2, C: Gur sgom sgra po
51. A, B2, C: Lha rje ston me; B: Lha rje me ston
52. A: Bar tang zhang ston; B, C: Bar thang zhang ston; B2: Par thang zhang ston
53. A: Sum pa dbu gar; B, B2, C: Sum pa dbu dkar
54. Khro tshang 'brug lha
55. A: Mi la ras pa; B: Mi la ris pa; C: Mu la ras pa
56. Gling rje ras pa
57. Zhu sgom 'khrul zhig
58. A: Mi sgom zhig po; B, B2: Me bsgom zhig po; C: Me sgom zhig po
59. Kun dga' zhig po
60. Bon zhig
61. A: 'Khrul zhig ldom bu; B, B2, C: 'Khrul zhig ldam bu
62. Dam pa g.yu zhig
63. A: Bod rbar zhig po; B: Bod ber zhigs po; B2, C: Bo rbar zhig po
64. Gnyos tshul khrims rgyal mtshan
65. Tre ston go cha
66. Jo gdung
67. Jo g.yung
68. A: 'Gu ru rno rtse; B: Gu ru rno rtse; B2: Gu ru non rtse; C: Ghu ru rnon rtse
69. A: Rma ston srid 'dzin; B2, C: Rme ston srol 'dzin
70. Bdud rtsi rgyal mtshan
71. A, B2: Dgongs mdzad chen po; B: Dgongs mdzad ri khrod chen po; C: Dgongs mdzod chen po
72. A: Dmu tsa gyer med; B, B2, C: Dmu tsha gyer med
73. A: Zhu g.yas legs po; B: Zhu yas lod po; B2: Zhu g.yas led po; C: zhu yas legs po
74. A, B: Sprul sku klu dga'; C: Sprul sku klu rga
75. A: Nag pa ral pa can; B, C: Nag po ral pa can; B2: Nag po ral pa can
76. Bon zhig
77. Dbang ldan gshen sras
78. A: Spyang 'phag; B: Skyang 'phag; B2: Skyang 'phyag; C: Spyang 'phags

Appendix 5: Names of Ḍākinīs with Spelling Variants

Here follows a list of the names of the ḍākinīs quoted in *The Precious Golden Lamp, Advice from Eighty Ḍākinīs* (*Mkha' 'gro brgya bcu'i zhal gdams rin chen gser gyi sgron ma*), with the spelling variations presented in the different editions of the text. See appendix 1 or the bibliography for explanations of the letters indicating the various editions of the *Dran pa gser gdams*.

1. Skal bzang
2. 'Od ldan 'bar ma
3. Nyi ma 'od ldan
4. Srid rgyal
5. Thugs rje kun grol
6. Rgod lcam 'bar ma
7. Tshogs bdag dkar mo
8. Nyi ma stong khyab
9. Nyi 'od 'bar ma
10. Nyi 'od mdangs ldan
11. 'Bum bsgyur ma
12. A, B: 'Od zer mdangs ldan; C: 'Od zer mdangs ldan ma
13. Gsal sgron rgyan gcig ma
14. Gsal ldan 'od 'phro ma
15. A: Klong ma; B, C: Klong brtan ma
16. A, C: Rgod lcam g.yu mthing ma; B: Rgod lcam 'thing ma
17. Rgyan ldan ma
18. Rgyan gcig ma
19. Rgyan drug ma
20. Chu lcam rgyal mo
21. A, C: Chu lcam 'od 'phro ma; B: Lcam gcig 'od 'phro ma

22. Nyi 'od gsal ldan ma
23. Zer ldan sring gcig ma
24. Dri med 'od ldan ma
25. Seng gdong ma
26. Glog lcam nyi 'od ma
27. Rgod lcam gtsug gtor ma
28. Bdud rtsi 'char 'bebs ma
29. Rgyan ldan zer 'phro ma
30. Gsal ba'i sgron ma can
31. Glog lcam 'od 'gyu ma
32. A, B: Sna tshogs rgyan ldan ma; C: Sna tshogs rgyal ldan ma
33. Don 'bar ma
34. A: Nyi 'od gsal 'tsher ma; B, C: Nyi ma gsar 'tsher ma
35. Kun 'bum ma
36. Kun mkhyen zer ldan ma
37. A: Dkar gsal mdangs ldan ma; B: Dkar gsal ldan ma; C: A dkar gsal ldan ma
38. Thugs rje lcags kyu ma
39. Unnamed ḍākinī
40. Klong khyab ma
41. A, C: Byams pa kun gsal ma; B: Byams pa kun ldan ma
42. A: Yongs khyab ma; B, C: Yongs su khyab pa ma
43. Yongs khyab chen mo
44. A: Kun shes zer ldan ma; B, C: Kun shes zer ldan
45. A: Kun snang ma; B: Kun tu snang ma; C: Kun du snang ma
46. A: Thogs med 'od ldan ma; B, C; Thog med 'od ldan ma
47. A: Thogs med mi 'gyur ma; B, C: Thog med mi 'gyur ma
48. Sgron me mdangs ldan ma
49. A: Dbyings phyugs rgyal mtshan ma; B, C: Dbyings phyugs rgyan ldan ma
50. Dbang phyug sgron ma
51. Kun 'byung ma
52. Kun shes ma
53. 'Od 'phro ma
54. Gsal 'bar ma
55. Kun 'dus ma
56. Kun dga' ma
57. Kun mkhyen ma

58. Dbyings gsal ma
59. Dbyings grol ma
60. A: Su ka si ti; B, C: Su ka si ti ma
61. Mtha' yas ma
62. A: 'Od 'bar ma; B, C: 'Od gsal ma
63. Zer ldan ma
64. Bde ldan ma
65. Blo ldan ma
66. Thogs med ma
67. Mdangs ldan ma
68. Ye gsal ma
69. Ye 'byung ma
70. Ye khyab ma
71. Ye mkhyen ma
72. A: Ye dag ma; B: Yid dga' ma; C: Yi dag ma
73. Dbyings gsal ma
74. A: Dbyings bzhugs ma; B: Dbyings khyab ma; C: Dbyings phyug ma
75. Don ldan ma
76. A, C: Don grub ma; B: Don 'grub ma
77. Don ston ma
78. A, C: 'Od gsal bde ldan ma; B: Bde ldan ma
79. A: Rin chen don gsal ma; B, C: Rin chen 'od gsal ma
80. A, C: Zer ldan nyi ma 'od; B: Zer ldan nyi 'od ma; B2: Zer ldan nyid 'od ma
81. A: Dmar mo khrag skam; B: Dmar mo khrag rkang ma; B2: Dmar mo khrag skam ma; C: Dmar mo khrag skom ma
82. G.yung drung gtsug gtor ma
83. A: Rin chen nor bu 'byung ma; B, C: Rin chen nor 'byung ma

Appendix 6: The Translated Texts' Main Textual Variants in Two Editions of the *Dran pa gser gdams*

The following shows the main textual variants which I found in editions A (Delhi 1972) and B (Bka' brten, vol. 39) of the four texts translated in this book. The original spellings have not been corrected.

Chapter 1. *Rig 'dzin mkha' 'gro'i mjal snang*

A: 27/8 mtha' ba bcad cing
B: 36/6 ka ba bcad cing

A: 28/5 rgya yan shes na bon sku'i ngang du skyongs
B: 37/6 rgya yan gyi shes pa bon sku'i ngang du skyongs

A: 30/1 'phar ba gsum
B: 40/3 'phar ba gcig

A: 31/6 g.yo med ngang du gtan med gnas par mdzod
B: 42/5 g.yo med ngang du gtad med gnas par mdzod

A: 31/7 yang tig don gyi
B: 42/6 yang dag don gyi

A: 32/4 sprang mo gcig la
B: 43/6 sprang po gcig la

APPENDIX 6

A: 32/8 *one line missing after* mi bzad pa gcig bzhugs yin
B: 44/4: g.yon gral gyi mgor bu med mun nag rngam la 'jigs pa gcig bzhugs

A: 33/5 de la sogs pa'i rnams ni 'jig rten mkha' 'gro'i tshog gral chen po yin
B: 45/6 de la sogs pa'i rnams ni rig 'dzin mkha' 'gro'i tshog gral chen po yin

A: 39/8 blo 'das mnyam nyid bde chen klong/ma yin gang dang bral ba'i/ byil chung 'dzin ma 'phur du chug
B: 55/5 blo 'das mnyan nyid bde chen klong/ ma yin gang dang bral ba yin/byil chung 'dzin ma 'phur du tshul

A: 40/2 bdag gis ni phyi pa e mi yin
B: 56/2 bdag gis ni khyi yang e shu yin

A: 40/4 rig 'dzin gshen phran bco brgyad
B: 56/5 rig 'dzin gshen phran brgyad

A: 43/7 ma tar phyin pa yar bltas
B: 62/1 ma ltar phyi mas yar bltas

A: 52/2 bdag gis de la the tshom yid zos nges
B: 76/5 bdag gis de la tshe tshom mi za nges

A: 54/1 sems can bu med la sbrum ma ci 'byung
B: 80/1 sems can bu med la bu gcig 'byung ba

A: 54/4 yag par ma 'dzin lta mkhan sems la bltos
B: 80/4 yag par ma 'dzin 'dzin mkhan sems la bltos

A: 55/4 nyams dga' dang phro
B: 82/5 nyams dga' dngos spros

A: 57/4 byar med spros bral gyi yul du rjes med khrol
B: 85/5 dbyer med spros bral gyi ngang du 'dzin med khrol

A: 57/9 dran pa rigs lnga yab yum
B: 86/4 dran pa'i thugs kar rigs lnga yab yum

A: 59/9 skyes bu ljar nyal ma byed cog bzhugs mdzod
B: 90/2 skyes bu ljang nyal mdzad chog bzhugs pa mdzod

A: 61/1 rtogs pa'i bsam mno rang sar ma zin pas
B: 92/2 rtogs pa'i ma bsam mno rang sar ma zad pas

A: 63/8 phyogs kun nas ban bon rje dpon gsum
B: 97/1 phyogs nas ban skya bon gsum

A: 68/4 stag go ba tsam du
B: 104/6 stag bong ba tsam

A: 68/6 bdag kyang rig pa bud nas song ba
B: 105/3 bdag kyang ri la bud la song ba

A: 69/4 sku lus khro bo'i chen por sprul/ mthe bong bzhi rgyal chen rigs bzhir sprul
B: 106/5 sku lus sdong po khro bo chen por sprul/ rkang lag bzhi de rgyal chen rigs bzhir sprul

A: 71/4 lags pas gar stabs byas shing
B: 110/2 langs pa'i gar stabs byas shing

A: 72/5 mi bcad gzhal yas khang
B: 112/1 mi mdzes gzhal yas

A: 72/8 skyes bu grub pa mthar thug gnas su skyol med skyong
B: 112/5 skyes bu grub pa mthar thug gnas su skyol mod kyang

A: 72/9 yang snang ba ru logs phyi bu'i mthong ngam
B: 113/1 yang nas snang du log phyin ci'i mthong snang ngam

A: 73/8 pho skor gang la yang par ma byung na
B: 114/4 yo skol gang la yung sar ma byung nas

A: 76/5 spyan bcu gnyis yod pa
B: 119/2 spyan bcu yod pa

A: 78/6 'jang nas byung zhing bzhin/rin po che'i rtags bzhin
B: 122/5 'jang nas 'byung bzhin rin po che bzhin

A: 78/6 'gro rnams mun pa'i smag rum 'thib pa la/ 'jal ba'i rig 'dzin sprin ltar bab ba 'dra
B: 122/5 'gro rnams mun rgyug rum 'thib pa la/ mjal pa'i rig 'dzin sprin char 'thib pa 'dra

Chapter 2. *Man ngag don gyi ga dar*

A: 147/5 bcas bcos blo dang bral na de ka yin
B: 240/2 ma bcos blo dang bral na de ka yin

A: 138/2 mi yeng sgom du med pa la
B: 240/6 ci yang sgom rgyu med pa la

A: 144/4 re dog med pas rang sems sangs rgyas sku
B: 250/3 re dog med pas rang sems sangs rgyas yin

A: 145/1 rig pa phyi nas yin te
B: 251/4 rig pa phye ba yin te

A: 145/4 bag chags rang das su song na/ blo dang rtogs pa'i yul las 'das pa yin/ blo dang rtogs pa'i yul las 'das na/ dri ma dang bral ba'i sangs rgyas de ka yin
B: 252/3 *four lines missing after* bag chags rang dag su 'gro ba yin

A: 148/7 gnyis med byang chub sems su mnyam par bya
B: 257/5 gnyis med byang chub sems su myong bar bya

A: 148/8 yengs med shes pas sems la bya ra byed
B: 257/5 yengs med shes pa sa le sems la bya ra byed

A: 149/1 sus kyang ma bsgrub
B: 258/4 sus kyang ma bsgrib

A: 149/2 dran pa'i snying po ye shes don du gsal
B: 258/4 dran pa'i snying po yes shes 'od du gsal

A: 149/3 ye stong ye bdal nam mkha'i sems nyid can
B: 258/5 ye stong ye bdal nam mkha'i rang bzhin te

A: 149/7 nyid ni stong pa'i snying por rang bzhin med pas gsal
B: 259/2 nyid pa stong pa'i snying po rigs pa gsal

CHAPTER 3. *RIG 'DZIN BRGYA BCU'I ZHU LEN*

A: 361/2 ma g.yos mtha' bral kun bzang dgongs pa'i mchog
B: 586/1 ma g.yos mtha' bral kun bzang dgongs pa'i ngang

A: 361/2 rtsol med nang nas rang rig ye shes rtsal
B: 586/1 rtsal med nang gnas rang bzhin ye shes rtsal

A: 361/3 kun bzang ngo bo tshad med 'od ldan
B: 586/3 kun tu bzang po tshad med 'od ldan

A: 361/5 rang la rtogs tshad zur ma
B: 587/1 rang la spang rtogs tsha zur ma

A: 362/2 gzhan ma rnams gang lags zhus tsa msthan gsang ngo
B: 588/3 gzhan ma rnams gang lags zhus tsa mtshan gsungs ngo

A: 363/3 lam la ma bsgrod/ bsgrod mkhan rang sar shog
B: 590/3 lam la ma bgrod bgrod sa gnas su phyin par shog

A: 363/9 mtha' bral gnas lugs don dam rtogs mi myed
B: 591/4 mtha' bral gnas lugs don chen rtog mi med

A: 363/9 yang dag don gyi gnas lam mkhan
B: 591/4 yang dag gzhi'i lam mkhan

A: 363/9 'dzin pa rang grol gyi sgom pa
B: 591/4 *one line missing after* yang dag gzhi'i lam mkhan

A: 364/5 gang zag yar 'dzegs rnams kyi dgos 'dod gegs sel phyir
B: 592/4 gang zag yer 'dzegs rnams gegs bsal bog 'don phyir

A: 364/6 'dir gnas cha med kyi gzhi stong khyab brdal la
B: 592/4 'gnas 'dir cha med kyis gzhi stong ye bdal la

A: 364/7 bu bzung du med pa'i ngo bo stong pa la/ 'khrul pa med pa'i yi ge phyogs med 'char
B: 592/6 bu bdag 'dzin med pa'i ngo bo stong pa la/ 'khrul pa med pas ye shes phyogs med 'char

A: 364/8 btang snyoms med par rgyun du gnas par mdzod
B: 593/1 btang snyoms med par rgyun du bya ra mdzod

A: 364/9 du ma ro gcig lta ba ma yengs mdzod
B: 593/3 du ma ro gcig lta ba la ma spangs mdzod

A: 365/6 kun gzhi skye med gdod dag la
B: 594/4 kun gzhi skye med stong pa la

A: 365/8 ci snang grogs su 'char na spyod pa yin/ ngo no mtha' dbus bral na 'bras bu yin gsungs/ a nu 'phrag thag la zhus pas/ sems ngo no stong zhing bdag 'dzin bral
B: 595/1 *the above four lines are missing after* bdag gzhan 'dzin pa bral na sgom pa yin

A: 365/9 *one line missing after* sems ngo bo stong zhing bdag 'dzin bral
B: 595/1 *the line missing above:* rig pa rang gsal zhen chag bral

A: 366/1 sku gsum ngo bo sems su myong
B: 595/2 sku gsum ngo bo nyams su long

A: 366/3 stong nyid rang sar grol dgos pa yin
B: 595/4 stong nyid rig pa rang sar grol dgos pa yin

A: 366/3 sems nyid ye shes ngar dang bcas pa la
B: 595/4 stong nyid ye shes ngar dang chas pa la

A: 366/3 'phro med bde ba lding pos sangs mi rgyas
B: 595/5 'phro med bde ba kher bu'i sangs mi rgyas

A: 366/6 gling 'dir 'khor ba mi spang sdug bsngal chad kyis bsgrub
B: 596/2 gling 'dir mi rnams 'khor ba yang sdug bsngal ched kyis bsgrub

A: 366/7 bag chags bdud kyis khyer dog yod
B: 596/4 chags zhen bdud kyi khyer dog yod

A: 366/7 bu rmed sha nye la ma gdung gcig
B: 596/4 bu smad sha nye la ma sdang

A: 367/2 'gag med kyi phyam la yar ba bsrid
B: 597/3 'gags med kyi 'phrang la yar ba srid

A: 367/4 kha spyang sgros 'dog ma mang gol yin
B: 597/5 kha spyang sgro 'dog ma long go bar gyi

A: 367/5 kun gzhi mtha' dang bral na bon sku de ka yin
B: 597/6 kun gzhi mtha' bral na bon nyid de ga yin

A: 367/9 rjen par sa le bzhag sin na/ bde chen ngang nas 'char bas
B: 598/5 rjen par sa le ma bzhag na/ bde chen nang nas mi 'char bar

A: 368/1 rig 'dzin grangs med byon te/ zhal 'tsho mi 'tsho mang do
B: 598/6 rig 'dzin grangs mang byin te zhal 'tsho mi mang po gda'o

A: 368/2 gnyis 'dzin ma yin ro gcig ngang
B: 599/1 gnyis 'dzin ma byed ro gcig ngang

A: 368/2 *two lines missing after* rgya mtsho rba rlab med pa 'dra
B: 599/1 sku gsum lhun gyis grub pa de/ sprin med nam mkha'i ngog dang 'dra gsungs

A: 368/4 skye med klong nas 'gag med 'phyo
B: 599/3 skye med dbyings nas 'gag med 'phyo

A: 369/4 bu lha 'dre gnyis med sems su myong ba yin
B: 601/2 bu lha 'dre gnyis med sems su mnyam pa yin

A: 369/5 *seven lines missing after* gur sgom da res
B: 601/3 bu da lta'i dran rig gsal ba de/ bon sku yin pa ngo shes pa gyis/ phyi snang ba sna tshogs 'di/ rang mdangs yin ngo shes pa gyis/ snang sems gnyis med nang du ltos/ blo 'das gnyis med ngang la zhog gsungs

A: 369/6 bu lha 'dres kun rang sems 'di ka yin
B: 601/6 bu lha kun bzang rang sems 'di ga yin

A: 369/7 bder gshegs rgyun chad me na bon sku yin
B: 602/2 bde chen rgyun chad med na bon sku yin

A: 369/9 bu kun gzhi rig pa dbyings su 'dres/ snang sems gnyid med klong du sangs par gyis/ 'khor 'das byar med gcig du rdzogs par gyis
B: 602/5 bu kun gzhi'i rig pa dbyings su bsres/ snang sems dbyer med klong du 'dres pa gyis/ 'khor 'das gnyis med gcig tu rdzogs pa gyis

A: 370/1 bu 'dzin med kyi snang ba thad gtor gyis
B: 602/6 bu 'jig rten gyis snang ba thag gtor gyis

A: 370/4 de la sangs rgyas rang nyid yin
B: 603/4 de bas sangs rgyas rang rig yin

A: 370/7 lta ltangs bzang kyang sa mi chod
B: 604/1 lta stangs bral ba'i sa mi chod

A: 370/7 dran pa yengs med kyi gsal btab gces
B: 604/1 dran pa yengs med kyi go ba gces

A: 370/8 sna tshogs snang ba brid mkhan la/ zhe sdang ran grol gyi lta ba gces
B: 604/1 sna tshogs snang ba khrid mkhan la/ zhen med rang grol gyi lta ba gces

A: 370/9 sku dang ye shes phyogs med rgyas
B: 604/2 sku dang ye shes phyogs med sangs rgyas

A: 371/5 yang dag slob spong sems la chod/ skye med stong pa'i gzhal yas nas
B: 605/3 yang dag slob dpon sems la chos/ sems skye ba med pa stong pa'i zhal yas nas

A: 372/2 re dog med/ ye shes nyi ma 'dra na 'khrul rtogs skyon dang bral/ mi bskyod rgya mtsho 'dra na
B: 606/4 *two and a half lines missing after* dgongs pa nam mkha' dra na

A: 372/4 ma chags ma zhen rang sar shogs
B: 606/6 bag chags ma zhan rang sar shogs

A: 372/5 zad med don chen 'byung
B: 606/6 zag med don chen 'byung

A: 372/6 gtad bcas bzung po ma sdam la/ gtad med rgya yan gyi btab pa gces
B: 607/6 gtad bcas bzang par ma bsdam la/ gtad med rgya yi gtab par gces

A: 373/6 rig 'dzin mkha' 'gro gong ma rnams kyi bka' chad chod/ mkha' 'gro dbal mo rnams kyis snying khrag drong
B: 609/1 rig 'dzin gong ma rnams kyi bka' chad chod/ mkha' 'gro dpa' bo dpa' mo rnams kyis snying khrag drang

A: 373/5 rang nyid bde chen gnas mchog sleb nas kyang
B: 609/4 rang nyid rig 'dzin gnas mchog sleb nas kyang

CHAPTER 4. *MKHA' 'GRO BRGYAD BCU'I ZHAL GDAMS*

A: 375/5 mchog mthun kun gyis yum gcig dbang mzad ma
B: 612/2 mchog mthun gyi pang mzod yum gcig ma

A: 375/8 rig 'dzin sras yum yum chen rje la bstod
B: 613/1 rig 'dzin gsang yum yum chen rje la bstod

188 — APPENDIX 6

A: 377/1 mi spyod mtha' bral sa le shog
B: 615/4 ma skyod mtha' bral sa le shog

A: 377/9 ye stong nam mkha' stong pa la
B: 617/1 sems ye stong nam mkha' stong pa la

A: 378/1 dug lnga nyon mongs pa'i khyer na
B: 617/2 dug lnga nyon mongs ma spangs na

A: 378/5 ma sgribs kyi mun khang
B: 618/1 ma bsgrubs kyi mun khang

A: 378/6 sgo dgu so sor 'das nas snang
B: 618/2 *one line missing after* ma sang yi mi gcig 'tshub cing snang

A: 378/8 sems gsal stong blo dang bral ba de
B: 618/4 sems gsal rtogs blo dang bral ba de

A: 380/2 sems g.yeng ba skyur dang
B: 620/6 sems g.yeng ba la ma bskur dang

A: 380/7 rgod lcam gtsug gtor mas 'di skad gsungs/ rang sems sangs rgyas kun bzang 'di/ lta rtogs mkhan gyis mthong mi 'gyur/ mi rtogs mi 'bral yengs su med/ skyes bu de don rtogs kyis thob pa yin gsungs
B: 622/1 *five lines missing after* klang 'das gsung

A: 380/8 rtog tshad mtshan ma ma spangs rang sar grol
B: 622/1 rtag chad mtshan ma ma spangs rang sar grol

A: 381/2 mdzes la 'bral mi phod pa/ sku lus bshen la ldem pa/ zhal ngo ni nyi ma'i snying po dang 'dra bag cig byon nas/ bdag gis g.yas phyogs su bzhugs pa dang bdag la 'di skad gsungs
B: 622/4 *four lines missing after* gsal ba'i sgron ma can yin zer ba'i

A: 381/4 thams cad sems kyi rang mdangs 'char ba la
B: 622/5 thams cad sems kyi rang snang 'char la ba

A: 381/4 bdag bzang ma byed phyogs ris bral bar mdzod
B: 623/3 bdag bzungs ma byed phyogs ris bral bar gyis

A: 381/9 ye nas gsal la dri med bde stong ngang/ 'di gsum dbyer med sems su grol bar mdzod
B: 624/1 ye nas gsal la sgrib med bde stong pa/ de gsum dbyer med grol bar mdzod

A: 382/6 *three lines missing after* ye nas med gsungs
B: 625/2 yang mkha' 'gro ma dar nag gi nab bza' la/ stag gi tshar tshar gyi rgyan pa/ cig gis 'di skad gsungs

A: 382/6 don ldan g.yung drung 'od kyi gzhal yas nas
B: 625/3 *one line missing after* 'di skad gsungs

A: 382/5 rtsal grol ma 'gags rang la shar ba de
B: 625/4 rtsal bral ma 'gags rang la shar ba de

A: 382/8 yang dag gis don chen mi 'grub/ dug lnga rang sar ma grol tshe/ ye shes rgyud la mi gnas/ snyams byed blo dang ma bral tshe
B: 625/5 *four lines missing after* 'jig rten gyi snang ba ma spang tshe

A: 382/9 phyi dngos med du shes na stong nyid de ka yin/ sems nyid bon skur shes na de ka yin/ 'dzin pa rang sar grol la don dam de ka yin
B: 625/6 phyi nang dngos med du shes na stong nyid de ga yin/ sems nyid bon skur shes na sangs rgyas da ga yin/ 'dzin pa rang sar grol na don chen de ga yin

A: 383/1 sems la yeng med rtag na lta ba thag chod yin
B: 626/2 sems la yengs med lta na lta ba thag chod yin

A: 383/1 ngang la rgyun du gnas na sgom pa thag chod yin
B: 626/2 *one line missing after* lta ba yin thag chod yin

A: 383/4 ma brtsal ngang gis brjed na
B: 626/4 bya rtsal ngang gis brjed na

190 — APPENDIX 6

A: 383/3 ci spyod rang sar grol na spyod mkhan stong pa yin
B: 626/6 ci spyod rang sar grol na spyod mkhan gtor ba yin

A: 383/8 gter chen zad med snang ste spyod mi shes
B: 627/4 gter chen rang la yod ste spyod mi shes

A: 383/9 rang gi rang la rgyas pa'i dmag mi gdab
B: 627/5 rang gi rang la bgyag pas dmag mi 'ga'

A: 384/2 byar med kyi ri dwags mgo 'khor/ skyon med kyi brag la a 'thas
B: 628/2 dbyings kyi ri dwags mgo 'khor nas/ skyobs med kyi brag la a 'thas

A: 384/3 kun khyab nam mkha' la mu mtha' med
B: 628/4 kun gzhi nam mkha' mu mtha' med

A: 384/5 cha med rgyu med kyi mi gcig snang
B: 629/1 cha med rgyu med kyi yul na mi gcig snang

A: 384/6 mgon med skyabs med dgra yul dmags nang du 'thum
B: 629/1 mgon med skyabs med kyi dgra dmag nang du 'thum

A: 384/9 dmag gis sod rdo rang la yod ste zlog mi med/ go khrab rang la yod ste gon shes med
B: 629/5 dmag stor rang la yod ste zlog mi med/ go khrab rang ya yod ste gyon mi med

A: 385/3 bu lus po phag tshang snying po yin
B: 630/3 bu lus po phag tshang rnying pa yin

A: 386/1 sems nyid gsal stong mtha' dang ma bral ba'i
B: 631/5 sems nyid gsal stong mtha' dang bral na

A: 386/2 bu mi ldan 'gyur ba'i sa cha na
B: 632/1 bu yis dbyings su rgya spa cha nas

A: 386/5 *four lines missing after* ye khyab ma la zhus pa
B: 632/5 bu don gyi ngo bo ma mthong pas/ tha snyad tshig la mkhas pas long pa'i glu dang 'dra/ dmar thag sgros 'dog nang du ma chod na/ phyi'i bshad mkhan phal yang ne tso'i rgyu 'bras yin

A: 386/6 spyod pa byung rgyal rgod pos dkyus mo byed
B: 632/6 spyod pa byung rgyal yi rgo ba dkyus mo byed

A: 386/6 bang rtsal lus la rdzogs pas snying re gling
B: 633/1 dpa' rtsal lus la rdzogs pa'i yi re gsungs

A: 386/7 ngo bo mtha' dang bral ste mu mtha' med
B: 633/3 ngo bo mtha' dbus bral te mu mtha' med

A: 387/1 mi rtog pa la slebs na
B: 633/6 mi rtog pa la gnas na

A: 387/1 'khrul pa'i snang ba bstod na
B: 634/1 'khrul pas snang ba gtor na

A: 387/9 ma rmos yong khyab
B: 635/5 ma rmongs yong khyab

A: 388/6 mkha' 'gro brgya bcu'i zhu len 'di/ sems bskyed rnam dag 'gro ba'i don du bsngo
B: 637/1 *two lines missing at the beginning*

A: 388/9 'gro don ma rdzogs pa'i skye mched kyis/ ma'i lhums su yang zhugs dgos byung
B: 637/4 'gro don ma rdzogs pas skyes mchog kyis/ mi yi lhums su yang yang zhugs dgos byung

Appendix 7: A List of Gshen sras lha rje's Works in the Bönpo Canon

Works Contained in the Bka' 'gyur

What follows is a list of the works of gShen sras lha rje contained in the Bönpo Kangyur, the *G.yung drung bon gyi bka' 'gyur*, published in 1999 in Sichuan by Kun grol lha sras mi pham rnam rgyal in 179 volumes.

Go lde bskal bzang / Go sde'i bskal bzang 'gro ba 'dren pa'i mdo, in twenty chapters, volumes 8 (pp. 1–505) and 9 (pp. 1–526), *gter ma* rediscovered under the name Go sde 'phags sgom g.yung drung ye shes.

Rnam rgyal gzungs chen / Gshen rab rnam par rgyal ba'i yid bzhin nor bu rin po che dpal mgon rgyal po'i gzungs, in fifty-five chapters, volume 59, pp. 1–375, *gter ma* rediscovered under the name Dbang ldan gshen sras.

Works Contained in the Bka' brten

What follows is a list of the works of gShen sras lha rje contained in the *G.yung drung bon gyi bka' brten*, compiled by and published in Lhasa by Sog sde sprul sku bstan pa'i nyi ma in 1998 in three hundred volumes. Spelling mistakes in the original have been corrected in brackets.

Dran pa gser gdams, in volume 39, pp. 1–864. Snyan rgyud *et alia*.
Dkyil 'khor me lha'i sgo dbye, in volume 47, pp. 145–147. Composed by Dbang ldan gshen sras.
Rig 'dzin mkha' 'gro'i zhus len, in volume 61, pp. 1–22. Snyan rgyud.

Ma gcig skal bzang gis [gi] zhus len, in volume 61, pp. 23–37. Snyan rgyud.
Bla chen yi [gyi] zhus len, in volume 61, pp. 39–53. Snyan rgyud.
Ri khrod chen po'i zhus len, in volume 61, pp. 55–64. Snyan rgyud.
'Od ldan 'bar ma'i zhus len, in volume 61, pp. 65–85. Snyan rgyud.
Rig 'dzin brgya cu'i zhu lan snyan rgyud zhal gdams bdud rtsi'i 'phreng ba gdams pa, in volume 61, pp. 87–108. Snyan rgyud.
Go bde'i 'khrug bcos bca' thabs, in volume 84, pp. 521–523 and pp. 525–527. Two copies of the same text without colophon, probably composed by Gshen sras lha rje.
Sa bdag 'khrug bcos bya ba'i bon, in volume 84, pp. 529–584, *gter ma* rediscovered under the name Go sde 'phags pa at Pha bong g.yag ro.
Man ngag gser gdams, in volume 86, pp. 61–102.
'Khrug bcos rin chen 'phring [phreng] ba, in volume 87, pp. 903–925, *gter ma* rediscovered with the name Go bde 'phags pa at Pha 'ong g.yag ro.
Gshen rab rnam par rgyal ba'i mchod skong chen mo, in volume 88, pp. 719–745. Composed by Kong tse 'phrul rgyal, put into *gter ma* by Gyim tsha rma chung and rediscovered by Go lde 'phags pa at Rag phrom brag.
Rnam rgyal gyi bar phud kha bskang [skong], in volume 104, pp. 221–225. *Gter ma* rediscovered under the name Gshen sras lha rje.
Gshen rab rnam par rgyal ba'i mchod gzhung nges pa'i thig le, in volume 104, pp. 231–425. Arranged by Rgya nag Legs tang rmang po at Bdud 'dul ru tra'i gling, *gter ma* rediscovered by Go lde 'phags pa at Rag phrom gyi brag and decoded at Rke phu na ro'i gong sangs.
Gshen rab rnam par rgyal ba'i mchod bskangs, in volume 104, pp. 427–447. Composed by Kong rtse 'phrul rgyal, *gter ma* rediscovered by Go lde 'phags pa at Rag phrom gyi brag and decoded at Ke phu na ro.
Rnam par rgyal ba'i smon lam bsam pa don ldan, in volume 104, pp. 575–585. Translated by Legs tang rmang po, rediscovered by Gshen sras lha rje under the name Nyi ma shes rab.
Gshen rab kyi dka' thub nyon mongs drung byin, in volume 108, pp. 79–103, *gter ma* rediscovered by Go lde 'phags pa from the mountain of G.yung drung seng ge mchog in northern Tsang.
Man ngag gser gdam, in volume 191, pp. 287–319.
Go sde 'khrug bcos kyi bca' thabs dang 'don zin, in volume 232, pp. 501–506. No colophon.

Works Published Separately

This list is mainly based on Karmay 1977 and O thog bstan 'dzin dbang rgyal, op. 24.

Man ngag rin po che dran pa gser gyi gdams pa. Tibetan Bonpo Monastic Centre, Dolanji, 1972.

Gshen rab rnam par rgyal ba'i yid bzhin nor bu rin po che dpal mgon rgyal po'i gzungs in *Rnam rgyal gzungs chen*, pp. 1–464. Tibetan Bonpo Monastic Centre, Dolanji, 1972.

Gshen rab rnam par rgyal ba las zhang zhung ma'i mchod gzhung nges pa'i thig le, in *Rnam par rgyal ba'i sgrub skor gyi cha lag cha rkyen dang bcas pa*, pp. 255–510. Tibetan Bonpo Monastic Centre, Delhi, 1967.

Rnam par rgyal ba'i mchod bskang kong tses mdzad pa, in *Rnam par rgyal ba'i sgrub skor gyi cha lag cha rkyen dang bcas pa*, pp. 577–602. Tibetan Bonpo Monastic Centre, Delhi, 1967.

Rnam par rgyal ba'i phywa tshe g.yang gi bsgrub pa, in *Rnam par rgyal ba'i sgrub skor gyi cha lag cha rkyen dang bcas pa*, pp. 603–622. Tibetan Bonpo Monastic Centre, Delhi, 1967.

Rnam rgyal smon lam bsam pa don ldan ma, in *Rnam par rgyal ba'i sgrub skor gyi cha lag cha rkyen dang bcas pa*, pp. 715–725. Tibetan Bonpo Monastic Centre, Delhi, 1967.

Gshen rab rnam par rgyal ba las gzungs sde rin chen phreng ba, in *Rnam par rgyal ba'i sgrub skor gyi cha lag cha rkyen dang bcas pa*, pp. 733–784. Tibetan Bonpo Monastic Centre, Delhi, 1967.

Legs tang rmang pos mdzad pa'i sngags sgrub, in *Rnam par rgyal ba'i sgrub skor gyi cha lag cha rkyen dang bcas pa*, pp. 951–986. Tibetan Bonpo Monastic Centre, Delhi, 1967.

Gshen rab rnam par rgyal ba'i rgyud las bstan srung gcan lha'i sgos sgrub, in *Rnam par rgyal ba'i bsgrub skor gyi cha lag cha rkyen dang bcas pa*, pp. 918–1002. Tibetan Bonpo Monastic Centre, Delhi, 1967.

Bum mgon, in *Rnam par rgyal ba'i sgrub skor gyi cha lag cha rkyen dang bcas pa*, pp. 901–916. Tibetan Bonpo Monastic Centre, Delhi, 1967.

Rnam par rgyal ba'i mchod bskang, in *Bskang 'bum*, vol. 1, pp. 431–449. Tibetan Bonpo Monastic Centre, Delhi, 1973.

Glossary of Tibetan Terms and Expressions

Note the following abbreviations for glossary explanations:

CHNN Chögyal Namkhai Norbu
TN   Lopön Tenzin Namdak

ka dag. Primordial purity, pure from the beginning, the real condition of emptiness of all phenomena, inseparable from the aspect of *lhun grub* or self-perfection in the Dzogchen view of the base.

kun tu bzang po. Skt. Samantabhadra; literally, "ever good." The primordial buddha symbolizing the state of dharmakāya.

kun gzhi. The all-ground, universal base, original condition of existence prior to the division into samsara and nirvana.

klong. The primordial expanse from which phenomena originate.

sku gsum. The three dimensions of enlightenment: dharmakāya, saṃbhogakāya, nirmāṇakāya.

skye med. Birthless, meaning the unborn, empty, and ineffable condition of being.

khra ther. Tent, in Khams dialect.

'khrul pa. Illusion, delusion, mistaken view. The fundamental illusion is the nonrecognition of the nature of one's mind, which causes the dualism of subject and object.

dge sbyor. Literally, "the practice of virtue," in this text used to denote spiritual practice or meditation.

dgongs pa. The state of knowledge, the state of the mind of a buddha, corresponding to the state of contemplation.

'gyu ba. The movement or arising of thoughts in a wavelike fashion.

rgod pa. Agitation, one of the main defects in the practice of contemplation.

rgya yan. Spontaneous freedom beyond all limitations, which is a natural aspect of wisdom—such as the freedom of wild animals—and a result of the real knowledge of one's primordial state. (CHNN) *sgom pa.* Meditation or application, one of the three aspects of Dzogchen practice together with view and conduct. It means the continuous flow of the natural state of the mind, beyond any effort-based meditation.

ngang. The natural condition.

ngo bo. The essence, or ultimate nature.

bcos med. Impossible to modify or to correct, referring to the natural condition of the mind that cannot be altered by thoughts.

nyams. The signs of experience in the practice of contemplation.

nyon mongs pa. Emotions. In Tibetan this expression is originally a verb whose meaning implies the perturbation of the natural state of the mind, in the same way that the sky is obscured by the clouds. (CHNN)

gnyis 'dzin. Dualism, the consideration of a subject distinct from its object, the primary cause of attachment.

gnyug ma. The authentic condition of the mind, untainted by thoughts and emotions.

mnyam nyid. Absolute equality, the state beyond dualism.

mnyam bzhag. Contemplation; literally, "settling or relaxing into equanimity."

snyam byed. Literally, "thought-creating"; the intention of the mind while following a thought with a specific purpose, without letting it dissolve by itself.

rtog pa. Thoughts, concepts.

rtogs pa. Real knowledge or understanding, the recognition of one's natural state and its continuous experience as something alive.

lta ba. The view, the understanding of the real principle of the teaching through experiential recognition of one's natural state.

stong pa nyid. Emptiness, the ultimate condition of the mind and of all phenomena of existence.

thig le. Sphere, the primordial monad, archetypal structure of every being, from which all the elements of existence arise.

thugs. Primordial state of mind, wisdom mind.

mtha' bral. Beyond the conceptual extremes or limitations of the mind.

mthar thug. The final accomplishment or realization of enlightenment.

don. The real meaning, the essence. It also refers to the natural state that the practitioner has to continue. (TN)

dran pa. Presence or attention; thoughts or mind activity in the expression *dran rig*.

drod tshad. Literally, "the measure of heat," referring generally to the signs of practice.

gdangs. Primordial energy, the primary energy or natural luminosity of consciousness.

bdud. Demon, or any kind or beings or negative forces that obstruct the spiritual path.

nags 'ug. Forest, in Khams dialect.

nam mkha'. The sky or the outer space where all phenomena manifest.

gnas lugs. The natural state of the mind.
rnam rtog. Conceptual thought.
snang ba. Vision, in the sense of any object perceived by the five senses.
spyod pa. Conduct, behavior; one of the three aspects of practice, referring in Dzogchen to the integration of the state of contemplation in daily activities.
sprul sku. Nirmāṇakāya, the dimension of emanation in which an enlightened being can manifest in order to train beings in samsara.
spros pa. Conceptual constructs, mental elaborations, meaning any conclusion the intellect can reach (CHNN). The opposite of *stong pa* (empty), in the sense of the lack of any concept or material phenomenon (TN).
bag chags. Latent tendencies, karmic traces that present themselves in the form of habits and mental inclinations.
bon sku. Equivalent to *chos sku*, dharmakāya, the dimension of the essence of all phenomena, the primordial condition of consciousness in the manifestation of enlightenment.
bon nyid. Equivalent to *chos nyid*, dharmatā, the real condition of existence, ultimate nature of phenomena and of the individual consciousness.
byang chub sems. Bodhichitta, the primordially enlightened nature of the mind as pure and total consciousness; the primordial state.
bying ba. Drowsiness or torpor, one of the main defects in the practice of contemplation. It denotes a state in which there is no clarity but which is often mistaken for contemplation. (TN)
blo. Mind, conceptual mind, intellect.
dbang, dbang bskur. Initiation, empowerment. Fundamental in the Tantric tradition, it includes the transmission of the empowering energy from master to student.
dbyings. Basic space, the ultimate dimension or condition of phenomena in which the visionary experience manifests; also, the space of the sky.
'bras bu. The fruit or result, corresponding to the realization of the state of enlightenment.
ma rig pa. Ignorance, in the sense of nonrecognition of the real nature of the mind, which causes transmigration in samsara.
man ngag. Skt. *upadeśa*, essential instructions or methods based on particular experiences of realized masters.
rtsal. Energy, energy display, the natural power of the primordial state to objectify itself through the energy of the five elements.
rtsis rdab. Mental consideration or judgment.
'dzin pa. As a verb, to grasp at, to cling to, to seize, referring to the characteristic function of dualistic thought; as a noun, the subject or perceiver.
rdzu 'phrul. Miraculous power.
rdzogs sku. Saṃbhogakāya, the perfection or wealth of all the natural qualities of the primordial state manifesting through the pure dimension of the five elements.

gzhi. The base, original condition of existence, source of both samsara and nirvana.

gza' gtad. Conceptual fixation or consideration about the ultimate nature, the main mistake in the Dzogchen view.

'od gsal. Clear light or luminosity, the natural clarity of consciousness prior to the formation of dualistic thoughts.

ye shes. Wisdom, primordial wisdom inherent in all beings, temporarily obscured by thoughts and emotions.

rang grol. Self-liberation, the main practice of Dzogchen contemplation of abiding in one's real nature while letting thoughts effortlessly arise and dissolve in their natural condition of emptiness.

rang bzhin med pa. Without substance or self-nature, the real condition of all phenomena.

rang sa zin. Literally, "to take hold, or to resume, one's natural place," referring to abiding in the recognition of one's natural state.

rig pa. Instant presence, pure nondual awareness, the real nature of consciousness introduced by the master, and the heart of Dzogchen practice; also, consciousness.

rig pa hur. The state of *rig pa* "awakened" or experienced as intensely clear and strong.

sems. Mind as the base of dualistic thinking.

sems nyid. Mind-essence or the nature of mind, the original condition beyond duality.

gsal ba. Clarity, the aspect of luminosity of the primordial state inseparable from its empty essence.

bsam mno. Thoughts.

lhag mthong. Literally, "further seeing": clear insight, contemplation, the real vision of emptiness. In Dzogchen contemplation it denotes the recognition and integration of thoughts as an aspect of clarity.

lhun grub. Self-perfection as one of the two aspects—together with *ka dag*, or primordial purity—of the view of the base in Dzogchen; self-perfected, naturally existing, denoting the original qualities of the primordial state that manifest once real knowledge has been achieved.

a 'thas. The attachment of thoughts, the fixation of the mind on illusory phenomena; as an adjective, severe, hard, solidified.

a wa re. Hello, in Khams dialect.

Notes

Epigraph
   Op. 36: 788/1.

Preface
1. The *Klong chen 'od gsal mkha' 'gro'i snying thig*, containing many teachings that Chögyal Namkhai Norbu has transmitted in the context of the Dzogchen Community.
2. The Zhang zhung kingdom, predating the Tibetan kingdom by many centuries, had its center in western Tibet but its domain extended to most of the regions of greater Tibet and even further. After about two thousand five hundred years it was annexed to Tibet by the king Srong btsan sgam po (617–650). See Karmay 1972: xxx, 27.
3. *Bod kyi lo rgyus las 'phros pa'i gtam g.yung drung nor bu'i do shal* (Dharamsala: 1981), and *Bod rigs gzhon mi rnams la gros su 'debs pa gzi yi phreng ba* (Dharamsala: 1980). The latter has been translated and published in English as *The Necklace of Zi* (see Chögyal Namkhai Norbu 2004).
4. Shar rdza bkra shis rgyal mtshan (1859–1934) was the most important Bönpo master and scholar of the last century. His life story has been studied and translated in Achard 2008 and in an unpublished dissertation by William M. Gorvine (see Gorvine 2006). According to the biography of Byang chub rdo rje written by his grandson Gar dbang rin po che, called *Rig 'dzin chen po byang chub rdo rje'i rnam thar dad ldan thar lam 'dren pa'i shing rta*, Byang chub rdo rje met Shar rdza bkra shis rgyal mtshan in 1898, when the latter was forty, and received many teachings from him. Gorvine (p. 209, nn. 305 and 306) mistakenly suggests that Tshe dbang 'gyur med byang chub rdo rje rtsal, one of Shar rdza bkra shis rgyal mtshan's main students (quoted for example in op. 22: 435–436) could be the same person as Byang chub rdo rje. See also Achard 2008: 113.
5. *Sgrung lde'u bon gsum gyi gtam e ma ho* (Dharamsala: 1989), translated into English as *Drung, Deu and Bön*. See Chögyal Namkhai Norbu 1995.
6. *Zhang bod lo rgyus ti se'i 'od* (1996), translated into English and published as *The Light of Kailash, A History of Zhang Zhung and Tibet*, volume 1 (2009); volume 2 (2013); volume 3 (2015).

Introduction

1. Oḍḍiyāna (O rgyan), present-day Swat in Pakistan, is considered to be the source of the Dzogchen teachings of Buddhist tradition and also of many tantric cycles.
2. For a presentation of the origins of Dzogchen in the Buddhist tradition, see Clemente and Chögyal Namkhai Norbu 1999.
3. A third type of Bön, known as New Bön (*bon gsar ma*) is generally accepted by Bönpo scholars. It started around the fourteenth century with the rediscovery of *gter ma*s in which the influence of the Rnying ma tradition is very strong.
4. See Chögyal Namkhai Norbu 1995: 156–158.
5. For 'Chi med gtsug phud (Immortal Topknot), see Karmay 1972: xxi; Achard 2004: 252.
6. The *Gzi brjid*, whose complete title is *'Dus pa rin po che dri ma med pa gzi brjid rab tu 'bar ba'i mdo*, is a biography in twelve volumes of gShen rab mi bo. It was transmitted from Stang chen Dmu tsha gyer med to Blo ldan snying po (fourteenth century). Some parts of this text have been translated in Snellgrove 1967.
7. See also Lopön Tenzin Namdak 2006: 11–12; Chögyal Namkhai Norbu 1995: 37–38.
8. See Karmay 1972: 51.
9. The term "buddha" (*sangs rgyas*) is used in the Bön tradition to denote an enlightened being in the same way as in Buddhism. In the Bön tradition Gshen rab mi bo is considered a buddha, and Shakyamuni is simply viewed as a buddha who came later in time.
10. For the *Zhang zhung snyan rgyud* cycle and biographies of its masters, see Reynolds 2005.
11. Snya chen li shu stag ring is an important siddha in the Bönpo tradition. He is credited with many translations from the language of Zhang zhung into Tibetan. He lived at the time of the Tibetan king Khri srong lde'u btsan (742–797). Tradition says that he was born as a woman called Stag za li wer and then changed sex. For a brief story of his life, see Karmay 1972: 56–57; Achard 2004: 255 (under Stag za li wer); and op. 21: 149–150.
12. This cycle of teaching was originally discovered by the great *gter ston* Gshen chen klu dga' (b. 996); see Karmay 1972: 130. The second time it was discovered by Ra ston dngos grub 'bar (eleventh century); ibid.: 150. The third time it was discovered by Gnyan ston shes rab seng ge; ibid.: 153.
13. He compiled these teachings on the basis of the *Khro rgyud*, a cycle of teachings attributed to Gshen rab mi bo himself belonging to the *Spyi spungs*, and added instructions originating from his own mind-treasures. For a study of this system and partial translations of its teachings, as well as a biography of Dgongs mdzod ri khrod chen po, see Kvaerne 1973 and also Kvaerne and Rikey 1996.
14. For a biography of this important master see Reynolds 2011: 6–14.
15. The *Yang rtse klong chen* cycle, together with the *Bsgrags pa skor gsum* men-

tioned above, was rediscovered by Bzhod ston dngos grub grags pa in the temple of Khom mthing in Lho brag. See Karmay 1972: 154–156.

16. This very concise presentation of the fundamental principles of Dzogchen in the Bönpo tradition is mostly based on the *Phyi lta ba spyi gcod kyi man ngag lde'u bcu gnyis pa* (op. 18) and *Sgron ma'i 'grel pa nyi 'od rgyan* (op. 17), both from the *Zhang zhung snyan rgyud* cycle of teachings. For a more extensive explanation based on traditional texts, see Rossi 1999.

17. *Rigpa* is a key term in Dzogchen, where it represents the authentic nature of the mind introduced by the teacher. Here it has been rendered "instant presence," a special translation of this term devised by Chögyal Namkhai Norbu as an abbreviation of *skad cig ma'i rig pa*.

18. Op. 18: 84/7.

19. The analogy traditionally given for *lhun grub*, according to the explanation of Lopön Tenzin Namdak, is the following. Just as oil is potentially contained in a sesame seed, the vision of wisdom exists naturally inside oneself. Just as the seed needs to be squeezed in order for the oil to come out, it is necessary to devote oneself to practice for wisdom to manifest.

20. The term *sku* (Skt. *kāya*), literally "body" and here translated as "dimension," according to Chögyal Namkhai Norbu's explanations, indicates the enlightened dimension of both the material environment in which an individual lives and the individual him- or herself. This dimension has become material due to ignorance (*ma rig pa*) of one's real nature, which causes the dualistic condition of subject and object. When duality is overcome and one's real nature, or primordial state, is completely realized, this same karmic, material dimension manifests as the three dimensions, or *kāya*s, of enlightenment.

21. Op. 18: 84/18.

22. Samantabhadra or Kun tu bzang po, "Ever Good," is a name for the primordial buddha, symbol of the state of *dharmakāya*, and ultimate source of the Dzogchen teachings.

23. Op. 18: 85/6.

24. The six classes of beings are the main karmic dimensions of existence in samsara, caused by the predominance of one of the six fundamental emotions (pride, jealousy, dualism or a mixture of all emotions, ignorance, attachment, and anger): the devas or gods, the asuras or demigods, human beings, animals, pretas or hungry ghosts, and hell beings.

25. Op. 18: 85/18.

26. The term *dbyings*, in this context rendered "basic space," has a specific connotation in Dzogchen. It is generally also rendered as "space," but in Tibetan we have two other terms with similar meaning: *mkha'* (space) and *klong* (expanse). According to op. 17: 171ff., they are distinguished in the following way. *Mkha'* or *nam mkha'* is the general outer dimension or condition, where all things exist. This term is normally used to denote the space of the sky. As the text says: "Clear space (*mkha'*) is all-pervading: since the condition of the all-ground is

unimpeded clear light, the expression 'clear space' is used; since a single sphere (*thig le*) pervades all, it is all-pervading." About *dbyings,* or *bon nyid kyi dbyings,* the basic space or ultimate dimension of existence, we read, "In one single basic space all things abide: since the condition of the all-ground is the indivisibility of emptiness and clarity, it is also called 'the basic space of total equality.' In this dimension all of the outer and inner worlds, the universe and its beings, samsara and nirvana, abide." Chögyal Namkhai Norbu explains further that *dbyings* indicates the true empty condition of any phenomenon that appears material. When the practitioner reintegrates the physical body and the material dimension into the *dbyings*, the rainbow body is achieved.

Concerning *klong* we read, "From the total expanse (*klong*) everything arises: since the condition of the all-ground is empty and without a self, the expression 'total expanse' is used. Since from this primordial expanse all phenomena of samsara and nirvana arise, everything arises from it." *Klong* refers then to the primordial dimension of existence, corresponding to the empty condition of the mind. In the visualization practices of tantra the word *klong* is used to denote the imaginary space from which the form of the deity has to arise. Moreover, the term *klong chen*, or "total expanse," is used to mean the universe, in the originary sense of a dimension arising from one's real nature of mind.

27. There are two kinds of rainbow bodies (*'ja' lus*). One is attained during the present lifetime, without manifesting death, and is known as the great transference into the rainbow body (*'ja' lus pho ba chen po*). The second is attained usually one week after death, and has been widely witnessed in Tibet. For accounts of the latter type, see Chögyal Namkhai Norbu 2010a.

28. Both spellings *gshen sras* and *gshen gsas* are given in all the available sources, with a predominance of the former. *Gshen sras* would mean "son of a *gshen*," while *gshen gsas* means "divine *gshen*," *gsas* being an archaic term, originally from the language of Zhang zhung, equivalent to *lha* or deity. It is also found in expressions such as *gsas mkhar*, palace of the gods, meaning a temple or a maṇḍala.

29. The Secret or *Gsang* section of the *Brten 'gyur* contains exclusively Dzogchen scriptures, while in the *Bka' 'gyur* they are contained in the *Mdzod* or Treasury section. The Bönpo canon comprises two subdivisions, the *Bka' 'gyur*, containing scriptures taught by Gshen rab mi bo himself, and the *Brten 'gyur*, containing texts and commentaries on various aspects of the teachings. A similar distinction exists also in the Buddhist canon, but the Buddhist subdivision of texts and commentaries is called instead *Bstan 'gyur*. See Kvaerne 1974: 23–24. For a general history of the canon, see Martin, Kvaerne, and Nagano 2003.

30. Concerning the *snyan brgyud* category of Bönpo scriptures, see Kvaerne 1974: 35–36; and Karmay 1975: 188–189.

31. See the sections "The Visionary Dimension" and "The Origins of *The Golden Teaching*," below, for examples of how texts were received as *snyan brgyud* by Gshen sras lha rje.

32. The first *gter ma* discoveries in the Bönpo tradition are attributed to the A tsar a mi gsum at Bsam yas in 913 C.E. Concerning the Bönpo *gter ma* literature, see Kvaerne 1974: 31–40; Karmay 1975: 186–187, and also 1972: xxxiii–xxxix; and Martin 2001.
33. For a study of the *gter ma* tradition in Tibetan Buddhism, see Tulku Thondup Rinpoche 1986 and Doctor 2005.
34. See Kvaerne 1974: 36.
35. See Karmay 1972: 159. Gyer mi nyi 'od is one of the most important *gter ston* in the Bönpo tradition. He lived in the twelfth century and had direct contact with Dran pa nam mkha' through visions. For a short biography, see Karmay 1972: 156–160.
36. According to Bönpo historical texts there have been three periods of propagation of the Bön teachings in Tibet. The first propagation took place in a period of time beginning with the ascent of the first Tibetan king gNya' khri btsan po (circa second century B.C.E.) and lasting until the time of the eighth king Gri gum btsan po (circa first century C.E.). At this point there was a first persecution of Bön caused by this king, after which Bön flourished once again until the time of Khri srong lde'u btsan (742–797), who caused a second persecution. The period that goes from the end of the first persecution to the beginning of the second is known as the second propagation of Bön. The third stage of propagation begins with the rediscovery of *gter ma* scriptures and the revelations of *snyan brgyud* literature, starting from the tenth–eleventh century. See Kvaerne 1974: 27–30; Karmay 1975: 182ff., and 1972: 15ff., 72ff., 105ff.
37. Concerning Stag gzig and a possible geographical identification see Karmay 1975: 171–172; also 1972: xxvii ff.
38. See Karmay 1972: 90ff.
39. The following biography was orally abridged by Lopön Tenzin Namdak from *Rgyung yar khod spungs kyi lo rgyus*, op. 43.
40. For this important center of the ancient Zhang zhung kingdom and residence of some of its kings, see Chögyal Namkhai Norbu 2010b: 29–35.
41. The *Srid pa'i mdzod phug* is an important work on Bön cosmogony rediscovered by gShen chen klu dga' (996–1035), for the most part in a Zhang zhung–Tibetan bilingual version.
42. For an explanation of the terms *mkha'*, *klong*, and *dbyings*, see above, note 26.
43. The Mkha' 'gying are one of the main five *yi dam* deities, known as *gsas mkhar mchog lnga*, in the Bönpo tradition according to the *Spyi spungs* cycle. The five are Dbal gsas rnam pa (Body), Lha rgod thog pa (Voice), Gtso mchog mkha' 'gying (Mind), Dbal chen ge khod (Qualities), and 'Brug gsas chem pa (Activities). At times we find Phur pa for activities instead of the latter. See also Karmay 1972: 45, note 2.
44. The eight scholars or sages (*mkhas pa mi brgyad*), also known as the eight translators and scholars (*lo paṇ brgyad*), are eight knowledge-holders of paramount importance in the first propagation of Bön. They are Stong rgyung mthu chen

from Zhang zhung, Sha ri dbu chen from Tibet, Lde Gyim tsha rma chung, Lce tsha mkhar bu from Me nyag, Za rang (rangs) me 'bar from Stag gzig, Kha yam rlung lce from Sum pa, Ngam pa (also Rngam pa) lce ring from Ge sar, and Stang chen Dmu tsha gyer med. See op. 10: 7 and also op. 11: 2 where Ne rgyung 'phar bu is given instead of Lce tsha mkhar bu. The first four are known as the four scholars (*mkhas pa mi bzhi*).

45. Tha mi thad ke (Da mi thad ke in the text, but also spelled Thad mi thad ke and Tha mi dad ke) was an important scholar and siddha from Zhang zhung. See below, chapter 3, note 10.

46. The *Spyi spungs* is one of the most ancient and important tantric cycles of Bön. See Karmay 1972: 44–49. The *Zhi khro* cycle of teachings, dealing with the manifestation of deities as projections of one's consciousness during the intermediate state between death and rebirth, is paramount in both the Bön and Tibetan Buddhist traditions. In Bön they are related to the *Spyi spungs* cycle.

47. In Tibetan *mkha' 'gro ma'i phyag rgya mo*, a human ḍākinī, also known as *las kyi phyag rgya mo* or *karmamudrā*, who can assist practitioners in tantric sexual yoga.

48. One among the other signs was that the complexion of his body became blue, and this is how Dran pa nam mkha' is depicted in many traditional thangkas.

49. Usually the name of Dran pa nam mkha's consort is 'Od ldan 'bar ma and not Nyi ma 'od ldan, who is a different ḍākinī.

50. Tshe dbang rig 'dzin (Vidyādhara of Long Life) is an important siddha whose biography and prophecies are contained in two collections, the *Tshe dbang bod yul ma* and the *Tshe dbang rgya gar ma*.

51. The continuation of the story of the two twins is found in *Lung bstan 'khol du phyung ba*, op. 45. For an English translation of a similar version by 'Jam dbyangs mkhyen brtse'i dbang po, called *Rgyal sras gu ru padma 'byung gnas kyi rnam par thar pa mdor dril ba bsgrags pa bon lugs ltar bstan pa*, contained in the Rin chen gter mdzod (Bhutanese edition, 1976, vol. 39: 229–245), see *The Bon Version of the Life of Guru Rinpoché* in Ngawang Zangpo 2002: 191–205.

52. Erroneously given as *Dbang ldan gshen gsas kyi rnam thar* in op. 9: 130. The text is translated in appendix 2.

53. Variants are *go sde* and *go bde*.

54. He is the sixty-first in the list given in the article *Gter ston brgya rtsa'i skor dpyad gleng* by Spu rgyal ba cang pa nyi ma rgyal mtshan, op. 20. For his works and *gter ma*s in the Bönpo canon, see appendix 7, and also Kvaerne 1974: 97, 100, 120.

55. Tib. *gling gi sprang po*. Op. 27A: 376.

56. I have not been able to identify the source for this date, as Gshen sras lha rje is not mentioned in the *Bstan rtsis* by Nyi ma bstan 'dzin or in other chronological documents. Apparently the source for this date is the preface to the *Dran pa gser gdams* edition A (Delhi, 1972), which says:

The manuscript collection reproduced in this volume of Bönpo texts comes from the monastery of Bsam gling in Dol po [northwestern Nepal]. We do not know when this manuscript was written, but the style of writing suggests some antiquity. The religious instructions contained in this collection belong to the class of teachings known as *snyan rgyud*, or "oral transmissions." Our tradition says that the *snyan rgyud* precepts included in this volume were given by Dran pa nam mkha' to Gshen gsas Lha rje [Go lde 'Phags pa G.yung drung ye shes]. Gshen gsas Lha rje is also known by the name Gnyos Nyi ma shes rab (b. 1215). We hope these teachings will be of benefit to all sentient creatures. Mutsuk Maro!

This date has been repeated in Karmay 1977: 107.

57. Me shod is an area in Derge, eastern Tibet, where the famous Rdzong gsar monastery is located.
58. I have not been able to identify the place that is called Klag in the *Dran pa gser gdams*, although it is probably in the area of Derge. A word spelled *glag* is found in the names of two monasteries there: Glag tshang dgon (the monastery of the Glag family) in Dkar mdzes district, and Glag tha dgon in Dar rtse mdo district.
59. From op. 27A: 388/9; 27B: 637/4.
60. Stong rgyung mthu chen (the great magician Stong rgyung), from Zhang zhung, is one of the most important siddhas in the Bönpo tradition. Known also as "the great scholar" (*mkhas pa chen po*), he is one of the four scholars (*mkhas pa mi bzhi*) who were teachers of Dran pa nam mkha'. In biographical accounts it is said that he was the son of a king. At the moment of death he wanted to transfer his consciousness into another body, according to the *grong 'jug* method, but he could only find a horse, which he entered. Afterward he found the body of an Indian brahmin who had just died, and transferred his consciousness into it. For this reason he is depicted as having brown skin and dressed in brahmin attire. See also Karmay 1972: 49; Achard 2004: 271.
61. *Sugata* (*bder gshegs*), or "gone to bliss," is an epithet of the buddhas.
62. *Siddhi* (*dngos grub*) denotes the attainment of a spiritual accomplishment. Siddhis are generally classified as supreme siddhi (*mchog gi dngos grub*) and ordinary siddhis (*thun mong gi dngos grub*). The first one is the same as final realization of enlightenment, manifesting in the five aspects of enlightened Body, Voice, Mind, Qualities, and Activities. The ordinary siddhis are specific powers acquired while on the path, in the Bönpo tradition often listed as the five siddhis of long life, wealth, activity, capacity, and magical power. See op. 21: 163.
63. Op. 27A: 389/2; 27B: 638/1.
64. Op. 38: 21/2.
65. Op. 30A: 442/1; 30B: 674/1.
66. Op. 27A: 375/8; 27B: 613/1.
67. See, for example, Harding 2003 and Gyatso 1999.

68. Khyung po snang chen grags pa (rgyal mtshan), Shes rab dpal, Zha gar or Rdzogs chen zha gar ba, Ye shes sgom pa, Shes rab dpal, and 'Brug ris Shes rab grags pa are those most often mentioned.
69. Concerning Khyung po snang chen grags pa, see op. 19, vol. 2: 475/3, where he is mentioned as the owner of the teachings (*bon bdag*) of Gshen sras lha rje together with Dpon dge dpon 'ud and Shar khyung bsod nams rgyal mtshan. According to Karmay 1972: 178, he was also a student of Glang 'od la thung.
70. Op. 32: 352/5.
71. Bön *gter ma*s are classified into five categories: northern treasures (*byang gter*), southern treasures (*lho gter*), central treasures (*dbus gter*), treasures from Khams (*khams gter*), and modern treasures (*gter gsar*).
72. The *Rgyal kun spyi gzugs dran pa nam mkha' rje'i rnam thar g.yung drung gsang ba'i mdzod chen*, a *gter ma* rediscovery by Nyag rong gter ston Gsang sngags gling pa (b. 1864).
73. Op. 42, vol. 298: 352/2.
74. Op. 4: 430/7. The Tibetan is *nga'i mchog gis [gi] sprul pa las/ dbang ldan gshen sras bya ba 'byung/ spyod pa 'gag med rgyan shar ngang/ gsang sder [sde'i] bon gyis 'gro ba 'dren*.
75. This is probably the text *Sa lam don gsal rin chen sgron me* contained in the *Dran pa gser gdams*.
76. Op. 1: 336/3.
77. The *Rnam rgyal rgya nag ma* is considered to have originated in the Chinese language and to have been translated into Tibetan by Legs tang rmang po. See Karmay 1972: 26.
78. Lde Gyim tsha rma chung, one of the four great scholars (*mkhas pa mi bzhi*). See Achard 2004: 258–259; op. 21: 54–55.
79. This is the same quotation from the *Srid pa rgyud kyi kha byang*, although there are variants in the spellings. The Tibetan transliteration is *nga yi mchog gi sprul pa ni/ dbang ldan gshen sras bya ba 'byung/ spyod pa chags med rgyan shar ba/ gsang gter bon gyis 'gro ba 'dren*.
80. The *gshang* is a flat cymbal used by Bönpo practitioners in the left hand, in much the same way that Tibetan Buddhists use the *dril bu* or bell.
81. Op. 26: 304–305; see also Karmay 1972: 174–175.
82. Op. 19A, vol. 2: 225/3; 19B: 259, line 5 from bottom.
83. *Mtshan ldan khye'u bzhi*, the four main students of gShen rab mi bo: Yid kyi khye'u chung, Gto bu 'bum sangs, Rma lo, and G.yu lo.
84. Op. 23: 80/7.
85. Op. 23: 82/5. See also op. 44: 13/5, where this lineage is given for the *Rnam rgyal zhang zhung ma* cycle.
86. *Gong ma che drug*, same as *bla ma che drug*: Gsang ba 'dus pa, Stag la me 'bar, Yongs su dag pa, Mi lus bsam legs, Ye shes snying po, and Snang ba mdog can. Sometimes Rma lo dar dpyangs is listed instead of Stag la me 'bar. See Karmay 1972: 58.

87. *Gdung rgyud bcu gnyis*, which could be a mistake for the thirteen lineage descendants (*gdung brgyud bcu gsum*) listed in historical texts: Mu khri btsan po, Ha ra ci par, Stag wer li wer, A nu phrag thag, Sad ne ga'u, Tha mi thad ke, Shad bu ra khug, Zing pa mthu chen, Spe bon thog rtse, Spe bon thog 'phrul, Hring ni mu ting, Sum pa lbu kha, and Glang chen mu wer. See op. 26: 182; Karmay 1972: 58.
88. Lha bdag sngags 'gro, Gser thog lce 'byams, and Legs tang rmang po are respectively known as the scholar from India, the scholar from Phrom (or Khrom, a country vaguely located to the north of Tibet), and the scholar from China.
89. Op. 44: 133/1.
90. *G.yung drung sems dpa'*, a Bönpo expression equivalent to the Buddhist *byang chub sems dpa'*.
91. Mu cho ldem drug, son of Gshen rab mi bo and regent of his teachings.
92. The *dbal mo* are female deities akin to the ḍākinīs.
93. Op. 23: 37/5.
94. Op. 28, vol. 2: 526/2.
95. See op. 25: 192/5.
96. These rediscoveries by Gshen sras lha rje are classified as "northern treasure" (*byang gter*) in op. 26: 322; Karmay 1972: 190–191.
97. In volume 108: 79–103.
98. Op. 40: 93.
99. Sad kun Ratna, one of the three *gter ston*s known as *a tsa ra mi gsum*; see Martin 2003: 170–177.
100. See op. 44: 135–136. However, Achard quotes it as a discovery of Gshen sras lha rje: Achard 2004: xiv.
101. In vol. 47: 145–147.
102. Op. 42, vol. 298: 302/1.
103. Op. 8: 419/3.
104. Op. 5: 502–503.
105. Op. 3: 269/2; see also Jamgön Kongtrul Lodrö Thaye 2011: 188.
106. Tulku Thondup places Gnyal pa nyi ma shes rab in the twelfth century; see Tulku Thondup Rinpoche 1986: 192.
107. The title page of this volume reads: Gshen gsas lha rje / *Drung mu gcod chen* / *Zab lam gnad kyi gdams pa drung mu gcod chen gyi gsung pod* / A collection of Bönpo *Gcod* texts: tantras, rituals, and *khrid yig* / Received in a vision from Stong rgyung mthu chen by Gshen gsas Lha rje / Reproduced from an ancient manuscript preserved at Bsam gling Monastery in Dolpo / Tshultrim Tashi, TBMC / Dolanji, 1973. See also Martin 2003: 731; Achard 2008: 398.
108. The *Dri med shel gyi phreng ba* by Dbra ston ngag dbang bskal bzang bstan pa'i rgyal mtshan (1897–1959).
109. Op. 23: 38/4.
110. The *Bka' lung dri ma med pa'i mdo drung mu bskal bzang sangs rgyas stong gi mtshan brjod*. See Martin 2003: 80–82.

111. Op. 19A, vol. 2: 431/1; 19B: 327/14.
112. Op. 12: 7/5.
113. William Blake claimed to have had his first vision at the age of four and his visions continued until the day he died. Most of his paintings and poetry originate from visions he actually saw, and when asked about where he saw all this, he pointed to his forehead saying that anybody could have this capacity. At times he would simply state that an "elph" had sat on his shoulder and dictated a poem to him. His poetry is full of symbols and imagery that he had to fit somehow into the Judeo-Christian tradition in which he was raised, as he had no knowledge of Buddhism. Nevertheless some of his ideas, such as the principle of energy as being the source of eternal delight, as explained in *The Marriage of Heaven and Hell*, bear comparison to ideas that underlie tantric teachings, such as the transformation of emotions and sexual energy. For him the visionary dimension was the ultimate reality, which he called "Imagination or the Divine Body in Every Man," the human divinity or the divine body of Jesus, and he considered our material vision as a pale shadow of that reality. When he was on his deathbed he started to sing hymns to God with tears of joy, saying that he was going to that country where he had always wished to go. One of his most striking visionary accounts is the description of his "first vision of light" that he had on the seashore at Felpham, a small village in West Sussex, England. It is contained in a letter to his friend Thomas Butts. I remember reading it to Lopön Tenzin Namdak in Dolanji, and the happy, surprised smile on his face while he repeated "beneath my bright feet," and "like dross purg'd away all my mire and my clay."

> To my Friend Butts I write/ My first vision of light,/ On the yellow sands sitting./ The sun was emitting/ His glorious beams/ From heaven's high streams./ Over sea, over land,/ My eyes did expand/ Into regions of air,/ Away from all care;/ Into regions of fire/ Remote from desire:/ The light of the morning/ Heaven's mountains adorning./ In particles bright,/ The jewels of light/ Distinct shone and clear./ Amazed and in fear/ I each particle gazed,/ Astonished, amazed;/ For each was a man/ Human-formed. Swift I ran,/ For they beckoned to me,/ Remote by the sea,/ Saying: "Each grain of sand,/ Every stone on the land,/ Each rock and each hill,/ Each fountain and rill,/ Each herb and each tree,/ Mountain, hill, earth, and sea,/ Cloud, meteor, and star,/ Are men seen afar."/ I stood in the streams/ Of heaven's bright beams,/ And saw Felpham sweet/ Beneath my bright feet,/ In soft female charms;/ And in her fair arms/ My shadow I knew,/ And my wife's shadow too,/ And my sister and friend./ We like infants descend/ In our shadows on earth,/ Like a weak mortal birth./ My eyes more and more/ Like a sea without shore,/ Continue expanding,/ The heavens commanding,/ Till the jewels of light,/ Heavenly men beaming bright,/ Appeared as one man,/ Who complacent began/ My limbs to infold/ In his beams of bright gold;/ Like dross purged away/ All my mire and my clay./ Soft consumed in delight,/ In his bosom sun-bright/ I remained. Soft he smiled,/ And I heard his voice mild,/ Saying: "This is my

fold,/ O thou ram horned with gold,/ Who awakest from sleep/ On the sides of the deep./ On the mountains around/ The roarings resound/ Of the lion and wolf,/ The loud sea and deep gulf./ These are guards of my fold,/ O thou ram horned with gold!"/ And the voice faded mild,/ I remained as a child;/ All I ever had known/ Before me bright shone:/ I saw you your wife/ By the fountains of life./ Such the vision to me/ Appeared on the sea. (E. J. Ellis and W. B. Yeats, *The Works of William Blake, Poetic, Symbolic, and Critical* [London, 1893]: 64–65)

114. This Tiger year could correspond to 1242 (Water-Tiger) or 1254 (Wood-Tiger). The Bka' brten edition gives instead *rta lo*, a Horse year, which could correspond to 1246 (Fire-Horse) or 1258 (Earth-Horse). The Tibetan year starts either in February or March; thus the seventh month, for example, can be either August or September.

115. Shen (*gshen*) or shenpo (*gshen po*) is a characteristic term of the Bön tradition. Originally the name of a clan (Dmu gshen) from whom Gshen rab mi bo ("the great man, supreme *gshen*") descended, in historical texts it is used for Bönpo priests, such as in the term *sku gshen* or royal priest. In later times it came to be equivalent with Bönpo practitioner.

116. The *gaṇacakra* (*tshogs kyi 'khor lo*), or tantric feast, is performed by knowledge-holders and ḍākinīs in pure nirmāṇakāya dimensions known as *mkha' spyod*, which are invisible to ordinary human beings. This ritual, whose counterpart at the level of ordinary practitioners is also called *gaṇapūja*, consists in transforming all sense enjoyments, such as eating and drinking, into spiritual power, or siddhi, by means of offering them to one's own body as a pure maṇḍala of deities and integrating everything in nondual awareness.

117. The Tibetan expression used in the text is *gshen phran*, denoting practitioners or followers of the teaching of Gshen rab who are not at the level of highly realized siddhas.

118. The practice of circumambulation (*skor ba*), in which the practitioner walks counterclockwise (clockwise in the Buddhist tradition) around the object of veneration, is a means for accumulating merit and purifying negative karma.

119. Tib. *rig 'dzin snying po zhi byed*.

120. *Mudrās* (*phyag rgya*) are symbolic hand gestures used in tantric practice for a variety of purposes, such as communicating with deities and guardians, making offerings, dispelling negative energies, and so forth.

121. Mkhyen brtse chen po (Great Wise and Compassionate) is another name for Tse dbang rig 'dzin.

122. Tib. *sha chen*, literally "great meat," generally includes five types of meat—cow, dog, horse, elephant, and human—considered to be endowed with special spiritual qualities for *gaṇacakra* rituals. Tenzin Namdak reads the term in this context as a synonym for human flesh.

123. *Chang* is Tibetan beer, fermented from barley, or in some cases, from rice.

124. Op. 35A: 309/3; 35B: 508/2.

125. This Horse year could be identified as 1246, the Fire-Horse year, or 1258, the Earth-Horse year.
126. Tib. *g.yung drung sum brtsegs*.
127. Op. 31: 863/5.
128. Op. 36B: 762/2; 36C: 66/2.
129. In the text, *cha rkyen gser gdams nyer gcig*. I have not been able to identify these twenty-one secondary "golden teachings," although it may be assumed that they include some of the texts contained in the *Dran pa gser gdams* volume.
130. Thugs rje kun grol is an important ḍākinī, consort of Tshe dbang rig 'dzin.
131. Op. 19A, vol. 2: 402/5; 19B: 318/6.
132. Op. 19A, vol. 2: 233/6; 19B: 262/18.
133. Op. 44: 385/1.
134. Op. 29B: 86/8.
135. The Bka' brten edition has the first day instead of the eleventh.
136. Bya ri gtsug ldan is a mountain near Mount Kailash in western Tibet, particularly linked to the figure of Dran pa nam mkha'.
137. A *gtor ma* (sometimes rendered as "sacrificial cake") is a ritual object that can be made of dough, clay, or similar material and whose functions can be offering, dispelling obstructing forces, establishing protective or divine energies, and so on.
138. Op. 34A: 303/3; 34B: 499/4.
139. The full title reads: Gshen gsas Lha rje / *Man ngag rin po che dran pa gser gyi gdams pa* / *sNyan rgyud man ngag rin po che dran pa gser gyi gdams pa* / Bönpo oral transmission precepts granted by Dran pa nam mkha' to Gshen gsas Lha rje / Reproduced from a rare manuscript from Bsam gling Monastery in Dolpo / TBMC / Delhi / 1972.
140. *G.yung drung bon gyi bka' brten*, compiled by and published in Lhasa by Sog sde sprul sku bstan pa'i nyi ma in 1998, in three hundred volumes.
141. The chapters are listed as *Ngo sprod ye shes mdzub tshug*; *Man ngag bon sku gcer mthong*; *Man ngag rig pa don 'dus*; *Man ngag don gyi ga dar*; *Man ngag kun 'dus mthong grol*; *Man ngag ngo sprod thig gdabs*; *Man ngag don gyi yang tigs*; *Man ngag gnad kyi gzer bu*; *Man ngag drod tshad tha ma'i 'byung bsgyur*; *Man ngag mthar thugs gnad kyi lde mig*; *Man ngag bar do cig chod*; *Man ngag gis rgyal po las rgyud kyi tshogs skong*; *Man ngag rgyal po las rig 'dzin mkha' 'gro'i mjal snang*; *Man ngag rgyal po sngon 'gro mun sel sgron ma*; *Thig chen kun gyis yang bcud man ngag gsal ba'i sgron me*; *Man ngag rgyal po gnad kyi zhal gdams bsdus pa*; *Rig 'dzin brgya cu'i zhu len zhal gdams bdud rtsi phreng ba*; *Gdams pa rin chen gser gyi sgron me*; *Bla chen dran pa'i zhu len*; *Bla chen tshe dbang gi zhu len*; *Bla chen yab sras lha rje'i dge sdig bcum thug*; *Sa lam don gsal rin chen sgron ma*; *Ma cig bskal pa bzang mo'i zhu len*; *'Od ldan 'bar ma thugs kyi yang snying skal ldan skyes bu'i zhu len*; *Rje stong rgyung rin po che zhu len*; *Srid rgyal zhu len*; *Bar do gsal ba'i sgron me*. From *Rgyal ba'i bka' dang bka' rten rmad 'byung dgos 'dod yid bzhin gter gyi bang mdzod la dkar chag blo'i tha ram bkrol byel 'phrul gyi lde mig*, op. 25: 1185/2.

142. For an analysis of the various aspects of the meaning of *lde'u* in the Tibetan culture and literature, see Chögyal Namkhai Norbu 1995: 30–31.

CHAPTER 1: VISIONARY ENCOUNTERS WITH KNOWLEDGE-HOLDERS AND DAKINIS

1. Tshad med 'od ldan (Infinite Light) is one of the nine buddhas of the direct transmission of the *Zhang zhung snyan rgyud*. See Reynolds 2011: 43; Achard 2004: 273.
2. Co za bon mo, an important ḍākinī originally from Dwags po, closely related to the Tibetan Dran pa nam mkha' and to Li shu stag ring. For a short biography, see Lopön Tenzin Namdak 2012: 135–156.
3. The four goddesses of flowers (*me tog lha mo bzhi*) are usually listed as Lha mo dkar mo pad ma'i spyan, Lha mo dmar mo 'bar ma'i lcags, Lha mo sngon mo chu rkang ma, and Lha mo ser mo thor tshugs can. They are peaceful ḍākinīs belonging to a group of forty-five peaceful deities from the *Spyi spungs* cycle called *Zhi ba g.yung drung yongs rdzogs* (*gter ma* of Rma ston shes rab seng ge, alias Rma lha rgod thog pa, rediscovered at Yar la sham po in the twelfth century). Usually in the maṇḍala of the *Gsas mkhar zhi khro* there are forty-five peaceful deities and eighty-six wrathful deities.
4. In Tibetan *mtshams med*, literally "without interval," referring to five heavy actions known as *mtshams med lnga* that cause immediate rebirth in the hell realm. They are (1) killing one's master, (2) killing one's student, (3) killing one's mother, (4) killing one's child, and (5) killing one's father. Or, (1) killing one's master or student, (2) killing one's friend or spiritual companion, (3) killing one's father or mother, (4) killing one's sibling or child, and (5) taking one's own life or killing one's servant. Op. 21: 364.
5. Four classes of ḍākinīs are generally recognized: wisdom ḍākinīs (*ye shes mkha' 'gro*), who are enlightened beings; miracle ḍākinīs (*rdzu 'phrul mkha' 'gro*), who have a certain degree of realization and the capacity to display supernatural powers; action ḍākinīs (*las kyi mkha' 'gro*), who are of various types and act as assistants of yogins and siddhas; worldly ḍākinīs (*'jig rten gyi mkha' 'gro*), who are in human form and often unaware of their nature.
6. This is a possible translation of *mtha' ba bcad* in the Delhi edition (p. 27), which according to Lopön Tenzin Namdak could be taken as *mtha' bcad* ("resolved beyond the extremes"), in the sense of being in a state of meditation free from the limitations of permanence (*rtag pa*) and annihilation (*chad pa*). The Bka' brten (p. 36) and Steng chen (p. 39) editions have respectively *ka ba bcad* and *ka [dka'] ba bcad*, emended in the Sichuan edition (p. 22) as *dka' ba spyad* ("performing asceticism").
7. Tshe dbang ri khrod, another name for Tshe dbang rig 'dzin.
8. The arura or myrobalan (*Terminalia chebula*) is the drupe-like fruit of a medicinal tree, which is used in Tibetan medicine as a remedy for many disorders.

9. The swastika (*g.yung drung*) is the symbol of Bön, and like the vajra in the Buddhist tradition, it denotes the immortal or indestructible nature of existence.
10. In Tibetan, *dge sbyor*, literally "virtuous application," but generally used as a synonym for spiritual practice and meditation.
11. Srid pa'i rgyal mo is the most important ḍākinī in the Bönpo tradition, and especially the supreme guardian of the teachings of Bön. She is also known as the consort of Gtso mchog mkha' 'gying. See Achard 2004: 263. The abbreviated form *srid rgyal* is often found in our text.
12. In Tibetan *mtha' khob*, denoting a border region or country in which the teachings have not yet arrived.
13. Prostrations (*phyag 'tshal*) offered to masters, stupas, sacred objects, and so forth, are performed in order to purify negative karma.
14. It is considered that an enlightened being has five kinds of emanations: of the body (*sku*), of the voice (*gsung*), of the mind (*thugs*), of qualities (*yon tan*), and of activities (*phrin las*). In the translation I have capitalized Body, Voice, and Mind (*sku gsung thugs*), in the sense of their primordially enlightened condition, to distinguish them from the ordinary body, voice, and mind (*lus ngag yid*) of an individual.
15. Gnam phyi gung rgyal (the ancestor queen of the sky) is one of the most ancient goddesses in the Bönpo pantheon, in later times identified as Srid pa'i rgyal mo. See Karmay 1972: 135; Dell'Angelo,1982: 158–162.
16. In Tibetan *bde drod nyams kyi drod tshad*. Although in general inner heat (*drod*) and bliss (*bde ba*) are the specific result of the yogic practices of gtum mo, they also manifest naturally as signs of the experience (*nyams*) of the practice of contemplation, due to the relaxation of the energy of the practitioner. (Oral explanation by Chögyal Namkhai Norbu.)
17. This is a possible translation of *ma yin gang dang bral ba yin*. The Sichuan edition (p. 35) has *ma yengs* ("undistracted") instead of *ma yin* ("it is not").
18. Tib. *rig 'dzin gshen phran brgyad*, according to the Bka' brten edition (p. 56), while the Delhi edition has eighteen (*gshen phran bco brgyad*) instead of eight.
19. Se Sha ri dbu chen, an important siddha and one of the four scholars (*mkhas pa mi bzhi*). See Achard 2004: 274; op. 21: 440–441.
20. *Thug pa* is the staple Tibetan soup, of which many varieties exist.
21. Stang chen Dmu tsha gyer med, an important master who lived at the time of the eighth Tibetan king Gri gum btsan po, and a student of Dran pa nam mkha'. See Achard 2004: 264.
22. The outer, inner, and secret initiations are three kinds of initiation corresponding respectively to the body, voice, and mind of the individual. Their function is to empower and authorize the practitioner to apply the tantric methods of visualization, mantra recitation, and channels and prāṇas contained in the two stages of *bskyed rim* and *rdzogs rim*.
23. Here there is a pun between the term *dbang* (empowerment or initiation) and *rang dbang*, literally "power over itself," or freedom.

NOTES — 215

24. The *sil snyan* is a kind of smaller *gshang* cymbal used in the Bön tradition.
25. In Tibetan *byang chub sems*, corresponding to the Sanskrit *bodhicitta*, literally the mind (*citta*) of enlightenment (*bodhi*). According to the Dzogchen teachings, the Tibetan translation expresses three principles: purified or pure (*byang*), total or perfected (*chub*), and mind or consciousness (*sems*). Throughout the text this term has been rendered "primordially enlightened mind."
26. Tib. *sgo ba yab yum brgyad*, the four wrathful guardians with their consorts at the four gates of the maṇḍala, belonging to the eighty-six wrathful deities.
27. The essences of the lunar and solar energies, and of males and females respectively, in their material form corresponding to sperm and blood.
28. Basic space (*dbyings*) and primordial wisdom (*ye shes*), corresponding to the aspects of emptiness and clarity of the primordial state, are two important principles of the view and meditation, especially emphasized in the Anuyoga Buddhist tradition of Vajrayāna.
29. In ritual practices this has the purpose of removing the outer and inner obstacles and securing the place where the practice is performed.
30. The letter A is the symbol of the primordial state of Dzogchen transmitted by the master.
31. According to the oral explanation of Lopön Tenzin Namdak, the clouds symbolize thoughts; the jewel, emotions; killing the otter in the water, eliminating negativities from thoughts; and stripping the child naked, achieving total purification.
32. Yongs su dag pa, a Bönpo belonging to the Devas of the Thirty-Three, the first in the lineage of the *Zhang zhung snyan rgyud* after the nine primordial buddhas. See Achard 2004: 275.
33. Rgyung yar mu khod was a Zhang zhung king of Khyung lung, father of Dran pa nam mkha'. He received teachings from his son. Rje rgyal lha sgom, a student of Dran pa nam mkha', was also a minister of the latter's father Rgyung yar mu khod. See Achard 2004: 251.
34. The mythical bird *garuḍa* is usually represented with a flaming jewel at the forehead.
35. According to Lopön Tenzin Namdak's oral explanation, here the jewel of the garuḍa symbolizes the Dzogchen nature of primordial wisdom, while the remaining verses express the relation between thoughts and emotions, and the nature of wisdom.
36. Tib. *rigs lnga yab yum*, the five saṃbhogakāya buddhas with consorts personifying the pure aspect of the five *skandha*s (aggregates) and the five elements: (1) Kun snang khyab pa with Nam mkha'i lha mo (space goddess); (2) Gsal ba rang byung with Sa yi lha mo (earth goddess); (3) Bye brag dngos med with Me yi lha mo (fire goddess); (4) Dga' ba don grub with Chu yi lha mo (water goddess); and (5) Dge lha gar phyug with Rlung gi lha mo (air goddess).
37. See introduction, note 5.

38. According to Lopön Tenzin Namdak's oral explanation, the infant symbolizes the thought-free essence; the monkey, the arising of the manifestations of wisdom through the five elements; and the self-originated man, the unique sphere (*thig le nyag gcig*) of the wisdom of instant presence inside one's heart.
39. *Rtsa rlung* is a yogic system of practice dealing with the control of one's energy channels and prāṇas, related to bodily movements known as *'phrul 'khor* (also *'khrul 'khor*) or *yantras*. Yantra Yoga is a system of Tibetan yoga dealing with bodily movements and positions, breathing exercises, and mental visualization, widely developed in the practice of Tantra and Dzogchen. One of the most ancient systems of Yantra, codified by the eighth-century Tibetan master Vairocana, is the object of a detailed study in Chögyal Namkhai Norbu 2008.
40. In Tibetan, *chen po yab yum, rig pa yab yum, sgo ba yab yum*: all manifestations belonging to the eighty-six wrathful deities of the *Zhi khro* cycle.
41. On the five evil deeds that cause immediate retribution, see chapter 1, note 4.
42. Samayas (*dam tshig*) are generally commitments that a practitioner is bound to observe after receiving a Vajrayāna initiation.
43. In Tibetan, *du tri su'i bzlog pa*. This refers to a ritual related to the famous Bönpo mantra A DKAR A RMAD DU TRI SU NAG PO ZHI ZHI MAL MAL, which has the power to purify and block rebirth in the lower states of existence. According to Lopön Tenzin Namdak, the syllables of the mantra are explained as follows: A DKAR (white A), the pure nature of mind; A RMAD, the knowledge of this nature; DU, hell beings; TRI, the pretas; SU, the animals; NAG PO, negativities and karmic obscurations; ZHI ZHI, may they be purified; MAL MAL, may happiness be achieved. See also Reynolds 2011: 532.
44. *Stag bong ba* (in the Bka' brten and Steng chen editions), taken as *stag bung ba* (*stag chung bung ba*). The Delhi edition has *stag go ba*.
45. Tib. *mkhas pa mi gsum*, which I take to mean the four scholars excluding Stong rgyung mthu chen.
46. Tib. *rgyal chen rigs bzhi*, the guardians of the four directions of the universe.
47. This means that even a bad relation with a master is beneficial, since it plants the seed for joining the path in the future.
48. Rgyal gshen Mi lus bsam legs was a king of Stag gzig who wrote important commentaries on the *Ma rgyud* cycle of teachings. See Achard 2004: 251; op. 21: 297–298.
49. Stag la me 'bar was an important siddha from Stag gzig connected with the Phur pa cycle. For a short biography, see Karmay 1972: xxii; Achard 2004: 262; op. 21: 150–151.
50. Tib. *lha srin sde brgyad*, usually listed as *lha, gshin rje, ma mo, gza', klu, btsan, bdud, gnod sbyin*. See op. 21: 488.
51. The mantra Ā A DKAR SA LE 'OD A YAM OM 'DU is one of the most important mantras in the Bönpo tradition and is particularly linked with the principle of the Dzogchen teaching. According to Lopön Tenzin Namdak's explanation, the meaning of the syllables is the following: Ā, the immovable nature;

A, the unborn nature; DKAR (white), pure; SA LE (clarity), beyond doubts and concepts; 'OD (light), beyond thought; A, release from samsara; YAM, development of prāṇa energy; OM, the fruit of the five wisdoms; 'DU, wisdoms reabsorb in the unique *thig le*. See also Reynolds 2011: 531; Dell'Angelo 1982: 141.

52. Bon zhig khyung nag (1103–1183), an important master who received the famous Dzogchen cycle *Snyan rgyud rig pa gcer mthong*. For a biography, see Achard 1998; Martin 2001: 44.
53. Relics (*ring bsrel*) are spherical pills emanated from the body of a realized being at the time of cremation, several types of which exist. They are usually classified into five species: *sha ri ram, pa ri ram, chu ri ram, nya ri ram, pañca ram.*
54. A possible interpretation of the otherwise obscure *'jang nas* (read as *mjal snang* by Lopön Tenzin Namdak) *byung bzhin rin po che'i rtags bzhin*. "Preciousness" here denotes something truthful and trustworthy.

CHAPTER 3: THE GARLAND OF NECTAR: ORALLY TRANSMITTED ADVICE FROM EIGHTY KNOWLEDGE-HOLDERS IN THE FORM OF QUESTIONS AND ANSWERS

1. The Delhi edition (A: 364) has *yi ge phyogs med 'char*, "letters arise in all directions."
2. The six great lamas (*bla ma che drug*) are important siddhas in the Bön tradition. They are usually listed as Gsang ba 'dus pa, Rma lo dar dpyangs, Yongs su dag pa, Mi lus bsam legs, Ye shes snying po, and Snang ba mdog can. In this case, Stag la me 'bar is listed in place of Gsang ba 'dus pa. See Karmay 1972: 58.
3. Rma lo dar dpyangs was one of the teachers of Nam mkha' snang ba mdog can.
4. Klu grub ye shes snying po, the *gshen* of the nāgas. See Karmay 1972: xxii–xxiii; Achard 2004: 246; op. 21: 405.
5. Nam mkha' snang ba mdog can, an important *gshen* who acted as royal priest (*sku gshen*) at the time of the first Tibetan king Gnya' khri btsan po. See Karmay 1972: 32–34; Achard 2004: 259; op. 21: 220–221.
6. Mu khri btsan po (also Mu khri btsad po) was the second Tibetan king and a student of Nam mkha' snang ba mdog can. See Achard 2004: 264; op. 21: 299.
7. Ha ra ci par, or Mon bon ha ra ci par, was an important siddha in the early diffusion of Bön. His consort was Stag za li wer. See Karmay 1972: 46–47; Achard 2004: 264; op. 21: 485.
8. A nu 'phrag thag, student of Ha ra ci par. See Karmay 1972: 47; Achard 2004: 276; op. 21: 491–492.
9. Sad ne ga'u, student of A nu 'phrag thag. See Karmay 1972: 47; Achard 2004: 273; op. 21: 47.
10. Tha mi thad ke, student of Sad ne ga'u. See Karmay 1972: 47; Achard 2004: 257; op. 21: 158.
11. Hrin ni mu ting, one of the thirteen lineage descendants (*gdung brgyud bcu gsum*). See Karmay 1972: 58; op. 21: 487.

12. Glang chen mu wer, one of the thirteen lineage descendants (*gdung brgyud bcu gsum*). See Karmay 1972: 58; op. 21: 61.
13. Shad pu ra khug (variant Shad bu ra khug), student of Tha mi thad ke. See Karmay 1972: 47–48; Achard 2004: 272; op. 21: 441.
14. Zing pa mthu chen, a siddha from China and a student of Shad pu ra khug. See Karmay 1972: 48; Achard 2004: 267; op. 21: 387.
15. Spe bon thog 'phrul, student of Zing pa mthu chen. See Karmay 1972: 48; Achard 2004: 259–260; op. 21: 235.
16. Spe bon thog rtse, student of Spe bon thog 'phrul. See Karmay 1972: 48–49; Achard 2004: 260; op. 21: 235.
17. Lce tsha mkhar bu, one of the four great scholars (*mkhas pa mi bzhi*). See Achard 2004: 64; op. 21: 103.
18. Tib. *bon nyid*, corresponding to the Sanskrit *dharmatā*. The Delhi (A) edition has *bon sku* instead.
19. Ra sangs khod ram, a Bönpo minister at the time of the Tibetan king Gri gum bstan po. See Karmay 1972: 62–64.
20. Blon chen mu thur, a contemporary of Dran pa nam mkha', listed as one of the "eight gshen translators and scholars" (*lo paṇ gshen brgyad*) in Karmay 1972: 42.
21. Ngam pa lce ring of Ge sar, one of the eight great scholars (*mkhas pa mi brgyad*). See introduction, note 44; see also Karmay 1972: 42 and Achard 2004: 251.
22. Za rangs me 'bar, a siddha from Stag gzig. See introduction, note 44; also Karmay 1972: 42.
23. Mu spungs gsal tang, a siddha from Zhang zhung, listed as one of the "eight translators and scholars" (*lo paṇ gshen brgyad*) in Karmay 1972: 42.
24. In general the outer teachings of Bön are considered to cover the first to the fourth of the nine vehicles; the inner teachings, the fifth to the eighth vehicle; the secret teaching, corresponding to Dzogchen, the ninth vehicle.
25. Lha rje bar sgom, a student of Bru chen Nam mkha' g.yung drung (994–1054).
26. Gur sgom da re, possibly the same Gur sgom student of Sgom chen G.yung drung grags; see Karmay 1972: 170.
27. Gur sgom bsgras po. Same problem of identification as in the previous note.
28. Sum pa dbu dkar (also spelled Sum pa dbu kha and Sum pa sbu ga), a siddha from Sum pa and one of the thirteen lineage descendants (*gdung brgyud bcu gsum*). See Karmay 1972: 58; Achard 2004: 274; op. 21: 468.
29. Khro tshang 'brug lha (956–1077), an important *gter ston*. See Karmay 1972: 124–125; op. 21: 31–32.
30. Mi la ras pa (1040–1123), the Tibetan Buddhist yogin famous for his biography and spiritual songs.
31. The Bka' brten edition (B: 602) has '*jig rten gyi snang ba*, "the worldly vision."
32. Gling rje ras pa Pad ma rdo rje (1128–1188), a great Tibetan siddha, first in the lineage of the 'Brug pa bka' rgyud tradition.
33. Zhu sgom 'khrul zhig (eleventh–twelfth century), one of the main teachers of Bon zhig khyung nag. See Achard 1998: 29.

34. Mes sgom zhig po (also Me sgom zhig po, alias Me ston zhig po) (eleventh–twelfth century) was one of the main teachers of Bon zhig khyung nag. See Martin 2001: 44; Achard 1998.
35. Kun dga' zhig po, one of the main teachers of Bon zhig khyung nag. See Achard 1998: 30.
36. Bon zhig khyung nag; see chapter 2, note 52.
37. The Delhi edition has *zhe sdang rang grol*, "self-liberation of anger."
38. 'Khrul zhig ldom bu (also 'Khrul zhig ldong bu) was one of the main students of Bon zhig khyung nag. See Achard 1998: 33–35.
39. Dam pa g.yu zhig, student of 'Khrul zhig ldom bu. See Achard 1998: 35.
40. Gnyos Tshul khrims rgyal mtshan (born in 1144). See Karmay 1972: 140; op. 21: 128.
41. Dre ston go cha, a teacher of Rme'u dgongs mdzod ri khrod chen po (see note 46).
42. Jo gdung and Jo g.yung, two important masters in the *A khrid* tradition, students of Sgom chen 'bar ba (eleventh century). See Kvaerne 1973: 40. For Jo g.yung, alias Khyung sgom jo g.yung, see also op. 21: 113–115.
43. Gu ru rno rtse (also Gu ru rnon rtse), born in 1136, was an important *gter ston* who also discovered Buddhist texts. See Karmay 1972: 166–167.
44. Rma ston srol 'dzin, an important *gter ston* born in 1092. See Karmay 1972: 167–168.
45. 'A zha Bdud rtsi rgyal mtshan (twelfth century), a master in the lineage of the *A khrid* tradition. See Karmay 1972: 140; Kvaerne 1973: 47.
46. Rme'u dgongs mdzod (spelled *dgongs mdzad* in most editions of our text) ri khrod chen po (1038–1096), the founder of the *A khrid* tradition. For a biography, see Kvaerne 1973: 29–36.
47. Zhu g.yas legs po (1002–1081), the main student of Gshen chen klu dga'. For a biography, see Martin 2001: 81–92; also Karmay 1972: 136–137; and op. 21: 380.
48. The famous *gter ston* Gshen chen klu dga' (996–1035). For a detailed study of his life and works, see Martin 2001.
49. This Bon zhig could either be the same Bon zhig khyung nag quoted above at note 36, or Bon zhig nag po, which is one of the names of Gyer mi nyi 'od.
50. Dbang ldan gshen sras is one of the names of Gshen sras lha rje, but in this case it must obviously refer to some other master whom I have not identified.
51. Skyang 'phags mu la drung mu, a *gter ston* whose rediscoveries belong to the Khams treasures. See Karmay 1972: 172 and 191.
52. The Tibetan expression is *btsun chung*, a religious who keeps basic vows but is not a fully ordained monk.
53. The colophon in the Delhi (A) edition says: "The transmission lineage of these teachings is the following: the eighty knowledge-holders and sugatas transmitted them to Gshen sras, the savior of beings. Gshen sras transmitted them to the faithful beggar [Zha gar]. Skal bzang requested them from the faithful beggar Zha gar. Shes rab rgyal mtshan requested them from Skal bzang. I, Sos sems

skyed don ldan, for the benefit of beings, requested its authorization according to the scriptures, and was told, 'Explain these teachings without partiality! Teach these words of advice to the faithful ones! Give its authorization to all the meritorious ones!' According to the words of my teacher, I, Sems skyed, wrote down these words of advice, and I dedicate them to the benefit of all beings!" The Bka' brten (B) edition says: "The beggar Ye shes sgom pa with devotion requested this from the knowledge-holder Gshen sras. I, the faithful Nam mkha' rgyal mtshan, undertaking great hardship, requested them from the former." The B2 and C editions say: "The faithful Shes rab dpal requested this from the lord of beings Gshen sras lha rje. May all be auspicious!"

CHAPTER 4: THE PRECIOUS GOLDEN LAMP: ADVICE FROM EIGHTY DAKINIS

1. Skal pa bzang mo, same as its abbreviated forms Skal bzang and Skal bzang ma found throughout the text.
2. I have followed the Delhi edition (A: 376) which has *bu thog rdug[s] med na de'i bar pa mdzod*, the Tibetan term *bar pa* meaning someone who acts as peacemaker in a dispute. The other editions (B: 614; C: 643) have *thog rdug[s] med pa de'i bar so mdzad*, interpreted by Lopön Tenzin Namdak in his oral commentary at the Buddhas Weg, September 2014, in the sense of "passing unobstructed" through the soldiers.
3. Tib. *chu rkyal bshig pa* (also *bshigs pa*), that is to say, churning water instead of milk in order to make butter.
4. I have followed the Delhi edition (A: 378) which has *dug lnga nyon mongs pa'i khyer na*; the other editions (B: 617; D: 645) have *dug lnga nyon mongs ma spangs na*, "If you don't abandon . . ."
5. See chapter 1, note 3. The names given here do not correspond to those generally found.
6. Chu lcam rgyal mo, also known as Chu lcags rgyal mo, known as "the mother of existence" (*srid pa'i yum*). See Chögyal Namkhai Norbu 1995: 148.
7. The *mdzo mo* is the female offspring of a yak and a cow, or of an ox and a *'bri* (female yak). Her calves usually do not live long.
8. The Tibetan term *ri dwags*, in this and the next quatrain rendered as "deer," actually refers to all kinds of wild herbivores.
9. The colophon of the Delhi (A) edition says: "I [Zha gar ba] received this quintessential teaching, heart-blood of the ḍākinīs, from Gshen sras lha rje. Virtue! Bskal bzang [Bskal bzang ma in the text] received it from Rdzogs chen Zha gar ba, and I, Shes rab rgyal mtshan, received it from him. May all this be auspicious!" The Bka' brten (B) and Tengchen (C) editions say: "The faithful Shes rab dpal received it from Gshen sras lha rje, protector of beings. May all this be auspicious!"

Appendix 1: The *Dran pa gser gdams* in the Various Editions

1. See appendix 3.
2. Contained in volume 10 of the *gsung 'bum* in fifteen volumes of the Steng chen monastery (Rdza steng chen dgon) edition, TBRC W2CZ7988. The first text is quoted at f. 166b/5; the second at ff. 156b/5 and 170b/3.
3. For an example of *'das log* literature, see Delog Dawa Drolma 1995.
4. See note 2 above. The quotations are found at ff. 18/2, 143b/2, 145b/3, and 223b/5.
5. The chapters listed are *Rgyud kyi tshogs phyag*; *Rig 'dzin mkha' 'gro'i mjal snang*; *Rig 'dzin brgya bcu'i zhal gdams*; *Mkha' 'gro brgya bcu'i zhal gdams*; *Bla chen yab sras zhu len*; *Stong rgyung zhu len*; *'Od ldan 'bar ma'i zhal gdams*; *Srid rgyal zhu len*; *Skal pa bzang mo'i zhal gdams*; *Gser gdams le'u gcig pa*; *Man ngag gdams chung*; *Man ngag snying thig*; *Dge sdig 'bru thus*; *Sa lam don gsal*; *Sngon 'gro mun sel sgron ma*; *Rig 'dzin mkhas pa mi gsum dang mkha' 'gro gsum gyi zhu len*; *Man ngag rang rig sgron ma*; *Ngo sprod ye shes mdzub tshug*; *Man ngag bon sku gcer mthong*; *Rang rig don 'dus*; *Don gyi ga dar*; *Kun 'dus mthong grol*; *Don gyi yang thig*; *Gnad kyi gzer bu*; *Drod tshad tha ma'i 'bras bu*; *Mthar thug gnad kyi gdams pa*; *Man ngag bar do gcig chod*.
6. *Dran pa gser gdams*, A: 519/6. Then the lineage continues with Khyung po bsod nams rgyal mtshan, Mtha' bral bsod nams rgyal mtshan, 'Od ston tshul khrims 'od zer, Rnam rgyal ka ra, Rin chen blo gros, Shes rab rgyal mtshan, Bsod nams ye shes, Rnam dag 'od zer, Blo gros rgyal mtshan, Slob dpon bstan pa 'od zer, Dran chog nyi ma 'od zer, Wer yak khi khar, Bstan pa tshul khrims, Rme'u shes dpal, Nam mkha' lhun grub, Rtogs ldan blo gros grags pa, Grub chen g.yung drung rnam dag, Sprul sku rgyal ba blo gros, Mi 'gyur rgyal mtshan, Rnal 'byor pa dbang phyug drung mu rin chen. See also op. 19, vol. 2: 403/3; op. 44: 385/1.
7. The chapters listed are *Ye shes mdzub gstug ston pa'i le'u dang po*; *Bon sku rig pa gcer mthong sun go sprod pa'i le'u gnyis pa*; *Rang rig don 'dus kyi le'u gsum pa*; *Don gyi ga dar le'u bzhi pa*; *Kun 'dus mthong grol gyi le'u lnga pa*; *Ngo sprod thig 'debs kyi le'u drug pa*; *Don gyi yang tig le'u bdun pa*; *Gnad kyi gzer bu'i le'u brgyad pa*; *Nyams myong gi drod tshad bstan pa'i le'u dgu pa*; *Mthar thug gnad kyi lde mig le'u bcu pa*.
8. The Tibetan title gives *khro rgyal* ("wrathful") instead of *mkha' 'gro*.
9. In the Tibetan title the Zhang zhung word *mu la* ("space") is given instead of the Tibetan *nam mkha'*.
10. Page 662 contains a fragment of the beginning of this same chapter.

Appendix 2: The Previous Lives of Gshen sras lha rje

1. Actually forty-two lives can be counted, including Gshen sras lha rje.
2. The text says *tshe lo brgya pa'i dus*, the time of the life span of a hundred years, which seems to be contradictory in this case.

Bibliography

1. Tibetan Sources

Collections

Bon gyi bka' 'gyur / *G.yung drung bon gyi bka' 'gyur*. 179 volumes. Chengdu: Kun grol lha sras mi pham rnam rgyal, 1999.

Bon gyi bka' brten / *G.yung drung bon gyi bka' brten*. 300 volumes. Compiled and published by Sog sde sprul sku bstan pa'i nyi ma. Lhasa: 1998.

Dran pa gser gdams / Man ngag rin po che dran pa gser gyi gdams pa

A: Delhi: Tibetan Bonpo Monastic Centre, 1972.
B: In Bon gyi bka' brten, vol. 39.
B2: Additional texts in volumes 61, 86, and 191 of the Bon gyi bka' brten.
C: In Steng chen brten 'gyur, set from the Steng chen monastery, Khyung po, vol. 82.
D: In Sangs rgyas g.yung drung bon gyi dpe tshogs, vol. 21. Sichuan: Si khron mi rigs dpe skrun khang, 2013.

Single Works

Kun grol grags pa (b. 1700)
[Op. 1] *Sangs rgyas bstan pa spyi yi 'byung khungs yid bzhin nor bu 'dod pa 'jo ba'i gter mdzod*, in *Three Sources for a History of Bon*, pp. 197–552. Dolanji: Tibetan Bonpo Monastic Centre, 1974.
[Op. 2] *G.yung drung bon gyi bka' 'gyur dkar chag* (*Zab dang rgya che g.yung drung bon gyi bka' 'gyur dkar chag nyi ma 'bum gyi 'od zer*). Beijing: Krung go'i bod kyi shes rig dpe skrun khang, 1993.

Kong sprul blo gros mtha' yas (1813–1899)
[Op. 3] *Gter ston brgya rtsa'i rnam thar*. Tezu, Arunachal Pradesh: Tseten Dorji, 1973.

Khod po blo gros thogs med (*gter ston*, b. 1280)
[Op. 4] *Srid pa rgyud kyi kha byang chen mo*, in *Bon gyi bka' brten*, vol. 142, pp. 295–533.

Gu ru bkra shis (eighteenth–nineteenth century)
[Op. 5] *Gu bkra'i chos 'byung (Bstan pa'i snying po gsang chen snga' 'gyur nges don zab mo chos kyi byung ba gsal bar byed pa'i legs bshad mkhas pa dga' byed ngo mtshar gtam gyi rol mtsho)*. Beijing: Krung go'i bod kyi shes rig dpe skrun khang, 1990.

Sga ston tshul khrims rgyal mtshan (fourteenth century)
[Op. 6] *Gter gyi kha sbyang*, in *Bon gyi dpe bkod phyogs bsgrigs* (Collection of Rare Bonpo Texts), edited by Drang srong rnal rgyal, pp. 63–150. Kathmandu: Vajra Publications, 2003.

'Jam dbyangs mkhyen brtse'i dbang po (1820–1892)
[Op. 7] *Rgyal sras gu ru padma 'byung gnas kyi rnam par thar pa mdor dril ba bsgrags pa bon lugs ltar bstan pa*. In Kong sprul blo gros mtha' yas, *Rin chen gter mdzod*, vol. 39, pp. 229–245. Bhutanese edition, 1976.
[Op. 8] *Gangs can gyi yul du byon pa'i lo paṇ rnams kyi mtshan tho rags rim tshigs bcad du bsdebs pa ma hā paṇ di ta shī la ratna'i gsung*. In *Mkhyen-brtse on the History of the Dharma*, pp. 209–684. Leh: S. W. Tashigangpa, 1972.

Bstan pa'i nyi ma
[Op. 9] *Bon gyi brten 'gyur chen mo'i dkar chag*. Lhasa: Bod ljongs mi dmangs dpe skrun khang, 2011.

Bstan 'dzin rnam dag (b. 1926)
[Op. 10] (editor) *Dpal ldan bla ma'i rnam thar mu tig 'phreng ba*. Dolanji: Tibetan Bonpo Monastic Centre, 1981.

Dran pa nam mkha'
[Op. 11] *Bden pa bon gyi mdzod sgo sgra 'grel 'phrul gyi lde mig*. In *Mdzod phug: Basic Verse and Commentary*. Delhi: Tenzin Namdak, 1966.

Drung mu ha ra (thirteenth century)
[Op. 12] *Gcod gdams sngon byung lo rgyus don gsal sgron ma*. In *Drung mu gcod chen*, pp. 5–24. Dolanji: Tibetan Bonpo Monastic Centre, 1973. This text appears also in volume 203 of the *Bon gyi bka' brten*, pp. 207–240, with the title *Drung mu ha ra'i dngos grub thob tshul bzhugs pa dge legs 'phel*.

Nam mkha'i nor bu, Chos rgyal (b. 1938)
[Op. 13] *Bod kyi lo rgyus las 'phros pa'i gtam g.yung drung nor bu'i do shal*. Dharamsala: Library of Tibetan Works and Archives, 1981. Also in *Nam mkha'i nor bu'i gsung rtsom phyogs bsgrigs*, pp. 1–97. Beijing: Krung go'i bod kyi shes rig dpe skrun khang, 1994.
[Op. 14] *Bod rigs gzhon nu rnams la gros su 'debs pa gzi yi phreng ba*. Dharamsala: Library of Tibetan Works and Archives, 1982. Also in *Nam mkha'i nor bu'i gsung rtsom phyogs bsgrigs*, pp. 494–546. Beijing: Krung go'i bod kyi shes rig dpe skrun khang, 1994.
[Op. 15] *Sgrung lde'u bon gsum gyi gtam e ma ho*. Dharamsala: Library of Tibetan

Works and Archives, 1989. Also in *Nam mkha'i nor bu'i gsung rtsom phyogs bsgrigs*, pp. 233–483. Beijing: Krung go'i bod kyi shes rig dpe skrun khang, 1994.
[Op. 16] *Zhang bod lo rgyus ti se'i 'od*. Beijing: Krung go'i bod kyi shes rig dpe skrun khang, 1996.

Snang bzher lod po, Gyer spungs (seventh century)
[Op. 17] *Rdzogs pa chen po zhang zhung snyan rgyud las sgron ma'i 'grel pa nyi 'od rgyan*. In *Rdzogs pa chen po zhang zhung snyan rgyud bka' rgyud skor bzhi*, pp. 166–202. Kathmandu: Vajra Publications, 2006.
[Op. 18] *Rdzogs pa chen po zhang zhung snyan rgyud las phyi lta ba spyi gcod kyi man ngag lde'u bcu gnyis pa*. In *Rdzogs pa chen po zhang zhung snyan rgyud bka' rgyud skor bzhi*, pp. 84–97. Kathmandu: Vajra Publications, 2006.

Dpal ldan tshul khrims (1902–1973)
[Op. 19] *Sangs rgyas g.yung drung bon gyi bstan pa'i byung ba brjod pa'i legs bshad skal bzang po'i mgrin rgyan rab gsal chu shel nor bu'i do shal*. Published as *G.yung drung bon gyi bstan 'byung*, vols. 1 & 2. Dolanji: Tibetan Bonpo Monastic Centre, 1972. Also: *G.yung drung bon gyi bstan 'byung phyogs bstus*. Lhasa: Bod ljongs mi dmangs dpe skrun khang, 1988.

Spu rgyal ba cang pa nyi ma rgyal mtshan
[Op. 20] "Gter ston brgya rtsa'i skor dpyad gleng," in *Bgres po'i 'bel gtam* 3 (2003): 55–60. Kathmandu: Khri brtan nor bu rtse.

Blo gros rab gsal (b. 1971)
[Op. 21] *Gna' bo'i zhang bod tshig mdzod*. Lanzhou: Kan su'u mi rigs dpe skrun khang, 2010.

Dbra ston ngag dbang bskal bzang bstan pa'i rgyal mtshan (1897–1959)
[Op. 22] *Shar rdza bkra shis rgyal mtshan gyi rnam thar*. Beijing: Krung go'i bod kyi shes rig dpe skrun khang, 1990.
[Op. 23] *Sku gsum ston pa'i gsung rab bka' 'gyur rin po che'i lung rgyun ji snyed pa phyogs gcig tu bsdus pa'i bzhugs byang brgyud rim bcas pa dri med shel gyi phreng ba*. In *Bon gyi bka' 'gyur*, vol. 179.

O thog bstan 'dzin dbang rgyal (b. 1961)
[Op. 24] *Bod kyi dpe mdzod khang gi bod yig phyag dpe'i dkar chag mthong ba rang grol*. Catalogue of the Library of Tibetan Works and Archives, Manuscript Section, vol. 5, Bonpo Collection. Dharamsala: Library of Tibetan Works and Archives, 2001.

G.yung drung tshul khrims dbang drag (nineteenth century)
[Op. 25] *Rgyal ba'i bka' dang bka' rten rmad 'byung dgos 'dod yid bzhin gter gyi bang mdzod la dkar chag blo'i tha ram bkrol byel 'phrul gyi lde mig*. In *Bon gyi bka' brten*, vol. 234.

Shar rdza bkra shis rgyal mtshan (1859–1934)
[Op. 26] *Legs bshad rin po che'i gter mdzod*. Beijing: Mi rigs dpe skrun khang, 1985.

Gshen sras lha rje (b. 1215)
[Op. 27] *Mkha' 'gro brgyad [brgya] bcu'i zhal gdams rin chen gser gyi [gyis] sgron ma*. A: 375–390; B: 611–639.
[Op. 28] (*gter ma*) *Go lde'i bskal bzang 'gro ba 'dren pa'i mdo*. In *Bon gyi bka' 'gyur*, vols. 8, 9.
[Op. 29] *Ngo sprod ye shes mdzub tshugs*. A: 85–101.
[Op. 30] *Dran pa yab sras kyis sprul sku gshen sras lha rje la dge sdig shan 'byed gsung pa* (*Bla chen dran pa yab sras lha rje'i dge sdig 'bru thus*). A: 441–463, B: 673–713.
[Op. 31] *Bar do gsal ba'i sgron me*. B: 841–864.
[Op. 32] *Dbang ldan gshen gsas kyi skyes tshogs*. In *Bon gyi bka' brten*, vol. 203, pp. 345–353.
[Op. 33] *Man ngag don gyi ga dar* (*Lhag mthong ye shes gcer bur bstan pa'i man ngag don gyi ga dar*). A: 135–150; B: 235–259.
[Op. 34] *Man ngag bar do gcig chod*. A: 277–307; B: 459–505.
[Op. 35] *Man ngag rang rig sgron me* (*Theg [thig] chen kun gyi [gyis] man ngag gsal ba'i sgron me las rang rig [rigs] sgron me yang zer*). A: 309–332; B: 507–553.
[Op. 36] *'Od ldan 'bar ma thugs kyi yang snying skal ldan skyes bu'i zhu len*. In *Dran pa gser gdams*. B: 761–789.
[Op. 37] *Rig 'dzin mkha' 'gro'i mjal snang*. A: 25–78; B: 33–123.
[Op. 38] *Rig 'dzin mkha' 'gro'i zhus len*. In *Bon gyi bka' brten*, vol. 61, pp. 1–22.
[Op. 39] *Rig 'dzin brgyad [brgya] bcu'i zhu len snyan rgyud zhal gdams bdud rtsi'i 'phreng ba*. A: 361–374; B: 585–610; C: 87–108.
[Op. 40] *Gshen rab kyi dka' thub nyon mongs drung byin*. In *Bon gyi bka' brten*, vol. 108, pp. 79–103.
[Op. 41] *Rig 'dzin mkha' 'gro'i tshogs kyi rgyud phyag* (*Rgyud kyi tshogs skong*). A: 7–23; B: 3–31.

Gsang sngags gling pa, Nyag rong gter ston (b. 1864)
[Op. 42] *Rgyal kun spyi gzugs dran pa nam mkha' rje'i rnam thar g.yung drung gsang ba'i mdzod chen*. In *Bon gyi bka' brten*, vols. 291–298.

Various and Anonymous Authors
[Op. 43] *Rgyungs yar khod spungs kyi lo rgyus*. In *Dpal ldan bla ma'i rnam thar mu tig 'phreng ba*, pp. 1–35. Edited by Tenzin Namdak. Dolanji: Tibetan Bonpo Monastic Centre, 1981. Also in *Sources for a History of Bon*, pp. 142–164. Dolanji: Tibetan Bonpo Monastic Centre, 1972.
[Op. 44] *Mdo 'bum rgyud mdzod bzhi'i dbang lung khrid kyi brgyud rim gser gyi phreng ba*. Dolanji: Tibetan Bonpo Monastic Centre, 1973.
[Op. 45] *Lung bstan 'khol du phyung ba*. In *Dpal ldan bla ma'i rnam thar mu tig 'phreng ba*, pp. 35–58. Edited by Tenzin Namdak. Dolanji: Tibetan Bonpo Monastic Centre, 1981. Also in *Sources for a History of Bon*, pp. 167–183. Dolanji: Tibetan Bonpo Monastic Centre, 1972.

2. Works in Western Languages

Achard, Jean-Luc. 1998. "Bon zhig khyung nag and the Rig pa gcer mthong Tradition of Rdzogs chen." *Tibet Journal* 23 (4): 28–57.

———. 2004. *Bon Po Hidden Treasures. A Catalogue of gTer ston bDe chen gling pa's Collected Revelations.* Brill's Tibetan Studies Library, vol. 6. Leiden: Brill.

———. 2008. *Enlightened Rainbows: The Life and Works of Shardza Tashi Gyeltsen.* Brill's Tibetan Studies Library, vol. 18. Leiden: Brill.

Clemente, Adriano. 1983. "La dottrina Rdzogs chen nel ciclo di insegnamenti visionary *Dran pa gser gdams*." Unpublished dissertation. Istituto Universitario Orientale, Naples.

———. 1994. "The Sgra Bla, Gods of the Ancestors of Gshen-Rab Mi-Bo according to the *Sgra Bla Go Bsang* from the *Gzi Brjid*." In *Tibetan Studies, Proceedings of the 6th Seminar of the International Association for Tibetan Studies.* Oslo. Pp. 127–136.

———, and Chögyal Namkhai Norbu. 1999. *The Supreme Source: The Fundamental Tantra of the Dzogchen Semde, Kunjed Gyalpo.* Ithaca, N.Y.: Snow Lion Publications.

Dell'Angelo, Enrico. 1982. "Srid pa'i spyi mdos: Contributo allo studio dell' insegnamento di gShen rab mi bo che." Unpublished dissertation. Istituto Universitario Orientale, Naples.

Delog Dawa Drolma. 1995. *Delog: Journey to Realms Beyond Death.* Junction City, Calif.: Padma Publishing.

Doctor, Andreas. 2005. *Tibetan Treasure Literature: Revelation, Tradition, and Accomplishment in Visionary Buddhism.* Ithaca, N.Y.: Snow Lion Publications.

Gorvine, William M. 2006. "The Life of a Bonpo Luminary: Sainthood, Partisanship, and Literary Representation in a Twentieth-Century Tibetan Biography." PhD diss., University of Virginia. Based on two biographies of Shar-rdza Bkra-shis-rgyal-mtshan.

Gyatso, Janet. 1999. *Apparitions of the Self: The Secret Autobiographies of a Tibetan Visionary.* Princeton: Princeton University Press.

Harding, Sarah. 2003. *The Life and Revelations of Pema Lingpa.* Ithaca, N.Y.: Snow Lion Publications.

Jamgön Kongtrul Lodrö Taye. 2011. *The Hundred Tertöns: A Garland of Beryl: Brief Accounts of Profound Terma and the Siddhas Who Have Revealed It.* Translated by Yeshe Gyamtsho. Woodstock, N.Y.: KTD Publications.

Karmay, Samten Gyaltsen. 1972. *The Treasury of Good Sayings: A Tibetan History of Bon.* London Oriental Series 26. London: Oxford University Press.

———. 1975. "A General Introduction to the History and Doctrines of Bon." *Memoirs of the Research Department of the Toyo Bunko.* Tokyo. Pp. 172–218.

———. 1977. *A Catalogue of Bonpo Publications.* Tokyo: The Toyo Bunko.

———, and Yasuhiko Nagano. 2001. *A Catalogue of the New Collection of Bonpo Katen Texts.* Senri Ethnological Reports 24, 25; Bon Studies 4, 5. Osaka: National Museum of Ethnology.

———, and Yasuhiko Nagano, eds. 2008. *A Lexicon of Zhangzhung and Bonpo Terms*. Senri Ethnological Reports 76; Bon Studies 11. Osaka: National Museum of Ethnology.

Keutzer, K. and K. O'Neill. 2009. "A Handlist of the Bonpo Kangyur and Tengyur." *Revue d'Etudes Tibétaine* 17: 63–128.

Kvaerne, Per. 1971. "A Chronological Table of the Bon-po: The bsTan rcis of Nyi ma bstan 'jin." *Acta Orientialia* 33: 205–282.

———. 1973. "Bon po Studies I: The A-khrid System of Meditation." *Kailash* 1: 19–50.

———. 1974. "The Canon of the Tibetan Bonpos." *Indo-Iranian Journal* 16: 18–56, 96–144.

———, and Thupten K. Rikey, trans. 1996. *The Stages of A-Khrid Meditation: Dzogchen Practice of the Bon Tradition*. Text by Bru-sgom Rgyal-ba g.yung drung. Dharamsala: Library of Tibetan Works and Archives.

Martin, Dan. 2001. *Unearthing Bon Treasures: Life and Contested Legacy of a Tibetan Scripture Revealer with a General Bibliography of Bon*. Brill's Tibetan Studies Library 1. Leiden: Brill.

———, Per Kvaerne, and Yasuhiko Nagano. 2003. *A Catalogue of the Bon Kanjur*. Senri Ethnological Reports 40; Bon Studies 8. Osaka: National Museum of Ethnology.

Namkhai Norbu, Chögyal. 1995. *Drung, Deu and Bön: Narrations, Symbolic Languages and the Bön Tradition in Ancient Tibet*. Translated and annotated by Adriano Clemente. Dharamsala: Library of Tibetan Works and Archives.

———. 2004. *The Necklace of Zi: On the History and Culture of Tibet*. Translated by Adriano Clemente. Arcidosso: Shang Shung Publications.

———. 2008. *Yantra Yoga: The Tibetan Yoga of Movement*. Translated and annotated by Adriano Clemente. Ithaca, N.Y.: Snow Lion Publications.

———. 2009. *The Light of Kailash: A History of Zhang Zhung and Tibet. Volume One: The Early Period*. Translated by Donatella Rossi. Arcidosso: Shang Shung Publications. Revised edition, 2013. *A History of Zhang Zhung and Tibet: Volume One: The Early Period*. Berkeley: North Atlantic Books.

———. 2010a. *Rainbow Body: The Life and Realization of a Tibetan Yogin, Togden Ugyen Tendzin*. Translated and annotated by Adriano Clemente. Arcidosso: Shang Shung Publications.

———. 2010b. *Zhang Zhung: Images of a Lost Kingdom*. Translated by Adriano Clemente and compiled by Alex Siedlecki. Arcidosso: Shang Shung Publications.

———. 2013. *The Light of Kailash: A History of Zhang Zhung and Tibet. Volume Two: The Intermediate Period*. Translated by Donatella Rossi. Arcidosso: Shang Shung Publications.

———. 2015. *The Light of Kailash: A History of Zhang Zhung and Tibet. Volume Three: The Later Period*. Translated by Donatella Rossi. Arcidosso: Shang Shung Publications.

Ngawang Zangpo. 2002. *Guru Rinpoché: His Life and Times*. Ithaca, N.Y.: Snow Lion Publications.

Reynolds, John Myrdhin. 2005. *The Oral Tradition from Zhang-Zhung*. Kathmandu: Vajra Publications.

———. 2011. *The Practice of Dzogchen in the Zhang-Zhung Tradition of Tibet*. Kathmandu: Vajra Publications.

Rossi, Donatella. 1999. *The Philosophical View of the Great Perfection in the Tibetan Bon Religion*. Ithaca, N.Y.: Snow Lion Publications.

Shardza Tashi Gyaltsen. 1993. *Heart Drops of Dharmakaya: Dzogchen Practice of the Bön Tradition*. Translation and commentary by Lopon Tenzin Namdak. Ithaca, N.Y.: Snow Lion Publications.

Snellgrove, David. 1967. *The Nine Ways of Bon: Excerpts from the gZi brjid*. London: Oxford University Press.

Tenzin Namdak, Lopön. 2006. *Bönpo Dzogchen Teachings*. Edited by John Myrdhin Reynolds. Kathmandu: Vajra Publications.

———. 2012. *Heart Essence of the Khandro: Experiential Instructions on Bönpo Dzogchen*. New Delhi: Heritage Publishers.

———. 2015. *Drenpa Serdam: Oral Instructions of the Eighty Wrathful Khandro called The Precious Golden Lamp*. Root text by Shense Lhaje. Oral commentary by Yongdzin Lopön Tenzin Namdak Rinpoche. Transcribed and edited by Carol Ermakova and Dmitry Ermakov. Foundation for the Preservation of the Yundrung Bön. Buddhas Weg, Germany, 19–23 September 2014 and Shenten Dargye Ling, France, 11–13 September 2015.

Tulku Thondup Rinpoche. 1986. *Hidden Teachings of Tibet: An Explanation of the Terma Tradition of the Nyingma School of Buddhism*. Edited by Harold Talbott. London: Wisdom Publications.

Index of Tibetan, Sanskrit, and Zhang Zhung Names and Terms

NOTE: Phonetic renderings of Tibetan and Sanskrit terms in the text are followed here by their formal transcriptions in parentheses. For names and terms that recur frequently throughout the text, references are given only for the introduction and the notes where the reader can find detailed information about them.

A dkar theg pa, 3
A khrid, 4, 219n42, 219n45, 219n46
A nu rong tsa, 165
a rdzogs snyan gsum, 4
a 'thas, 200
a tsa ra mi gsum, 209n99
a wa re, 200
'A zha Bdud rtsi rgyal. See Dütsi Gyaltsen
Anu Tragthag (A nu phrag thag; A nu 'phrag thag), 31, 106, 168, 172, 209n87, 217n8
arura (a ru ra), 42, 45, 80, 169, 213n8
Azhang Sangthub ('A zhang gsang thub), 18

bag chags, 199
Ban ma bon, 165
bcos med, 198
bde drod nyams kyi drod tshad, 214n16
bder gshegs, 207n61
bdud, 198
Bha ta hor, 165
Bhisha (Bhi sha), 10
Bka' brgyud skor bzhi, 3
Bkra shis yon tan, 15
bla ma che drug, 208n86, 217n2
Bla med go 'phang sgrub thabs kyi mdo rgyud, 16, 19

blo, 6, 199
blo 'das, 95
Blo gros rgyal mtshan, 211n6
Blo ldan snying po, 202n6
bon bdag, 208n69
bon dbyings, 34
bon gsar ma, 202n3
bon nyid, 34, 199
bon nyid kyi dbyings, 4, 204n26
bon sku, 34, 199
Bon zhig nag po, 219n49
'bras bu, 199
Bru chen nam mkha' g.yung drung, 218n25
'Brug gsas chem pa, 205n43
'Brug ris Shes rab grags pa, 163, 208n68
bsam mno, 200
Bsgrags pa skor gsum, 4, 202n15
Bsod nams ye shes, 166, 221n6
Bstan pa tshul khrims, 221n6
btsun chung, 219n52
Btsun chung lo lo, 163–164
Bumgyurma ('Bum bsgyur ma), 127, 175
Bya bral dpal 'byor lhun grub, 155
byang chub sems, byang chub kyi sems, 4, 199, 215n25
Byang chub sems gab pa dgu skor, 4
byang gter, 208n71
byar med, 34

232 — INDEX

Chabkar (*Chab dkar*), 3
Chabnag (*Chab nag*), 3
chad pa, 213n6
Chagöshang, Chagöshong (Bya rgod gshang, Bya rgod gshong), 14, 20, 21
Champa Kunsalma (Byams pa kun gsal ma), 137, 176
Changchub Dorje (Byang chub rdo rje), x, 201n4
Chari Tsugden (Bya ri gtsug ldan), 31, 32, 44, 58, 153, 212n136
Chatsün Kungma (Phywa btsun gung ma), 9
Chenpo (*chen po, chen po yab yum*), 68, 216n40
Chetsa Kharbu (Lce tsa mkhar bu), 17, 18, 109, 172
Chime Tsugphü ('Chi med gtsug phud), 2, 39, 65, 112, 164, 167, 172, 202n5
chingwa (*bying ba*), xii, 199
Chipung (*Spyi spungs*), 9, 202n13, 205n43, 206n46, 213n3
Chöd (*Gcod*), 22, 209n107
Chodung (Jo gdung), 117, 173, 219n42
chos, 34
chos dbyings, 34
chos nyid, 34, 199
chos sku, 34, 199
Choyung (Jo g.yung), 117, 173, 219n42
Choza Bönmo (Co za bon mo), 40, 164, 213n2
Chucham Gyalmo (Chu lcam rgyal mo, Chu lcags rgyal mo), 39, 130, 168, 175, 220n6
Chucham Wöntroma (Chu lcam 'od 'phro ma), 130, 175

dam tshig, 216n42. See also samaya
Dangdenma (Mdangs ldan ma), 135, 144, 177
'das log, 221n3
Dbal chen ge khod, 205n43
Dbal gsas rnam pa, 205n43
dbang, dbang bskur, 199
Dbang gi gar ma byed, 164
Dbang phyug shes rab seng ge, 165
dbus gter, 208n71
dbyer med, 34
dbyings, 7, 199, 203–204n26, 205n42, 215n28

De Gyimtsa, De Gyimtsa Machung (Lde gyim tsha, Lde gyim tsha rma chung), 15–17, 19, 206n44, 208n78
Dedenma (Bde ldan ma), 143, 177
deu (*lde'u*), 34, 213n142
Dga' ba don grub, 215n36
Dge bsnyen theg pa, 3
Dge lha gar phyug, 215n36
dge sbyor, 197, 214n10
dgongs gter, 8
Dgongs mdzod ri khrod chen po. See Gongdzö Chenpo
dgongs pa, 197
Dgos 'dod kun 'byung gter sgo, 20
dharmakaya (*dharmakāya*), 5, 10, 34, 197, 199, 203n22
dharmata (*dharmatā*), 91, 199, 218n18
Dmu gshen, 211n115
dngos grub, 207n62
don, 198
Don la g.yung drung 'od gsal, 164
Don la 'gyur med g.yung drung, 164
Dori Kangkar (Rdo ri gangs dkar), 15
Dpon dge dpon 'ud, 208n69
Draké Bumgyur (Sgra skad 'bum bsgyur), 40, 169
Dran chog nyi ma 'od zer, 221n6
dran pa, 198
Drang ma, 164
Drang srong blo gros seng ge, 163
Drang srong theg pa, 3
drod tshad, 198
Drönme Dangdenma (Sgron me mdangs ldan ma), 139, 176
Druchen Gyalwa Yungdrung ('Bru chen rgyal ba g.yung drung), 4
Drung mu gcod chen, 21, 209n107
Düddul Yungdrung Tragpa (Bdud 'dul g.yung drung grags pa), 33
'dul ba gshen drug, 164
Dütsi Charbebma (Bdud rtsi 'char 'bebs ma), 132, 176
Dütsi Gyaltsen ('A zha Bdud rtsi rgyal mtshan), 118, 173, 219n45
Dwags po, 213n2
Dwang ma'i ding, 164
Dzö (*Mdzod*), 3, 204n29

ganachakra (*gaṇacakra*), 25, 165, 168, 211n116
ganapuja (*gaṇapūja*), 65, 116, 211n116

INDEX — 233

Gar dbang rin po che, 201n4
Gar gshen sras, 164
Garab Dorje (Dga' rab rdo rje), 1
garuda (*garuḍa*), 10, 55, 64, 167, 215n34
gdangs, 198
gdod ma'i gzhi, 4
gdung brgyud bcu gsum, 209n87, 217n11, 218n12, 218n28
gdung rgyud bcu gnyis, 209n87
Ge sar, 206n44, 218n21
Ghuhu Li Parya (Ghu hu li par ya), 17
Glang 'od la thung, 208n69
gnas lugs, 199
Gnya' khri btsan po, 205n36, 217n5
Gnyan ston shes rab seng ge, 202n12
gnyis 'dzin, 198
gnyug ma, 198
go yi pha bong g.yag, 19
Göcham Barma (Rgod lcam 'bar ma), 39, 43, 126, 168, 175
Göcham Tsugtorma (Rgod lcam gtsug gtor ma), 132, 176
Göcham Yuthingma (Rgod lcam g.yu mthing ma), 129, 175
gong ma che drug, 208n86
Gongdzö Chenpo, Gongdzö Ritrö Chenpo (Dgongs mdzod chen po, Dgongs mdzod ri khrod chen po, Rme'u dgongs mdzod ri khrod chen po), 4, 118, 172, 202n13, 219n41, 219n46
'gro ba'i don mdzad gshen po bzhi, 168
'Gro mgon bsod nams lhun grub, 166
Grub chen g.yung drung rnam dag, 221n6
Grub thob ko long lha gsas, 164
gsal ba, 5, 200
Gsal ba rang byung, 215n36
Gsang sngags gling pa, 208n72
gsas mkhar, 204n28
gsas mkhar mchog lnga, 205n43
Gshen chen klu dga'. *See* Luga
Gshen chen re thul, 165
Gshen gyi dka' thub, 16–17, 19
Gshen gyi dpyi bu, 163
gshen phran, 211n117
Gshen rab rnam rgyal gzungs chen sgrub pa, 20
gter gsar, 208n71
Gto bu 'bum sangs, 208n83
Gto gshen drangs dkar, 163
Gtsang ma gtsug phud, 163

Gtso mchog rnam 'joms, Gza' 'dul gtso mchog rnam 'joms, 14, 15, 16, 18, 20
Guru Notse (Gu ru rno rtse, Gu ru non rtse), 68, 173, 219n43
Guru Trashi (Gu ru bkra shis), 20
Gyaltheb Mucho Demdrug (Rgyal theb mu cho ldem drug), 17
G.yang sgrub, 16
Gyenchigma (Rgyan gcig ma), 129, 175
Gyenden Sertroma (Rgyan ldan zer 'phro ma), 133, 176
Gyendenma (Rgyan ldan ma), 129, 175
Gyendrugma (Rgyan drug ma), 130, 175
Gyenzangma (Rgyan bzang ma), 45, 49, 73
Gyermi Nyiwö (Gyer mi nyi 'od), 8, 205n35, 219n49
Gyerpung Nangzher Löpo (Gyer spungs snang bzher lod po), 3
'gyu ba, 197
G.yu lo, 208n83
g.yung drung, 214n9
G.yung drung gling, 163
G.yung drung klong rgyas le'u nyi shu rtsa brgyad pa, 16, 19
G.yung drung 'od 'bar ma, 164
g.yung drung sems dpa', 209n90
g.yung drung sum brstegs, 212n126
Gyungyar Khöpung (Rgyung yar khod spungs), 9, 25, 29, 30, 32, 54, 66, 69, 75, 76, 80, 93
Gyungyar Mukhö (Rgyung yar mu khod), 9, 26, 64, 69, 70, 110, 172, 215n33
Gza' 'dul, 20
gza' gtad, 200
gzhan snang, 6
gzhi, 200
Gzungs chen, 16
Gzungs sde le'u lnga bcu rtsa lnga pa, 15
Gzungs sde rin chen phreng ba, 17

Hara Chipar (Ha ra ci par, Mon bon ha ra ci par), 105, 172, 209n87, 217nn7–8
Horshig Lhaje (Hor shig lha rje), 11, 82
Hringni Muting (Hring ni mu ting), 106, 172, 209n87
Hripa Chosé (Hris pa jo sras), 99, 171

'ja' lus, 'ja' lus pho ba chen po, 7, 204n27
Jamgön Kongtrul Lodrö Thaye ('Jam mgon kong sprul blo gros mtha' yas), 20

Jegyal Lhagom (Rje rgyal lha sgom), 64, 109, 172, 215n33
'jig rten gyi mkha' 'gro, 213n5
Jongyulma (Ljong yul ma), 21

ka dag, 197, 200
Kalpa Zangmo, Kalzang, Kalzangma (Skal pa bzang mo, Skal bzang, Skal bzang ma), 39, 49, 123, 124, 125, 150
Kalzang (*Bskal bzang*), 22
karmamudra (*karmamudrā*), 10, 206n47
Karsal Dangdenma (Dkar gsal mdangs ldan ma), 135, 176
kaya (*kāya*), 5, 144, 147, 149, 203n20
Ke Ragtram, Kepu Ragtram (Ke rag phram, Ke pu rag phram), 20
Keru (Ke ru), 20
Kha Long Ying (*mkha' klong dbyings*), 9
Kha yam rlung lce, 206n44
khams gter, 208n71
Khanam Kyolpo (Mkha' nam skyol po), 10
Khangying (Mkha' 'gying, Khro rgyal gtso mchog mkha' 'gying), 9, 39, 167, 205n43, 214n11
Khöpo Lodrö Thogme (Khod po blo gros thogs med), 14
khra ther, 197
Khro phu lo tsa ba, 166
Khro rgyud, 202n13
'khrul pa, 6, 197
Khyangphag (Skyang 'phag, Skyang 'phags mu la drung mu), 120, 173, 219n51
Khyentse (Mkhyen brtse, Mkhyen brtse chen po), 26, 27, 29, 30, 31, 168, 211n121
Khye'u 'od gsal, 164
Khyunglung, Khyunglung Ngulkhar (Khyung lung, Khyung lung mngul mkhar), 9, 30, 32, 153, 215n33
Khyungpo Sögyal (Khyung po bsod rgyal, Khyung po bsod nams rgyal mtshan), 16, 208n69, 221n6
Khyungpo Tragpa, Khyungpo Nangchen Tragpa, Khyungpo Nangchen Tragpa Gyaltsen (Khyung po grags pa, Khyung po snang chen grags pa, Khyung po snang chen grags pa rgyal mtshan), 13, 16, 17, 18, 28, 29, 155, 166, 208nn68–69
klong, 197, 203–204n26, 205n42

Klong brten rin chen gsal sgron, 168
Klu bon gsang ba g.yung drung gtsug phud, 165
Ko Ragtrom, Kophu Ragtrom (Rko rag phrom, Rko phu rag phrom), 14
Kode Kalzang (*Go lde bskal bzang*), 18, 22, 23
Kode Nyima Sherab (Go bde nyi ma shes rab), 14
Kode Phagpa, Kode Phagpa Yungdrung Yeshe, Kode Phag Gom Yungdrung Yeshe (Go lde 'phags pa, Go lde 'phags pa g.yung drung ye shes, Go lde 'phags sgom g.yung drung ye shes), 11, 15–20, 22, 207n56
Kongtse (Kong tse), 17
kun gzhi, 4, 197
Kun 'joms khro bo'i rgyud, 18
Kun rigs, *Kun rig*, 16, 19
Kun snang khyab pa, 215n36
Kun tu bzang po, 167, 197, 203n22. See also Samantabhadra
Kunbumma (Kun 'bum ma), 135, 176
Kundrol Tragpa (Kun grol grags pa), 20, 21
Kundüma (Kun 'dus ma), 141, 176
Kunga Shigpo (Kun dga' zhig po), 115, 173, 219n33
Kunga Zangmo (Kun dga' bzang mo), 10
Kungama (Kun dga' ma), 141, 176
Kunjungma (Kun 'byung ma), 140, 176
Kunkhyen Serdenma (Kun mkhyen zer ldan ma), 135, 176
Kunkhyenma (Kun mkhyen ma), 141, 176
Kunshe Serden, Kunshe Serdenma (Kun shes zer ldan, Kun shes zer ldan ma), 73, 138, 169, 176
Kunshema (Kun shes ma), 140, 176
Kuntu Nangma (Kun tu snang ma), 138, 176
Kurgom Drepo (Gur sgom sgras po), 113, 173, 218n27
Kurgom Tare (Gur sgom da re), 113, 172, 218n26
Kyu ra rin chen, 165
Kyura Wözer Gyaltsen (Kyu ra 'od zer rgyal mtshan), 22

Lag (Klag), 11, 207n58
Langchen Muwer (Glang chen mu wer), 30, 172, 209n87, 218n12

las kyi mkha' 'gro, 211n5
las kyi phyag rgya mo, 206n47
Legs grub rin chen 'bar ba, 164
Legtang Mangpo (Legs tang rmang po), 15–18, 194, 208n77, 209n88
Lha mo dkar mo pad ma'i spyan, 213n3
Lha mo dmar mo 'bar ma'i lcags, 213n3
Lha mo ser mo thor tshugs can, 213n3
Lha mo sngon mo chu rkang ma, 213n3
Lha rgod thog pa, 205n43
lha ri pha 'ong g.yag 'dra, 18
lha srin sde brgyad, 216n50
Lhadag Nagdrol, Lhadag Ngagdro (Lha bdag sngags grol, Lha bdag sngags dro, Lha bdag sngags 'gro), 17, 18, 209n88
lhag mthong, 200
Lhaje Pargom (Lha rje bar sgom), 112, 172, 218n25
Lhaje Tönme (Lha rje ston me), 113, 173
Lhazang Lupal (Lha bzang klu dpal), 21
lho gter, 208n71
lhun grub, 5, 197, 200, 203n19
Li mun gtsug phud, 165
Ling, Lingtsang (Gling, Gling tshang), 11
Lingje Repa (Gling rje ras pa pad ma rdo rje), 114, 173, 218n32
Lishag Wönam (Li shag 'od nam), 98, 171
Lishu Tagring, Nyachen Lishu Tagring (Li shu stag ring, Snya chen li shu stag ring), 4, 164, 168, 172, 202n11, 213n2
lo paṇ brgyad, lo paṇ gshen brgyad, 168, 205n44, 218n20, 218n23
Lo tsa mchog sred, 165
Lodenma (Blo ldan ma), 144, 177
Logcham Nyiwöma (Glog lcam nyi 'od ma), 25, 132, 176
Logcham Wöngyuma (Glog lcam 'od 'gyu ma), 133, 176
Lönchen Muthur (Blon chen mu thur), 110, 172, 218n20
Longkhyabma (Klong khyab ma), 136, 176
Longtenma (Klong brtan ma), 129, 175
lta ba, 198
Ludrub Yeshe Nyingpo (Klu grub ye shes snying po, Ye shes snying po), 105, 172, 208n86, 217n2, 217n4
Luga (Gshen chen klu dga', Sprul sku klu dga'), 119, 173, 202n12, 205n41, 219nn47–48

Lungnön Wangdrub (Lung non dbang grub), 100, 171
Luza Thingtsün (Klu za mthing btsun), 9

Ma rgyud, 216n48
ma rig pa, 6, 199, 203n20
Malo Tarchang (Rma lo dar dpyang, Rma lo dar dpyangs), 104, 172, 208n86, 217nn2–3
man ngag, 199
mandala (*maṇḍala*), 49, 204n28, 211n116, 213n3, 215n26
Marmo Tragkam (Dmar mo khrag skam), 148, 177
Matön Soldzin (Rma ston srol 'dzin), 118, 173, 219n44
mchog gi dngos grub, 207n62
Mdo thung, 15, 16
Me nyag, 206n44
me tog lha mo bzhi, 213n3
Megom Shigpo (Mes sgom zhig po, Me sgom zhig po), 115, 173, 219n34
Meshö (Me shod), 11, 55, 207n57
Mi 'gyur rgyal mtshan, 221n6
Milarepa (Mi la ras pa), 114, 173, 218n30
Milü Samleg (Mi lus bsam legs, Rgyal gshen Mi lus bsam legs), 77, 104, 172, 208n86, 216n48, 217n2
Mingyur Tönsal (Mi 'gyur don gsal), 102, 171
mkha', 203n26, 205n42
mkha' gro ma'i phyag rgya mo, 206n47
mkhas pa mi brgyad, 205n44, 218n21
mkhas pa mi bzhi, 206n44, 207n60, 208n78, 214n19, 218n17
mkhas pa mi gsum, 216n45
mnyam bzhag, 198
mnyam nyid, 198
mtha' bcad, mtha' ba bcad, 213n6
mtha' bral, 198
Mtha' bral bsod nams rgyal mtshan, 221n6
mtha' khob, 214n12
Mtha' yas 'phags, 165
mtshams med, mtshams med lnga, 213n4
mtshan ldan khye'u bzhi, 208n83
mu la, 221n9
Mucho Demdrug (Mu cho ldem drug), 17, 18, 164, 209n91
Mula Barwa (Mu la 'bar ba), 99

Mula Chingchen (Mu la gying chen, Mu la gling chen), 25
Mula Yungdrung (Mu la g.yung drung), 26
Mupung Saltang (Mu spungs gsal tang), 17, 111, 172, 218n23
Mutri Tsenpo (Mu khri btsan po, Dmu khri btsan po), 105, 167, 172, 209n87, 217n6
Mutsa Gyerme (Dmu tsha gyer med, Stang chen Dmu tsha gyer med), 8, 53 63 119 173, 202n6, 206n44, 214n21
Mutsa Trahe (Dmu tsha tra he), 17, 18

Nad yams bzlog pa, 15
Nagpo Ralpachen (Nag po ral pa can), 119, 173
nags 'ug, 198
nam mkha', 198, 203n26
Nam mkha' klong chen, 164
Nam mkha' lhun grub, 221n6
Nam mkha' rgyal mtshan, 220n53
Namchi Kungyal (Gnam phyi gung rgyal), 47, 214n15
Namgyal, Nampar Gyalwa (Rnam rgyal, Rnam par rgyal ba), 15–17, 20
Nangwa Dogchen (Snang ba mdog can, Nam mkha' snang ba mdog can), 105, 172, 208n86, 217n2, 217nn5–6
Natsog Gyendenma (Sna tshogs rgyan ldan ma), 134, 176
Ne rgyung 'phar bu, 206n44
Ngampa Chering (Ngam pa lce ring, Rngam pa lce ring), 111, 172, 206n44, 218n21
ngang, 198
ngo bo, 198
nirmanakaya (*nirmāṇakāya*), 5, 197, 199, 211n116
Norzangmo (Nor bzang mo), 10
Nyag rong gter ston. *See* Gsang sngags gling pa
Nyal (Gnyal), 20, 21
Nyalpa Nyima Sherab (Gnyal pa nyi ma shes rab), 20, 21, 209n106
nyams, 198
nyengyü (*snyan brgyud*), 7, 151, 193, 194, 204n30, 205n36, 207n56
Nyigong Yungdrung (Nyi gong g.yung drung), 9

Nyila Shelwö (Nyid la shel 'od), 101, 171
Nyima Kyechig (Nyi ma skyes gcig), 52
Nyima Saltser (Nyi ma gsal 'tsher), 39, 54, 168
Nyima Tendzin (Nyi ma bstan 'dzin), 7, 206n56
Nyima Tongkhyab (Nyi ma stong khyab), 39, 63, 127, 168, 175
Nyima Wöden (Nyi ma 'od ldan), 10, 12, 23, 124, 150, 152, 168, 206n49
Nyingma (Rnying ma), 1, 8, 202n3
Nyisal Wötse (Nyi gsal 'od rtse), 100, 171
Nyiwö Barma (Nyi 'od 'bar ma), 39, 127, 169, 175
Nyiwö Dangden (Nyi 'od mdangs ldan), 39, 127, 169, 175
Nyiwö Saldenma (Nyi 'od gsal ldan ma), 131, 176
Nyiwö Saltserma (Nyi 'od gsal 'tsher ma), 134, 176
Nyö (Gnyos), 21
Nyö Nyima Sherab (Gnyos Nyi ma shes rab), 11, 15–17, 207n56
Nyö Tsultrim Gyaltsen (Gnyos Tshul khrims rgyal mtshan), 117, 173, 219n40
nyon mongs pa, 198
Nyong ri khrod pa, 165

'od gsal, 200
'od lnga, 5
'Od ston tshul khrims 'od zer, 221n6
Oddiyana (Oḍḍiyāna), 1, 43, 169, 202n1
'Ol phug, 166
'Or phug btsun ching, 166

Padma Thongdrol (Pad ma mthong grol), 10
Padmasambhava (Padmasaṃbhava), 1, 9, 10, 164, 166
Palden Tsultrim (Dpal ldan tshul khrims), 16, 19, 22, 28
Partang Shangtön (Bar tang zhang ston), 113, 173
Pebön Thogtrul (Spe bon thog 'phrul), 108, 172, 209n87, 218nn15–16
Pebön Thogtse (Spe bon thog rtse), 108, 172, 209n87, 218n16
Pha dam pa, 165
Phagpa Sherab ('Phags pa shes rab), 21

INDEX — 237

Phenyul (*'Phan yul*), 3
'Phrul gshen theg pa, 2
'phrul 'khor, 'khrul 'khor, 216n39
Phur pa, 205n43, 216n49
Phya, 163, 164
phyag 'tshal, 214n13
Phywa gshen theg pa, 2
Phywa g.yang gi sgrub pa, 15
Phywa rje Keng tse len med, 164
Pöbar Shigpo (Bod rbar zhig po), 116, 173
Pönge (Dpon dge, Dpon dge dpon 'ud), 16, 208n69
Pönse (*Dpon gsas*), 3
Pönzhig (Bon zhig khyung nag), 60, 76, 173, 217n52, 218n33, 219n34
Pude Kungyal (Spu sde gung rgyal), 9
Pungnam Chergyung (Spungs nam gyer rgyung), 99, 171

Ra ston dngos grub 'bar, 202n12
Ragtrom (Rag phrom, Rag phrom brag, Rag phrom gyi brag), 14–16, 194
Ragya Yeshe (Ra rgya ye shes), 31, 168
rang bzhin med pa, 200
rang grol, 7, 200
rang sa zin, 200
rang snang, 5
Rasang Khöram (Ra sangs khod ram), 110, 172, 218n19
rdzogs sku, 5, 199
rdzu 'phrul, 199
rdzu 'phrul mkha' 'gro, 213n5
rgod pa, 197
rgya yan, 197
rgya yi mchod rten ka ru, 14
Rgyal ba blo gros, 164
Rgyal bu grol ldan, 165
rgyal chen rigs bzhi, 216n46
Rgyal 'phel slob dpon, 166
Ri bo rtse lnga, 165
rig 'dzin gshen phran brgyad, 214n18
Rig 'dzin gshen sgom, 155
Rig 'dzin G.yung drung 'od gsal, 165
rig 'dzin snying po zhi byed, 211n119
rig pa, 200, 203n17
rig pa hur, 200
rig pa'i ye shes kyi rtsal, 5
Rigpa (*rig pa, rig pa yab yum*), 68, 216n40
rigs drug, 6
Rigs drung 'od nam gstug phud, 164

rigs lnga yab yum, 167, 215n36
Rin chen blo gros, 221n6
Rinchen Norjungma (Rin chen nor 'byung ma), 149, 177
Rinchen Tönsalma (Rin chen don gsal ma), 148, 177
Rma gnyan pom ra, 165
Rma lo, 208n83
Rme'u dgongs mdzod ri khrod chen po. *See* Gongdzö Chenpo
Rme'u shes dpal, 221n6
Rnal 'byor pa dbang phyug drung mu rin chen, 221n6
Rnam dag 'od zer, 221n6
Rnam rgyal ka ra, 221n6
Rnam rgyal rgya nag ma, Rnam rgyal rgya nag ma'i ma'i sgrub pa, 14, 15, 208n77
Rnam rgyal rtsa sgrub, 15
Rnam rgyal zhang zhung ma, 15, 208n85
rnam rtog, 199
Rnam sras mdung dmar can, Rnam sras dmar po yang gsang mdung dmar po, Rnam sras mdung dmar can gyi sku skor, 14, 20, 21
rtag pa, 213n6
rtsis rdab, 199
rtog pa, 198
Rtogs ldan blo gros grags pa, 221n6
rtogs pa, 5, 198
rtsal, 5, 199

Sa bdag go lde ma, 19
Sa bdag 'khrug bcos, 16, 19
sa gter, 8
Sad kun Ratna, 209n99
Salbarma (Gsal 'bar ma), 140, 176
Salden Wöntroma (Gsal ldan 'od 'phro ma), 128, 175
Saldrön Gyenchigma (Gsal sgron rgyan gcig ma), 128, 175
Salwa Wöden (Gsal ba 'od ldan), 102, 171
Salwai Drönmachen (Gsal ba'i sgron ma can), 133, 176
Samantabhadra, 6, 10, 28–30, 32, 197, 203n22. *See also* Kun tu bzang po
samaya, 73, 216n42. See also *dam tshig*
sambhogakaya (*saṃbhogakāya*), 5, 197, 199, 215n36
Sangkar (Zangs dkar), 21
Sangs rgyas tshab, 165

238 — INDEX

Sangwa Düpa (Gsang ba 'dus pa), 18, 164, 208n86, 217n2
Sarang Menbar (Za rangs me 'bar, Za rang me 'bar), 111, 206n44, 218n22
Sas jo 'bum me, 165
sems, 6, 200, 215n25
sems nyid, 95, 200
sems phyogs, 2
Sems smad sde dgu, 4
Sene Gau (Sad ne ga'u), 106, 172, 209n87, 217nn9–10
Sengdongma (Seng gdong ma), 131, 176
Senkhar Shitro (*Gsas mkhar zhi khro*), 44, 213n3
Serden Nyima Wö (Zer ldan nyi ma 'od), 148, 177
Serden Singchigma (Zer ldan sring gcig ma), 131, 176
Serdenma (Zer ldan ma), 143, 177
Serthog Chejam (Gser thog lce 'byams), 17, 18, 209n88
sgo ba yab yum, sgo ba yab yum brgyad, 215n26, 216n39
Sgo bzhi mdzod lnga, 3
Sgom chen 'bar ba, 219n42
Sgom chen G.yung drung grags, 218n26
sgom pa, 198
sha chen, 211n122
Sha kya srid 'khor, 165
Shampo Lhatse (Sham po lha rtse), 18
shang (*gshang*), 15, 16, 167, 208n80, 215n24
Shang Shung (Zhang zhung), x, 2, 9, 201n2, 202n11, 204n28, 205n40, 206n45, 207n60, 215n33, 218n23, 221n9
Shar khyung bsod nams rgyal mtshan. See Khyungpo Sögyal
Shardza Trashi Gyaltsen (Shar rdza bkra shis rgyal mtshan), x, 3, 15, 19, 153, 154, 201n4
Shari Uchen (Sha ri dbu chen), 17, 18, 51, 75, 108, 172, 206n44, 214n19
shen, shenpo (*gshen, gshen po*), 25, 26, 204n28, 211n115, 217nn4–5, 218n20
Shenla Wökar (Gshen lha 'od dkar), 2, 167
Shenrab Miwo (Gshen rab mi bo), 2, 8, 15, 202n6, 202n13, 202n9, 204n29, 208n83, 209n91, 211n115, 211n117
Shepu Rakhug (Shad pu ra khug, Shad bu ra khug), 107, 172, 218nn13–14

Sherab Pal (Shes rab dpal), 13, 208n68, 220n53, 220n9
Shes rab rgyal mtshan, 219n53, 220n9, 221n6
Shes rab seng ge, 165
Shes rab snying po, 164
Shitro (*Zhi khro*), 9, 206n46, 216n40
Shugom Trulzhig (Zhu sgom 'khrul zhig), 115, 173, 218n33
Shuye Legpo (Zhu g.yas legs po), 119, 173, 219n47
siddhi, 12, 207n62, 211n116
silnyen (*sil snyan*), 54, 58, 63, 215n24
Singpa Thuchen (Zing pa mthu chen), 107, 172, 209n87, 218nn14–15
Sipai Gyalmo (Srid pa'i rgyal mo), 45, 168, 214n11, 214n15
Skal bzang gi mdo, 16
skor ba, 211n118
sku, 203n20, 214n14
sku gshen, 211n115, 217n5
sku gsum, 5, 197
sku gsung thugs, 214n14
skye med, 197
Skyi rong zhig po, 166
Slob dpon bstan pa 'od zer, 221n6
Sman rgyal rang grol, 166
snang ba, 199
Snang dang g.yu rtse, 163
Snang gshen theg pa, 2
snyam byed, 198
Sos sems skyed don ldan, 219n53
spros pa, 199
sprul sku, 5, 199
Sprul sku rgyal ba blo gros, 221n6
spyod pa, 199
Srid gshen theg pa, 2
Srid pa'i mdzod phug, 9, 205n41
srid pa'i yum, 220n6
Srong btsan sgam po, 201n2
Stag wer li wer, 209n87
Stag za li wer, 202n11, 217n7
stong nyid, stong pa nyid, 95, 198
stong pa, 5, 199
sugata, 12, 207n61, 219n53
Sukasiti (Su ka si ti), 26, 40, 49, 112, 142, 169, 177
Sum pa, 206n44, 218n28
Sumpa Ukar (Sum pa dbu dkar, Sum pa lbu kha), 114, 173, 209n87, 218n28

Tagla Menbar (Stag la me 'bar), 79, 104, 112, 167, 172, 208n86, 216n49, 217n2
Tagzig (Stag gzig), 8, 10, 169, 205n37, 206n44, 216n48, 218n22
Tampa Yuzhig (Dam pa g.yu zhig), 116, 173, 219n39
Tapihritsa, 3
terma (*gter ma*), 4, 7, 8, 202n3, 205nn32–33, 205n36, 206n54, 208nn71–72, 213n3
tertön (*gter ston*), 13, 14, 15, 19, 20, 21, 24
Thami Teke (Tha mi dad ke, Ta mi thad ke, Thad mi thad ke), 9, 106, 172, 206n45, 209n87, 217n10, 218n13
Thayema (Mtha' yas ma), 143, 177
theg pa rim dgu, 2
thig le, 198, 204n26, 217n51
thig le nyag gcig, 216n38
Thogme Mingyurma (Thogs med mi 'gyur ma), 139, 176
Thogme Wödenma (Thogs med 'od ldan ma), 138, 176
Thogmema (Thogs med ma), 144, 177
Thugje Chagkyuma (Thugs rje lcags kyu ma), 136, 176
Thugje Kundrol (Thugs rje kun grol), 28, 29, 31, 126, 155, 168, 175, 212n130
thugpa (*thug pa*), 52, 214n20
thugs, 198
thun mong gi dngos grub, 207n62
Tönbarma (Don 'bar ma), 134, 176
Töndenma (Don ldan ma), 146, 177
Töndrubma (Don grub ma), 147, 177
Tongyung Thuchen (Stong rgyung mthu chen), 8, 11, 12, 18, 22, 168, 205n44, 207n60, 209n107, 216n45
Töntönma (Don ston ma), 147, 177
torma (*gtor ma*), 31, 55, 62, 63, 72, 73, 212n137
Trangje Tsünpa Sermig (Drang rje btsun pa gser mig), 19
Trenpa Namkha (Dran pa nam mkha'), 8
Tretön Kocha (Dre ston go cha), 65, 219n41
Trigum Tsenpo (Gri gum bstan po), 8, 9, 205n36, 214n21, 218n19
Trigyer Tongnam (Khri gyer stong nam), 9
Trilo Namdrag (Khri lo gnam grags), 15, 16

Trime Wödenma (Dri med 'od ldan ma), 131, 176
Trimön Gyalzhe (Khri smon rgyal bzhad), 18
Trisong Deutsen (Khri srong lde'u btsan), 8, 9, 202n11, 205n36
Trithog Partsa (Khri thog spar tsha), 17, 18
Trom (Phrom, Khrom), 17, 18, 209n88
Trotsang Druglha (Khro tshang 'brug lha), 114, 165, 173, 218n29
Trulzhig Dombu ('Khrul zhig ldom bu, 'Khrul zhig ldong bu), 116, 173, 219n38
Trungmu Hara, Tsenden Trungmu Hara (Drung mu ha ra, Mtshan ldan Drung mu ha ra), 21–22
Trungmu Kalzang (Drung mu bskal bzang), 22
tsalung (*rtsa rlung*), 67, 216n39
Tsangpo (Gtsang po), 19
Tsangpo Dong (Gtsang po dong), 21
Tseme Wöden (Tshad med 'od ldan), 3, 39, 98, 167, 171, 213n1
Tsensher Gyerchen (Btsan sher gyer chen), 9
Tsewang Rigdzin (Tshe dbang rig 'dzin), 7, 8, 10, 23, 168, 206n50, 212n129, 213n7
Tshe dbang 'gyur med byang chub rdo rje rtsal, 201n4
Tshe dbang ri khrod, 213n7. *See also* Tsewang Rigdzin
tshogs kyi 'khor lo, 211n116. *See also* ganachakra
Tsogdag Karmo (Tshogs bdag dkar mo), 39, 49, 59–60, 126, 168
Tsugshen Wönbar (Gtsug gshen 'od 'bar), 101, 171
tsünchung (*btsun chung*), 12, 219n52

Urgyen Hringni (U rgyan hring ni), 31
Utpala Dzepa (Utpa la mdzes pa), 10

Vairochana (Vairocana), 1, 164, 216n39
Vajrayāna, 215n28, 216n42
Vidyadhara (*vidyādhara*), 165, 167, 206n50
Vimalamitra, 1

walmo (*dbal mo*), 19, 121, 123, 150, 166, 209n92
Wangchug Drönma (Dbang phyug sgron ma), 39, 139, 169, 176

Wangchug Hringwö (Dbang phyug hring 'od), 100, 171
Wangden Shense (Dbang ldan gshen sras, Dbang ldan gshen gsas), 11, 14, 28, 120, 155, 163, 173, 193
Wer ya drung mu, 21
Wer yak khi khar, 221n6
Wöden Barma ('Od ldan 'bar ma), 7, 27, 124, 125, 150, 152, 158, 168, 206n49
Wönam Mupung ('Od nam mu spungs), 101, 171
Wönbarma ('Od 'bar ma), 143, 177
Wöntroma ('Od 'phro ma), 140, 176
Wösal Dedenma ('Od gsal bde ldan ma), 147, 177
Wözer Dangden ('Od zer mdangs ldan, 'Od zer mi 'gyur mdangs ldan), 40, 128, 169, 175

yang dag pa'i sems bon, 2
Yang rtse bla med theg pa, 3
Yangtse Longchen (*Yang rtse klong chen*), 4, 202n15
yantra, 67, 216n39. See also *'phrul 'khor*
Yarlha Shampo (Yar lha sham po), 9
Ye grol dam pa bi ti, 165
Ye gshen gstug phud, 164
Ye gshen theg pa, 3
Ye sangs dkar po, 164
ye shes, 95, 200, 215n28
ye shes mkha' 'gro, 213n5
Ye shes sgom pa, 208n68, 220n53
Yedagma (Ye dag ma), 146, 177
Yejungma (Ye 'byung ma), 145, 177
Yekhyabma (Ye khyab ma), 145, 177
Yekhyenma (Ye mkhyen ma), 145
Yelo (Ye blo), 76
Yesalma (Ye gsal ma), 144, 177
Yeshe Lama (Ye shes bla ma), 77

Yeshe Lhungyal (Ye shes lhung rgyal), 100, 171
Yeshe Sangthal (Ye shes zang thal), 22
Yetong Shangsal (Ye stong zhang gsal), 99, 171
Yid kyi khye'u chung, 208n83
Yingchug Gyaltsen (Dbyings phyug rgyal mtshan), 39, 63, 139, 169, 176
Yingdrolma (Dbyings grol ma), 142, 177
Yingsalma (Dbyings gsal ma), 142, 177
Yingzhugma (Dbyings bzhugs ma), 146, 177
Yogatantra, 20, 21
Yongkhyab Chenmo (Yongs khyab chen mo), 137, 169
Yongkhyabma (Yongs khyab ma), 137, 176
Yongsu Tagpa (Yongs su dag pa), 63, 104, 172, 208n86, 215n32, 217n2
Yungdrung Bön (G.yung drung bon), 2, 59, 164
Yungdrung Sengchong (G.yung drung seng mchong), 15
Yungdrung Tsugtorma (G.yung drung gtsug gtor ma), 148, 177
Yungdrung Tsultrim Wangdrag (G.yung drung tshul khrims dbang drag), 32
Yungdrung Wösal (G.yung drung 'od gsal), 27

Zha gar, Zha gar ba, Rdzogs chen Zha gar ba, 208n68, 219n53, 220n9
Zhang zhung snyan rgyud, ix, 2, 3, 202n10, 203n16, 213n1, 215n32
Zhig po a rgod, 166
Zhötön Ngödrub Tragpa (Bzhod ston dngos grub grags pa), 4, 203n15
Zhu g.yas, 154
Zhu g.yas rgyal mtshan mchog legs, 166
Zijid (*Gzi brjid*), 2, 8